HEALTHWISE HANDBOOK

A SELF-CARE MANUAL FOR YOU

Donald W. Kemper
Kathleen E. McIntosh
Toni M. Roberts

A Healthwise® Publication
Healthwise, Inc., Boise, Idaho
Ninth Edition

Standard Healthwise cover design by Beth Workman

Illustrations by Consuelo Udave, June Perry and Mac Browning

First Edition Printing, 1976
Second Edition Printing, 1978
Third Edition Printing, 1979
Fourth Edition Printing, 1983
Fifth Edition Printing, 1985
Sixth Edition Printing, 1986
Seventh Edition Printing, 1987
Eighth Edition, 1990
Ninth Edition, 1990

ISBN: 0-9612690-9-X
Library of Congress Catalog Card Number: 89-84789

Printed in the United States of America

TABLE OF CONTENTS

PART III: STAYING HEALTHY

PART IV: SELF-CARE RESOURCES

To Our Readers

Eighty percent of all health care problems are managed at home. The Healthwise Handbook was written to help you handle health problems effectively. The information includes specific self-care recommendations for home treatment of over 130 of the most common medical problems.

The guidelines are based on sound medical information provided by physicians, nurses, pharmacists, physical therapists and others. Where our medical consultants have disagreed, we have worked to find consensus guidelines best supported by medical research. We have also tried our best to present the information and guidelines in a no-nonsense style that is free from medical jargon and easy to use in the home treatment of health problems.

This book does not eliminate the need for professional medical help. Instead, it provides a better basis for you to work with your doctors to jointly care for and prevent health problems. Should you receive professional advice in conflict with this book, look first to your health professional. Because your doctor is able to take your specific history and needs into consideration, his or her recommendations may prove to be best. Likewise, should any self-care recommendations fail to provide positive results within a reasonable period, you should consult a health professional.

The book is as good as we can make it, but we cannot guarantee that it will work for you in every case. Nor will the authors or publishers accept responsibility for any problems that may develop from following its guidelines. The book is only a guide; your common sense and good judgment are also needed.

We wish you the best of health.

About HEALTHWISE

Healthwise is a nonprofit organization working to help people improve their health through healthy living and effective self-care. Since its founding in 1975, Healthwise has won awards of excellence and recognition from the Centers for Disease Control, the U.S. Department of Health and Human Services, the American Society on Aging and the World Health Organization.

Healthwise works with organizations wishing to enhance the individual's role in health care. Our clients range from volunteer organizations and church groups to Fortune 500 companies, major unions, state governments, hospitals, insurers and HMO's.

Healthwise has published four books, all with workshops and training to support them.

The *Healthwise Handbook* and the Healthwise Workshop.
The use of informed medical self-care to improve the quality of care given at home and to help reduce health care costs.

Pathways: A Success Guide for a Healthy Life and the Pathways to Health Workshop.
A guilt-free approach to health changes in ten areas, including stress, nutrition, fitness, smoking, alcohol and drugs and relationships. The book and workshops are designed to help people make the healthy changes they most want to make.

The *Growing Younger Handbook* and the Growing Younger Workshops.
Fitness, relaxation, nutrition and self-care for older adults aged 60 and better.

Growing Wiser: The Older Person's Guide to Mental Wellness and the Growing Wiser Workshops.
Memory improvement, mental vitality, coping with loss and life change, maintaining independence and self-esteem for older adults.

In addition to these books and workshops, Healthwise has produced videotapes and other instructional aids to support health promotion efforts.

For more information, contact Healthwise at P.O. Box 1989, Boise, Idaho, 83701, (208)345-1161.

Acknowledgments

The Healthwise Handbook made its first appearance in 1976, a long time ago in the fast-paced world of health information. The Healthwise Handbook is kept up-to-date in part by the efforts of our readers. Suggestions and comments we receive from readers lead to a fact search to determine if the new information can be documented and supported. This process helps keep us and the handbook fresh. We are grateful to our readers for that support and we encourage more of it.

Special thanks go to Molly Mettler and Cindy Krieg, senior members of the Healthwise staff. Together, they are responsible for design, format and editing. Other Healthwise staff members, Betty Matzek, Phyllis Tomlinson, and Gayle Earnest provided invaluable assistance.

This book would not have been possible without the extensive help and guidance we have received from health professionals. We depend upon them for accurate information, the latest medical developments and spirited debate. The following professionals have been particularly helpful:

Physicians

Steve Schneider, M.D., principal medical reviewer.

Elizabeth Abel, M.D.
Paul Creighton, M.D.
Gail Eberharter, M.D.
Tom Ferguson, M.D.
Mike Gibson, M.D.
Beverly Ludders, M.D.
Bruce Moody, M.D.
Keith Sehnert, M.D.
Don Vickery, M.D.
Allan J. Chernov, M.D.
Joseph Daglan, M.D
L.J. Fagnan, M.D.
Marty Gabica, M.D.
Dave Johnson, M.D.
Bob Mathies, M.D.
H.A.P. Myers, M.D.
Dick Starkey, M.D.

Dentists

Robert Collins, D.M.D., M.P.H.
Bob Gudmundsen, D.M.D.
Scott Presson, D.D.S., M.P.H.
Scott Freeman, D.M.D.
Edwin Matthes, D.D.S.

Dental Hygienists

Karen Slusser

Health Educators

Jim Giuffre', M.P.H.
Susan Gunn, Ph.D.
Bob Gorsky, Ph.D.
Richard Sager, M.P.H.

Home Economists

Joanne Graff

Nurses

Gene Drabinski, R.N.
Sharon Job, R.N.
Jane Mayfield, R.N.
Susan Short, R.N.

Nutritionists

Marsha Irvin, R.D.
Judy Peterson, R.D.
Ruth Schneider, R.D.

Pharmacists

Doris Denney, R.Ph.
John Rawlings, R.Ph.
Virginia Turner, R.Ph.

Physical Therapists

Lynn Johnson, P.T.
Anita Leccese, P.T.

Psychologists

Michael Eisenbeiss, Ph.D.
Francis Kirk, Ph.D.
Mark Mays, Ph.D.
Jim Read, Ph.D.
Martin Seidenfeld, Ph.D.

Consumers of Special Note

Dianne Barbosa
Judy Fuller
Pris Pontefract
Patricia Raino
Carolyn Rapp
Phyllis Salter
Marcia VanSkiver

Most of all we thank the hundreds of thousands of medical consumers who use the Healthwise Handbook. It is your actions that reward us the most and inspire us to constantly look for ways to improve this guide.

Funding for the original development of the Healthwise Handbook was provided by the W.K. Kellogg Foundation of Battle Creek, Michigan.

Donald W. Kemper

July, 1990

Introduction

The Healthwise Handbook can help you improve your health and lower your health care costs. It is a book you may turn to time and again as health problems arise.

The book is divided into four sections:

Self-Care Basics. What you need to know in order to be a wise medical consumer.

Health Problems. Prevention, treatment and when to call a doctor for over 130 common illnesses and injuries.

Staying Healthy. Tips and techniques for dental health, fitness, stress management, nutrition, and mental wellness.

Self-Care Resources. What you need to have on hand in your home to cope with health problems.

Most people will not read through the book from cover to cover in one sitting; it is more of a topic-by-topic book. Look up what you need when a problem or interest develops.

We do recommend that you read pages 1 and 2 and three special chapters right away.

Page 1 is the **"Healthwise Approach,"** a process to follow every time a health problem arises. Page 2, the **"Ask the Doctor Checklist"**, will help you get the most out of every doctor visit.

Chapter 1, **The New Medical Consumer**, offers important information that you can use to improve the quality and lower the cost of the professional care you need.

Chapter 2, **The Home Physical Exam**, will help you develop skills and awareness that will improve the quality of the self-care you provide when problems do arise.

Chapter 18, **Your Home Health Center**, lists medications, supplies and self-care equipment that you may wish to buy in advance.

The rest of the information in the book is there when you need it. We have enjoyed writing this book and keeping it up-to-date. We hope it will help you succeed in better managing your own health problems.

THE HEALTHWISE APPROACH

For use every time you have a health problem.

Step #1 - Observation

Describe the problem: ____________________

When did it begin? ____________________

Is it steady or periodic? __________ If periodic, how long does it last each time it comes? ____________________

What is its quality? (For pain, is it sharp, achy or dull?)____________________

What makes it better or worse? ____________________

Have you had it before? If so,what was done for it? Did it help?

____

Other symptoms? ____________________

Medications? ____________________

Possible reactions? ____________________

Personal or work habits that might be related to the problem?

____

Has anything unusual been happening, good or bad, to cause stress or change?

____

Anything else that seems important? ____________________

What has already been done for the problem? Results? ____________________

____

Record vital signs: Temperature ______________ Pulse __________/minute

Blood pressure ______/______ Respiration ______/minute

Other appropriate examination: ____________________

Step #2 - Learning More About It

Healthwise Handbook (note page numbers): ____________________

Other books and articles: ____________________

People --- lay or professional advice: ____________________

Step #3 - Thinking it Through and Taking Action

What's going on? (your tentative diagnosis): ____________________

Specific action plan: ____________________

General support plan: ____________________

When to see a health professional? ____________________

Step #4 - Follow-Up Evaluation

Are your actions working? ____________________

THE ASK-THE-DOCTOR CHECKLIST

BEFORE the visit (complete this along with the Healthwise Approach, page 1):

1. Why am I going to the doctor? (the main reason) ____________________

   ____

2. What else worries me about my health? ____________________

   ____

3. What do I expect the doctor to do for me today? ____________________

   ____

DURING the visit (complete with help of your doctor):

1. Show health professional your Healthwise Approach sheet.
2. Record: Temperature: ______________ Blood pressure ______________

   Other tests: ____________________________________

3. What is the health professional's diagnosis? ____________________

   ____

4. How can it be prevented? ____________________________

   ____

5. Medications? What? __________________ When? __________________

   For how long? ______________ Over-the-counter ____ Prescribed ____

   Generic name: ____________________ Possible concerns or side effects:

   ____

6. Are there any helpful patient education materials available for the condition?

   ____

7. What should I do at home? ____________________________

   Activity: ____________________________________

   Treatment: ____________________________________

   Precautions: ____________________________________

AFTER the visit (complete with help of your doctor):

1. Am I to return for another visit? ____No ____Yes - When? ______________

   Why? ____________________________________

2. Am I to phone in for test results? ____No ____Yes - When? ______________

   ____

3. What danger signs should I look for? ____________________

   ____

4. Should I report back to the doctor by phone for any reason? ____No ____Yes

   When? ____________________________________

5. What else should I know? ____________________________

   ____

   ____

You, the individual, can do more for your health and wellbeing than any doctor, any hospital, any drug and any exotic medical device.

Joseph Califano

Chapter 1

The New Medical Consumer

If you are an average American, you will buy over $200,000 worth of medical care in your lifetime. The consumer tips in this chapter will help you to get more for your money. With these few skills, you can:

1. Improve the quality of your care.
2. Avoid many risks of care.
3. Reduce the cost of care.

How much you can improve quality, avoid risks and reduce costs depends more on your relationship with your doctor than on anything else.

What Kind of Medical Consumer Are You?

The chart on the next page describes three models of typical medical consumers.

- Model #1: Doctor's Choice
- Model #2: Shared Choice
- Model #3: Consumer's Choice

Until recently, most Americans followed the Doctor's Choice model. They did what the doctor said with little question or concern. That model is still appropriate for many situations.

Today, however, many people are changing to "shared choice" relationships in which they and their doctors jointly decide on treatment plans. Some even move to the "consumers choice" model where they take full control of treatment decisions. The wise consumer learns when to use each model.

Why Choose a Consumer Model?

Most problems between doctors and patients happen because one does not know what the other expects. Don't make your doctor guess what you want. If he guesses wrong, the quality of your medical care will suffer.

MEDICAL CONSUMER MODELS

You may follow different models for different doctors or situations.

MODEL #1: Doctor's Choice

Description

You rely on the doctor's advice with little questioning.

Your trust in the doctor replaces the need to seek other alternatives.

You do not ask many questions or offer much information unless asked.

Message

"I'm looking for a doctor that will take charge of all my health problems. I plan to rely on your judgment in all medical decisions."

Situations

You have one main doctor you trust to provide or coordinate care.

In emergencies where split second decisions are critical.

MODEL #2: Shared Choice

Description

You expect your doctor to discuss alternatives and develop a shared treatment plan with you.

You are comfortable asking questions and expressing concerns or ideas.

You have a "working partnership" with your doctor.

Message

"I'm looking for a doctor who will involve me fully in treatment decisions and give me access to my medical records. I will share responsibility for choosing among treatment alternatives."

Situations

You are confident your ideas will improve the quality of care you get and believe your ideas will help keep costs down.

You do not have a regular doctor who provides or coordinates all your care.

MODEL #3: Consumer's Choice

Description

You listen to the doctor's assessment of alternatives but reserve the right to decide what to do yourself.

Message

"I like to make up my own mind about which tests and treatments are best for me, but I need your help to diagnose my problems and identify alternative treatments."

Situations

Fragmented Care: You are bounced from specialist to specialist with no one physician coordinating overall care.

Alternative Medicine: You wish to try a non-medical approach.

Consumer Model - continued

If you prefer the doctor to make all the decisions (Model #1), he needs to fully accept that responsibility. If you want to be more involved, asking for more involvement is the best way to get it. Talking about what you expect from your doctor and what he expects from you is the foundation of high quality medical care.

Finding the Right Doctor

No matter which consumer type you choose, you have to begin by finding a doctor that you can work with. Everyone wants a physician whose services are convenient, not too expensive and of top medical quality. You also want someone whose expectations of the doctor-patient relationship match yours.

Step One: Pick the kind of doctor you want.

If you want a generalist who can be a "family doctor" for you and your family, look for someone who is certified in family practice or perhaps a GP (General Practice). Other logical options are identified in the chart below.

Step Two: Find a few to choose from.

- Ask your friends how they like their doctors. Pay most attention to those friends who would choose the same consumer style as you.
- Ask any doctors or nurses that you know as friends whom they would recommend.
- Call your health plan office for recommendations.

Step Three: Call the office staff to ask about the doctor's qualifications and the convenience and costs of the care.

Tell the receptionist that you are trying to find a new regular doctor. Ask if the doctor is taking new patients. If yes, proceed with the following questions. If the receptionist seems too busy, suggest that she call you back when there is more time. You could also ask the same questions in a letter.

GOOD CANDIDATES FOR "MAIN" PHYSICIAN

Patient Descrip.	Family Practice	Internist	Pediatrician	Ob-Gyn	Geriatrician	Specialist
Anyone	X					
Family:						
Adults	X	X				
Kids	X		X			
Woman	X	X		X		
Older Adult	X	X			X	
Person with major chronic illness	X	X			X	X

Finding a Doctor - continued

Competence Questions

1. What special medical training does the doctor have?
   a. Residency programs
   b. Other special training in areas of concern to you.
2. Is the physician board certified? In what medical specialties?
3. At which hospitals does the physician have admitting privileges?

Convenience Questions

4. What are the office hours and average waiting times? "If I called today for a routine appointment, how soon could I be scheduled?"
5. What coverage is arranged for evenings and weekends?
6. Which insurance forms will the office fill out for me?
7. Will the doctor discuss problems over the phone?

Cost Questions

8. Is the doctor eligible for maximum payments under your health plan?
9. If you have often needed any particular procedure in the past, ask the cost of that.
10. What are the terms of payment? Is there a finance charge? If so, when does it start?

Step Four: Talk with the doctor.

Ask the office staff person if you can briefly meet with the doctor for no charge. If yes, schedule a meeting at the doctor's convenience. If no, ask if you can schedule a phone conversation.

- Say that the purpose of your visit is to see if what you want from a doctor and what he wants from a patient is a good match.

> **What Will the Doctor Think?**
>
> If you are worried that your doctor will think that talking about your expectations is a waste of time, you can relax. Most doctors today understand very well the importance of doctor-patient relationships. Most doctors work hard to establish good working relationships with their patients. In most cases, your doctor will appreciate your efforts and will feel better able to work with you in the future.

- Describe the consumer model that you want to follow. (See page 4).
- Ask if he will support the kind of physician-patient relationship you would like.
- Ask what the doctor expects from his patients.

Developing a Shared Choice Relationship with Your Doctor

Patient involvement in the treatment plan almost always results in better care. Here's how to do it.

1. *Tell your doctor(s) you want to be a partner in treatment decisions.*

Your doctor probably has lots of patients who don't want to share in the treatment plan. They just want the doctor to tell them what to do. If you say nothing, your doctor may well assume that you don't want to be involved either.

Tell your doctor that you want to share in decisions about tests, referrals and treatments. Also, indicate that you will want to have a good idea of the costs, benefits and risks of a service before going ahead.

2. Prepare for office visits.

Complete an "Ask the Doctor Checklist" like the one on page 2 before every visit. The checklist helps you to organize your observations and thoughts about the problem and to think about what you hope to gain from the visit.

Doctors know that 70% of correct diagnoses come from what the patient tells them. If you come in with a well-organized record of symptoms, history and concerns, most doctors will appreciate your effort.

3. Just ask "Why?"

For proposed medical tests, medications and treatment: ask "Why?"

By asking "Why?" you will often discover alternatives that may better meet your needs.

In asking "Why?" consider:

- Benefits: How will the service help me and what are the chances of success?
- Risks: What might go wrong? How likely are the risks and side effects?
- Costs: What are the total costs and how much will I have to pay?

4. Ask for alternatives.

Many people place too much faith in what medicine can do for them and too little faith in what they can do for themselves. When you are ill, it is easy to think, "Anything would be better than this." As a result people can often jump to the first treatment solution proposed.

There is always at least one alternative--to wait. Ask your doctor what the possible benefits, risks and costs of waiting a week, a month or a year might be. During that time three things can happen and two of them are good:

- You could improve on your own.
- You could find a better treatment alternative.
- Your condition could get worse.

A shared choice relationship is ideal for exploring alternatives such as outpatient surgery (see page 9) or other treatment options. If the treatment involves surgery, a second surgical opinion is often a good way to identify alternatives (see page 9).

5. Know where to look for help.

Smart consumers now have access to the same medical information as their physicians. If you have the time to do the basic research, you may find treatment ideas that you can bring to the doctor's attention.

Shared Choice - continued

Legal Rights in Health Care

In a legal sense you do have control over your treatment decisions. Except in emergencies or court imposed authority, no one can provide any medical test, medication, or treatment to you without your permission. You are also in charge of health care decisions about your children. If you ever disagree with your doctor about a treatment, you have the legal right to refuse it.

- Health Plan Resources

  Many health plans now offer medical information to consumers. Look at your health plan card. If there is a phone number to call if you need hospitalization, it may well be answered by a highly trained nurse with a great deal of information about treatment alternatives.

- Consumer Health Information Services

  Public libraries, bookstores, hospitals and community organizations make valuable medical information available to the public. A good place to start is by building your own home self-care library. Just keeping on hand a few books on medications, medical tests and any medical subject of importance to you can help you become an informed consumer. See page 268 for a listing of publications that are of particular value in a home health library.

If you can't find what you need locally, Planetree Health Resource Center in San Francisco may be able to help. Planetree is a non-profit consumer health organization that offers a health information-by-mail service. They will research any medical topic for you and prepare a comprehensive packet of information for a very reasonable charge. See page 268.

6. *Write it down.*

In a busy doctor's office or hospital, a written message can double the effectiveness of a conversation. For major medical procedures such as a childbirth or surgery, send a letter or birth plan to your doctor highlighting your concerns and desires regarding treatment. The letter will help you and your doctor develop a shared plan. If your plan involves anything that is not part of the standard procedure at the hospital, having a copy of it signed by your physician will help out whenever she is not present.

Make it clear that your plan is based on no complications. If an emergency situation arises, the plan should not restrict the physician from doing what she thinks is best.

A written note can also bring your frustrations to the doctor's attention. Long waits, lack of phone access to your doctor, or other concerns are best addressed in this way. Of course, complimentary notes are appropriate, too.

7. *Keep good medical records.*

Good home medical records will be helpful to your physician in diagnosing health problems. Most of all, records will help you to build confidence in your ability to care for similar problems in the future

For more information on home medical records, see page 264.

How to Buy a Good Operation

Surgery is something you buy only if you absolutely have to. It's not much fun, it usually involves both pain and risk, it costs a lot of money, and it's hard to tell exactly what you are buying. That is why it is so important to investigate the options before agreeing to have surgery.

When your doctor recommends surgery, it's smart to have some questions ready to make sure that what you think you are buying is in fact what you are most likely to get.

Outpatient Surgery

Outpatient surgery has been shown to be safe and effective for many common procedures, including:

- Breast biopsy
- Cataract surgery
- Cystoscopy
- Dilation and cutterage (D & C)
- Hernia repair
- Plastic surgery
- Skin biopsy

Many other outpatient surgeries are also common. Ask your doctor or health plan.

10 Questions to Ask Before Scheduling Surgery

About your Surgeon:

1. Are you board certified in your specialty?
2. How many similar surgeries have you performed?
3. Who would actually perform the surgery?

About the Surgery:

4. How new is this surgery? Is this the accepted treatment for this diagnosis?
5. What kind of anesthetic will be used? Are there alternatives?
6. What are the rates for mortality and other risks?
7. What is the success rate and will the surgery take care of the problem completely?

About You and Alternatives:

8. What are the likely consequences and alternatives if I decline or delay surgery?
9. Will I miss any work? How much?
10. How much will it cost and how much will my health plan pay?

Second Opinions

Before agreeing to any high risk procedure like surgery, it is often worthwhile to seek a second professional opinion. In one out of three cases, second opinions will uncover lower risk alternatives.

Second Opinions - continued

Many insurance plans now require second opinions on certain surgical procedures as a way to avoid unneeded risks and to reduce costs. Second opinions often are covered completely by health plans.

To get a second opinion:

- Don't ask the first surgeon to refer you for a second opinion; you are looking for independent thought. Your regular doctor or health care plan office can give you the names of appropriate physicians.
- Get a second opinion from a different type of physician. If the first doctor is a surgeon, go see a non-surgical specialist who treats similar problems.
- Focus the second opinion on looking for alternatives. It's not a matter of proving or disproving that the first physician was right.

Reducing the Cost of Care

Health care costs are high and there is no limit to how much higher they might go in the future. Skyrocketing costs have caused most insurance and HMO plans to raise deductibles and co-payments. Millions of Americans simply cannot afford to pay for either the insurance premium or the medical bills for services needed by their families.

New technology, higher wages for doctors and nurses, defensive medicine to protect doctors from malpractice claims, and an aging population all contribute to increases that can only lead to rationing of medical services in the future. You, the consumer, can play a very important role in keeping health care costs down.

Who Really Pays?

Most people think that their insurance pays for their health care. Actually, it is the consumer who pays. If your health care is covered by your employer, your medical costs are paid for in two ways:

- Your deductible and copayments.
- Your employer-paid premiums.

MEDICAL COST IMPACT ON WAGES

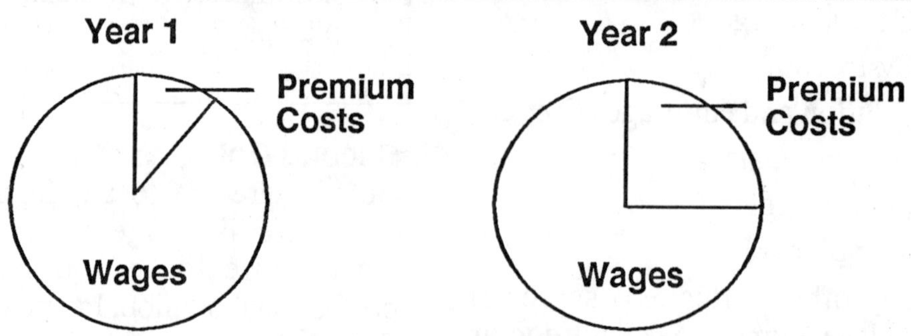

Medical premiums and wages come from the same budget. When premiums go up too fast, there is less money for wage increases.

Those premiums come out of the same budget that pays your wages. If medical costs or premiums go up, there is less money left over for wage increases. Increased premiums also force employers to raise deductibles and copayments.

While there is no guarantee that reducing health care costs will lead to higher wages, you can bet that major increases in costs will have a negative impact.

8 Ways to Cut Health Care Costs

1. *Give good home care.*

Eight out of ten health care problems are cared for at home, without the help of health professionals. By doing a good job of self-care, you are helping to reduce health care costs. By using medical self-care books like this one, you will be able to further improve your self-care skills and to better understand when to call a health professional.

2. *Assure good professional care.*

High quality care costs less than poor quality care. When you improve the quality of your shared treatment plan as described on page 4 you will be going a long way toward reducing the cost of care.

Every time you avoid an unneeded medical test, unneeded medication or an unneeded treatment, you will improve quality and reduce costs.

3. *Avoid hospitals as much as possible.*

Over half of all health care costs are for hospitalizations. A stay in a modern hospital costs far more than a stay at most luxury resorts. (And hospitals are a lot less fun than luxury resorts.)

When you do need hospital care, you are better off to minimize the time you stay in the hospital. With the right follow up support, you can often recover faster and with fewer risks in the comfort of your own home.

4. *Reduce your drug costs.*

Ask your doctor why you need the drug and what would happen if you choose not to take it. Because every drug carries with it the risks of some adverse reaction, your physician may be able to suggest a less risky drug.

A second way to lower medication costs is to ask for "generic equivalent" medications. Most drugs are marketed to physicians under a brand name. A generic equivalent is a drug with the same chemical formula as the name brand but without the name. Ask your physician or pharmacist if a high quality generic equivalent is available that will provide the same drug at a lower cost.

Finally, it often pays to comparison shop for medications which you will be using over an extended period. You may be amazed to find differences of up to 50% between stores for the exact same product.

Cut Health Care Costs - cont.

2 Ways to Reduce Hospital Risks and Costs:

1. Go as late as possible.
Ask for pre-admission testing. By having most medical tests done on an outpatient basis before going into the hospital, you can often avoid the costs and risks of one or more days of hospital care.

2. Go home early.
If you can arrange for good home care, either from your family or from paid nurses or attendants, you will often be able to both improve the quality and reduce the costs of your recovery.

Ask your doctor what kind of care you would need at home to assure a safe recovery? Also, call your health care plan office to ask if they will pay all or part of the home care costs. You may be saving yourself, the health plan and your co-workers a large amount of money without sacrificing one ounce of quality care.

You may even wish to consider mail-order catalogs for expensive drugs that you regularly use. If you do consider mail order, remember that the convenience and advice you get from your local pharmacist is worth a lot and should be considered in your decision.

5. Save emergency services for emergencies.

Emergency room services can cost two or three times what the same service costs in a doctor's office. What's worse is that you usually have to wait a long time; it is not on a first-come-first-served basis. Minor problems wait until all other problems are cared for. There is also little continuity of care. Your regular doctor has your records.

Ambulatory care centers have developed in many communities in recent years. These centers are often more expensive than a private physician but less expensive than a hospital emergency department. Because of their extended hours of service, they may be the best source of care for minor emergencies or trauma when your regular physician is not available.

6. Check your bills.

Hospitals and clinics are highly complex institutions. In some hospitals over half of all hospital bills have errors. In many cases, patients are inadvertently charged for services that they never received. If you check your bill carefully and notify the hospital and your health care plan office of any errors, you will be helping to reduce your health care costs.

7. Use your health plan resources.

Many health care plans now have highly specialized nurses or other professionals available to help you understand and explore alternative treatment plans for major health problems. These people can help you find out the cost, risk and benefit of most medical tests, surgeries, or other treatments that you may be considering. If you have access to a service like this, learn to use it to your benefit. It's a good way to become informed about health problems that go beyond the information in your home health library.

8. *Avoid defensive medicine.*

Defensive medicine refers to health care tests and services performed primarily to protect physicians from possible malpractice suits. In court, the physician will often have to show that he left no stone uncovered in trying to diagnose or treat the patient. Sometimes, what is good for the doctor's protection is not so good for the patient. Because every test and procedure has added costs and risks and many have little chance of helping you, you may prefer to take a more conservative approach.

You can avoid defensive medicine practices by developing a "Shared Choice" relationship with your physician as discussed on page 6. If you are actively involved in choosing tests and treatments, your physician will have less reason to order tests for primarily defensive purposes.

Currently, most malpractice cases are settled by tort law in which the physician is presumed to know what is best for the patient. By changing the relationship to one of collaboration or shared decision making, future cases may be decided more by contract law in which it is the agreement between the patient and physician that is most important. The "contract" does not need to be a written one. Any well-intended and clearly stated verbal agreement will do. By helping to shift medical relationships toward contract law, you will help to reduce the high cost of malpractice insurance and defensive medicine.

For more information on tort versus contract law and the models of physician-patient relationships see Resource #L2 on page 269.

The Rewards for a Healthwise Consumer

By using the communication tools in this chapter to develop good working partnerships with your doctors, you will help yourself become healthy, wealthy and wise.

- Healthy, because you will be getting a higher quality of medical care.
- Wealthy, because you will avoid the cost of much unnecessary care.
- And wise, because you will better understand that we are all responsible for our own health.

Each patient carries his own doctor inside him. We are at our best when the doctor who resides within each patient has the chance to go to work.

Albert Schweitzer, M.D.

Chapter 2

Home Physical Exam

Home physical examinations are the first step in taking responsibility for family health. You are the person who knows your family best; good home physicals help you learn what's normal for each family member so you can recognize a problem when it arises. This chapter outlines the steps in a home physical exam. Completing an exam is fun and easy, and after some practice, should take little more than half an hour.

The home exam creates a perfect atmosphere for introducing good health practices to your children, practices that may become lifelong habits. Plan to complete a thorough home physical of each family member once a year, perhaps on or near birthdays. Because infants and young children grow and change so quickly, they need more frequent exams. A complete check every month and a quick once-over at bath time is best for infants. Conduct exams every two months after the infant is six months old and twice a year thereafter until age five. As children grow, they will want to do parts of the physical for themselves, which is fine as long as good records are maintained.

The home physical is for more than just routine check-ups. When someone becomes ill, complete an exam and compare the results to a physical given when the person was well.

Record all your observations using something like the Home Physical Exam form found on the following pages. Good, clear, written records will help you remember the details.

Early Detection

By noticing health problems early, you can improve your family's health. Your observations, together with a recommended schedule of professional exams and

HOME PHYSICAL EXAM

Name: ________________ Date: ________________
Time of Day: __________ AM/PM

Vital Signs

1. Height: ______________ 2. Weight: ______________
3. Temperature:
   Oral ____________ Axillary ____________ Rectal ____________
4. Pulse:Beats/Min. ____________ Regular? ____________
5. Respiration: Breaths/Min. ________ Regular? ____________
6. Blood Pressure: ________________________
7. Reason for Physical Exam: ________________________
8. Overall Impression, Comments: ________________________
9. Mental Health Observations: ________________________
10. Skin: ________________________
11. Skull, Hair, Scalp: ________________________
12. Eyes: ________________________
    Pupil Constriction ________________________
13. Nose, Sinuses: ________________________
14. Ears: ________________________
    Hearing ________________________
15. Mouth, Teeth: ________________________

HOME PHYSICAL EXAM (continued)

16. Throat: ______

17. Neck, Lymph Nodes: ______
Chin to Chest ______

18. Chest, Breasts: ______
Breast Self-Exam (Women) ______

19. Spine: ______

20. Abdomen: ______

21. Genitals: ______

22. Anus: ______
Bowel Movements ______

23. Legs, Arms: ______

24. Hands, Nails: ______

25. Feet, Toenails: ______

26. Lungs, Heart: ______

Additional Comments: ______

Early Detection - continued

screening (see page 32), can identify many conditions while they are still easily treatable.

The home physical exam is an important part of any early detection program. Do the exam in a well-lighted room. Use toys, warm hands and self-confidence to help a child relax. Make the exam a time for fun and intimacy for you and your child.

Tools You'll Need

Doing a good, thorough home physical exam requires only a few tools:

- Penlight or flashlight
- Accurate thermometer
- Tongue depressor. Some people like clean popsicle sticks, but a butter knife or the end of a spoon also works well.
- Clock, stopwatch or watch
- Accurate bathroom scale and a tape measure
- Blood pressure cuff
- Stethoscope

See page 249 for descriptions.

The Exam Itself

In this section, each part of the home physical exam is numbered and described: how to do it, why, what you are looking for, and what to write down.

Vital Signs

Taking the vital signs is the easiest way to measure the life- sustaining functions of the body. Vital signs can tell us much more than simply if a person is alive. The three most essential vital signs are pulse (rate of heart beat), respiration (breath rate), and body temperature. Monitoring blood pressure, height, and weight is also valuable.

It is important to have records of a person's vital signs when the person is well. This will be a standard to compare against when the person falls ill.

1. - 2. Height and Weight

Height and weight, besides being a record of a child's growth, can be useful in diagnosing an illness. Sudden weight loss or gain accompanies some illnesses. Weigh at the same time of day, undressed. Measure height without shoes.

3. Temperature

Temperature, too, can be useful in diagnosis. Normal is 98.6° orally, but varies by individual, so it is important to determine a normal temperature for each person. Temperatures vary with time of day and other factors, so don't worry about minor changes.

Procedure:

Temperatures are commonly taken three ways:

1. Orally - in the mouth under the tongue
2. Axillary - under the armpit
3. Rectally - in the anus (a rectal thermometer is required.)

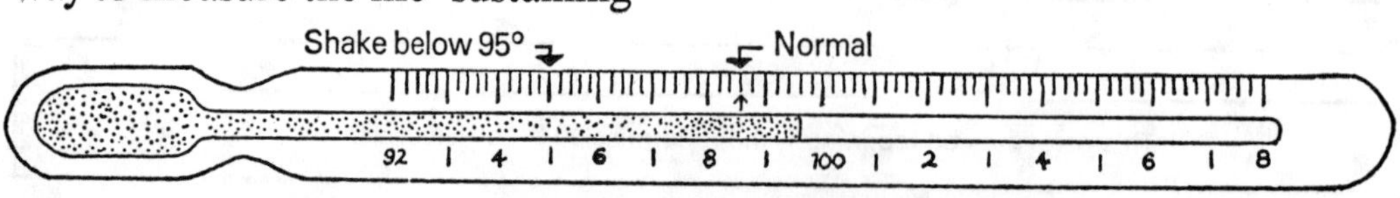

Temperature reading shows 99.6 degrees

To take an **oral temperature**, wash off the bulb, where the mercury is, and the lower part of the thermometer with cool, soapy water or rubbing alcohol.

Hold the thermometer tightly by the end opposite the bulb and "shake it down," to 95° or lower, as if you were trying to shake drops of water off the bulb.

Place the bulb under the tongue and be sure the lips are closed. Have the person breathe through the nose. Keep the thermometer in place for three minutes.

To read a thermometer, note that the thermometer is graduated from 92° degrees to 108° degrees. Each large mark indicates one degree of temperature. Between large marks are five small marks. Each small marks stands for 0.2°.

Read the thermometer in good light. Holding the end opposite the mercury bulb, rotate the thermometer slowly until you can see a silver (sometimes red) ribbon of mercury. The place where this ribbon stops indicates the temperature reading. Write it down, noting the time of day.

Axillary temperatures are less accurate and about 1° cooler than oral, but are safer for small children. Use an oral thermometer and place under the armpit for five minutes. New temperature strips are relatively fast and can be easily held under the arm and then read, but are not always accurate.

Rectal temperatures (1° hotter than oral) are very accurate but can cause injury if done improperly. Hold the rectal thermometer one inch from the silver bulb. Gently insert it no more than one inch and be absolutely sure to hold it right at the anus opening to protect the thermometer from breaking. Hold it in for three minutes.

The temperatures used in this book all refer to oral temperatures. Should you use one of the other methods, be sure to adjust the reading.

Fever

Fever is a symptom, not a disease. A fever is a body temperature that is abnormally high. Normal temperature can range from 97.6° to 99.6° with no cause for concern.

For an adult, fever up to 102° is generally beneficial. The higher temperature is one of your body's ways to fight infection.

Home Treatment

- Any person with a fever should drink more water or other liquids to avoid dehydration.
- Fevers above 103° or that cause discomfort can be reduced using sponging, light loose clothing and aspirin. (Use acetaminophen for children.)
- Retake and record the temperature often, particularly for fevers over 102°.

Fever - continued

When to Call a Health Professional

Fever, by itself, does not present a significant medical problem for adults until it reaches 105° or higher. Any fever of 105° that can not quickly be reduced to 104° or less should be brought to the attention of a health professional. Other guidelines for calling your doctor for fever include:

- High temperature and dry skin, even under the armpits. (Possible heat stroke, see page 191.)
- A fever of 100 ° or higher and a very stiff neck (to rule out meningitis).
- Any fever of 100 ° or higher in an infant under three months old.
- Any fever of 105° that cannot be reduced at least partially by home treatment.
- Any fever that lasts longer than three days.

4. Pulse

Measuring the pulse rate is one simple way to count a person's heartbeats. Contractions of the heart muscles as they force blood throughout the body cause a throbbing in the arteries. The pulse is actually the heartbeat.

A pulse can be taken wherever an artery comes close to the skin surface. Usually it is taken at the wrist, but often it's easier at the neck.

The pulse should be counted after the person has been resting quietly, or for a child, while asleep.

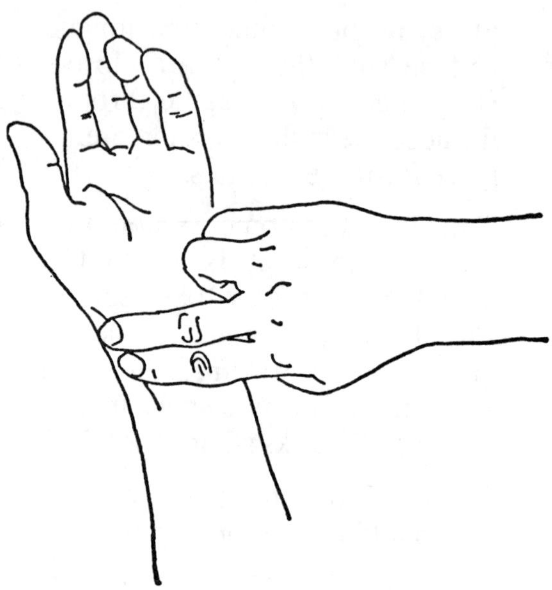

Taking a Pulse Rate

To take the pulse at the wrist, place two fingers against the wrist as shown (not the thumb, you may feel your pulse). Have the person raise the thumb to make a natural

NORMAL RESTING PULSE		NORMAL RESTING RESPIRATION	
Infant-1 yr.	70-150 beats/min.	Newborn	30-80 breaths/min.
6-10 years	70-110 beats/min.	One year	20-40 breaths/min.
Adults	60-100 beats/min.	Age 6	17-22 breaths/min.
		Age 10	12-19 breaths/min.
		Adult	10-20 breaths/min.

pocket for your fingers. Count the beats for 30 seconds, then double the results. The pulse is measured by beats per minute. After you count the pulse, keep your fingers on the artery and feel for regularity. Does the pulse speed up, or slow down or skip beats? Record the rate and regularity.

If it is hard to feel a throbbing at the wrist, place your fingers just below the jawline and to either side of the windpipe to feel the pulse. This is the carotid pulse. Count the beats for 30 seconds and double the result. The pulse rate is the same no matter where you feel it.

Pulse rate rises about ten beats per minute with each degree of fever.

5. Respiration

Respiration rate is how many breaths a person takes in a minute. The best time to count respiration is when the person is resting, perhaps after taking the pulse with fingers still at pulse. The person's breathing is apt to change on seeing you count it.

Count the rise and fall of the chest for one full minute. Also notice whether there is any "sucking-in" beneath the ribs or other abnormality.

Record the respiration rate.

As a person's temperature rises, respiration rates increase.

6. Blood Pressure

Blood pressure is the force of the flowing blood against the walls of the arteries. It is measured in two numbers, for example 120/80. The first number registers *systolic pressure*, the pressure when the heart contracts and pumps the blood through the body. The lower number registers *diastolic pressure*, the pressure between pumps, when the heart is relaxing.

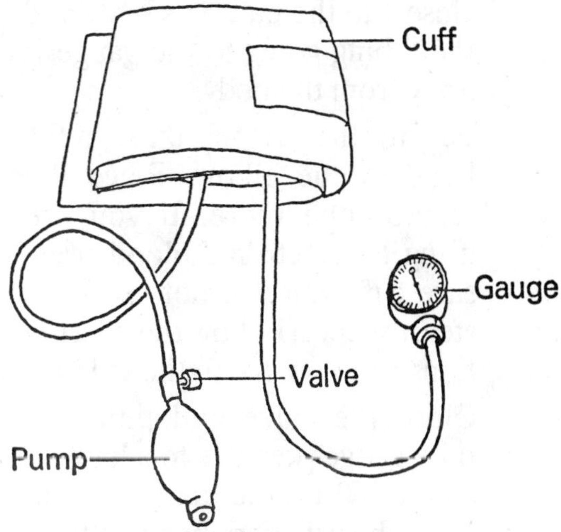

Blood Pressure Cuff

Blood pressure is measured by a blood pressure cuff. Most blood pressure cuffs are for adults and are too large for a child's small arm. When it is necessary to measure a child's blood pressure, your health professional has a child-sized cuff.

Procedure:

- Have your stethoscope ready. The ear pieces of the stethoscope need to point forward into your ears.
- Have the person seated beside a table with a bare arm outstretched and resting on the table. Loosen the valve near the

Blood Pressure - continued

pump by turning it counterclockwise. Deflate the cuff completely.

- Wrap the blood pressure cuff snugly but not too tightly around the person's arm with the lower edge of the cuff one inch above the crease at the elbow. Be sure the tubing going to the bulb is closest to the patient's body and the tubing going to the gauge is away from the body.
- Feel for the person's pulse in the bend of the elbow. Place the stethoscope there. If you are using an electronic blood pressure cuff, you will not need the stethoscope. (Follow the instructions that come with the cuff.)
- Close the valve and pump to raise gauge pressure to a level of about 160 on the gauge. If you hear a heartbeat right away, then pump it up higher. **Immediately** loosen the valve a bit so the needle starts dropping slowly. Don't leave the cuff pumped up; the pressure hurts.
- Watch the dial as you listen with the stethoscope. You will soon hear a tapping sound --- the pulse sounds. The number on the dial when you first hear the pulse sounds is the systolic pressure. A typical systolic pressure might range between 100 and 125.
- As air continues to escape from the cuff, the sounds will eventually disappear.
- Note where the needle is when the sounds disappear. This is the diastolic pressure. A typical reading would be 70 to 80.
- Open the valve completely, let the pressure fall to zero, and remove the cuff.
- Record the reading, systolic/diastolic (125/80 for above example).

If you need to recheck your measurement, be sure the cuff is entirely deflated before inflating it again. Otherwise, your new measurement will be inaccurate. If you cannot get a clear reading after two tries, use the other arm, or wait five full minutes.

Normal blood pressure for an adult under age 60 should be under 140/90. Report anything over that to a health professional.

Taking a blood pressure reading correctly requires practice. If you want further instruction and practice, review the procedure with your health professional.

High Blood Pressure

You have high blood pressure, or hypertension, if your blood pressure reading is over 140/90. It is quite possible to have high blood pressure without being aware of it; the first symptom may be sudden death. That is why a regular blood pressure check is so important. Shortness of breath, nosebleeds, headaches, and dizziness can be other warning signs. These are usually present only when high blood pressure becomes very severe. In most cases, high blood pressure is a lifelong condition. However, if you have it, you can control it.

Home Treatment

- Learn to measure your blood pressure. Keeping a record of your blood pressure will help you determine if your efforts to keep it down are really working.
- Lose weight. Weight reduction decreases the workload on your heart.
- Eat less salt. See page 225.
- Eat less fat. See page 223.
- Exercise for health. Regular aerobic exercise will gradually lower your blood pressure.
- Please stop smoking. See Resource #Q1 on page 270.

When to Call a Health Professional

If your self-care plan does not succeed in reducing your blood pressure.

7. Reason for Physical

Write here why the exam is being done: person is ill, or routine check.

8. Overall Impression, Comments

Include here a brief description of the person: attitude toward exam, general appearance, overall condition.

9. Mental Health Observations

Note the person's general outlook (anxious, cheerful, depressed, etc.). Describe any self-stimulating behaviors in children such as thumb-sucking, scratching, hair-sucking, clinging to a favorite toy or blanket, or head-banging. Going back to a behavior that has been given up earlier is of particular concern. Other behaviors or symptoms of mental health problems should be noted (see page 232).

10. Skin

Look at the skin for overall tone and color. Look for moles, warts, bruises, cuts, boils, lumps, rashes, birthmarks, insect bites, etc. Become familiar with the skin, so the next time you examine the person, you can note any changes. The first time write down the size and location of everything you observe. Better yet, draw a picture and mark any areas of concern. In subsequent exams, note any changes. Record the condition of the skin: dry, oily, sweaty, etc.

11. Skull, Hair, Scalp

Learn what is normal. Feel the skull for lumps, bumps, or tender areas. Check the hair for cleanliness, shininess and bounce. When normally healthy hair looks dull, make a note to mention it at your next doctor visit. Look for bald spots on the scalp, flakiness, or dandruff. Check for lice or other insects.

12. Eyes

Check for crustiness or flaking on eyebrows or eyelashes. Look for matter, bloodshot eyes, or excessive tearing. See page 70 for diagnosing these eye problems.

Pupil Constriction Test

Use to determine how a person's eyes ordinarily constrict, and after a head injury. In a darkened room, use a penlight. Direct the light from the right side into the right pupil. Watch the pupil constrict. Direct the light from the left side to the left pupil. Observe several times. Pupils should constrict to about the same size, at about the same rate. Some people normally have different-sized pupils. The importance is in establishing what is normal for each individual.

For a simple pupil constriction test on a child when there is no injury, play "anybody home?" Instruct your child to cover her eyes, then put hands down. Look at the pupils as soon as her hands are lowered.

13. Nose, Sinuses

Check to see that the person breathes through both nostrils. Examine discharge, if any. Write down the color, and whether it is thick or thin. To better see the inside of the nose, gently push it in and up. Use a penlight to examine the tissues inside the nose. Note whether they are pink and healthy-looking or gray, blue, red, or inflamed. In a child, look for sign of an object in the nose. If there is a foul odor from the nose, make a note of it. See Object in Nose, page 130, if any of these symptoms are found.

Apply firm pressure on the sinuses to test for tenderness.

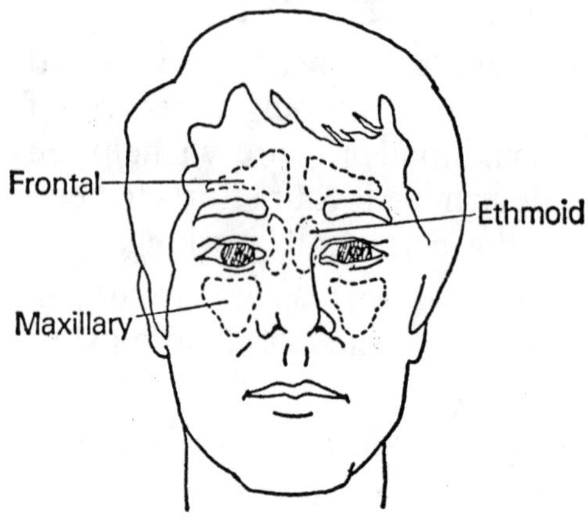

Sinus Cavities

14. Ears

Check the outer ear and behind the ear for crustiness, and wiggle the outer ear to test for tenderness. Use a penlight to look in the ear canal for wax. Gently pull the pinna (lobe) back and slightly down to see into the canal more clearly. Note if the wax is thin and runny, thick, brown, black, or whatever. Note, too, if there is a foul odor to the ear.

Your doctor uses an otoscope to examine your ears. You, too, can use an otoscope to monitor redness in the ear. The Earscope described on page 248, is inexpensive, comes with an instruction booklet and can become a useful tool, particularly for families with frequent ear problems. Ask your physician to show you how to do an ear exam and what to look for.

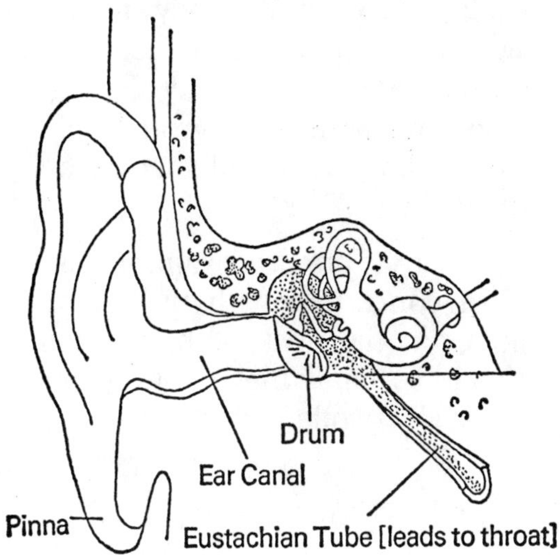

Ear

Hearing Test

The following simple test is a very rough check of hearing. Any possible problem discovered with this test should be thoroughly investigated by a health professional.

Use a clock, watch, or some other object which makes a stable, quiet sound. Hold the clock out of sight some distance from one side of the person's head. Slowly move closer. Ask the person to tell you when the ticking is first heard. Repeat for the other ear. The sound should be heard at about the same distance away from each ear.

If you suspect hearing problems in your child, ask a simple question such as, "Do you want to go the movie?" Try not to use a question that may be normally ignored, such as "Ready for your bath?" or "Would you pick up your toys?"

15. Mouth, Teeth

Using a penlight, check inside the mouth for sores or white spots on the tongue, cheeks, or lips. Look at the teeth and gums. Healthy gums are pink, sometimes grayish, firm and strong. They grow tightly around each tooth. Record any tenderness, puffiness or bleeding in the gums or if the seal around the base of each tooth appears to be pulling away. See page 205 for information on bleeding gums.

Examine the teeth for black or brown spots or holes (possible cavities). Check to see if the teeth are clean or if there is obvious plaque. For a discussion of plaque, see page 199. Note new arrivals of teeth for children.

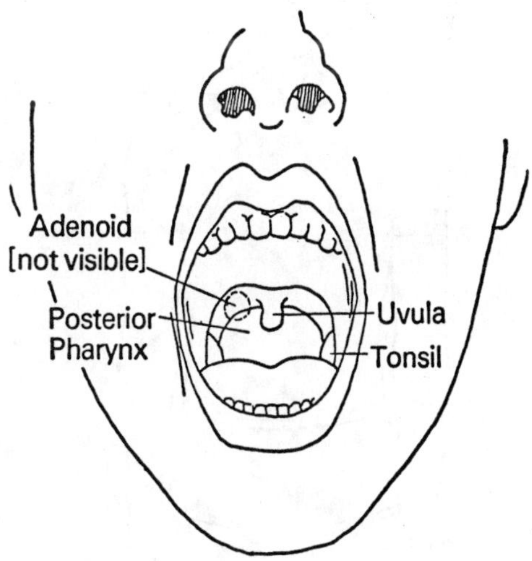

Mouth and Throat

Mouth, Teeth - continued

16. Throat

Have the person open the mouth as wide as possible. If necessary, push the tongue down with the end of a spoon or a butter knife to let you see way back in the throat. Put the spoon or depressor only as far back as the high point on the tongue. Having a small child "pant like a puppy when he's hot" sometimes helps.

Using a penlight, check for swollen or bright red tonsils (if they are there). Healthy throat tissue is pink and moist. Note anything red, swollen, white or yellow. Notice if there is yellow or white mucus draining down the back of the throat (the pharynx).

17. Neck, Lymph Nodes

Check the neck for swollen lymph nodes and for flexibility. The lymph system acts as a filter for infection, destroying bacteria brought to the nodes by white blood cells. Lymph nodes are located throughout the body and will swell when there is an infection in a nearby part of the body. For example, the node at the groin would swell if there was an infected cut on the thigh.

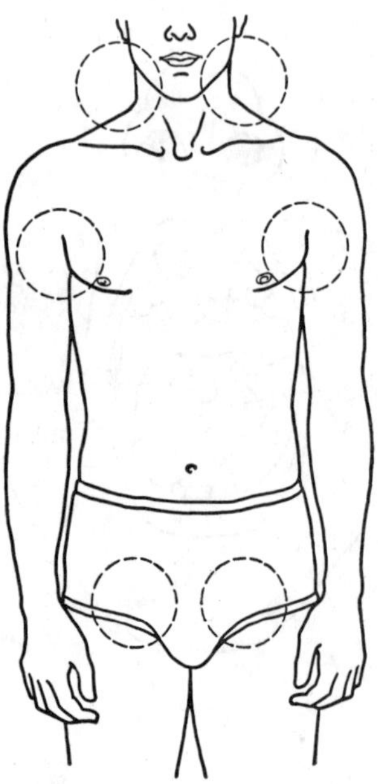

Lymph Nodes of the Body

In the home physical exam, you are most concerned with the lymph nodes in the neck, although you should certainly make note of any unusually swollen node.

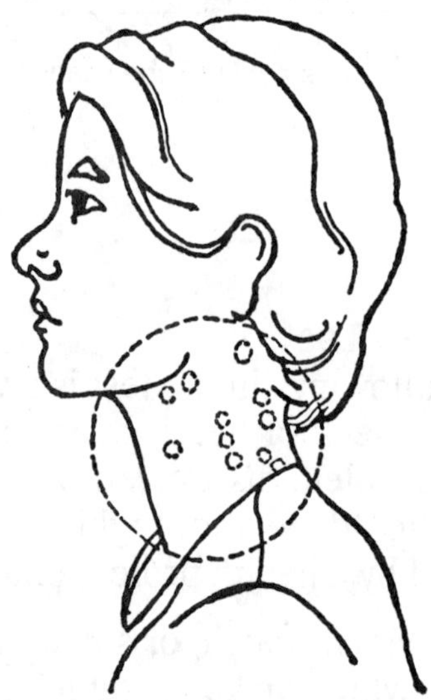

Lymph Nodes of the Neck

To examine the lymph nodes in the neck, place your hand directly under the person's left jaw. Have the person relax, then tilt the head slightly to the left. Start under the chin and feel gently with the fingertips for little lumps, the lymph nodes. Work up to under the ear and then do the same for the right side. Also work down, from the neck to shoulder, using the illustration as a guide. On a healthy adult, you won't feel the nodes. With a minor infection, the nodes may enlarge to the size of lima beans. Children's lymph nodes, however, may swell up enormously with an infection and not shrink for several weeks. History of past infections and knowing what's normal for your child are important in this case.

The neck should also be examined for any unusual lumps or bumps. Cysts on the neck are fairly common in babies and young children. A cyst is an enclosed pouch or sac of skin, often filled with mucus or oil-like material. Cysts are not serious, but need to be reported to your health professional at the next visit.

Any enlarged lymph node or unusual lump which persists over two months should be reported to a health professional.

Also check the neck for flexibility. Ask the person to touch chin to chest. If it cannot be done easily, this should be investigated.

18. Chest, Breasts

Look at the chest for symmetry (same on both sides) and to see how the person normally breathes --- with chest or abdomen. Listen to breathing sounds; harshness, irregularity, raspiness, whistling, dry crackling, or gurgling sounds are signs to discuss with your health professional.

Women over age 18 need to examine their breasts monthly. See breast self-exam on page 135.

See page 120 for information regarding breasts on infants.

19. Spine

In your home physical of a child, you'll be checking for any obvious curvature of the spine. Curvature can occur at any time during the growth years and the spine should be checked at each home physical. Curvature is most frequent in adolescent girls, and is usually caused by poor posture. Babies, before walking, have very straight spines. Normal curves develop after the child begins walking.

To check the spine, have the person bend over and touch the floor. Place a dot of ink on each vertebra that sticks out. When the person stands, the dots should form a straight line. If not, report it to your health professional. These problems can usually be corrected when detected early.

More information on special problems of the spine is in the chapter on Back and Neck Pain, page 47.

20. Abdomen

To check the abdomen, have the person lie down, hands resting on chest, knees slightly bent. The person should be undressed at least to the hairline of the pelvis. Make the person as comfortable as possible by putting a pillow under the head

Abdomen - continued

and keeping the room comfortably warm.

Notice whether the person's abdomen is normally flat or bulged out. Babies and young children often have pot-bellies. As the child grows, the abdomen no longer sticks out.

Mentally divide the abdomen into four quadrants.

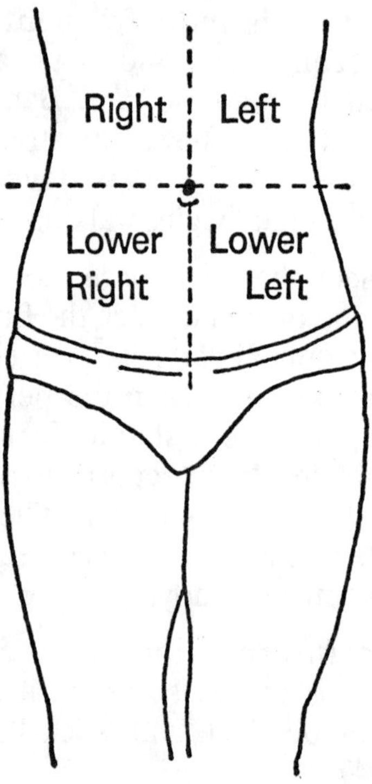

Abdominal Quadrants

Feel the abdomen in all four quadrants, using hands as shown in the following illustration.

Press gently, asking if there is pain, and watching for flinching. Normally you will not be able to feel any organs. Note if you do feel any masses. Also make a note of any hard or rigid surfaces. A hard smooth mass at the center of the bottom of the abdomen is probably only a full bladder.

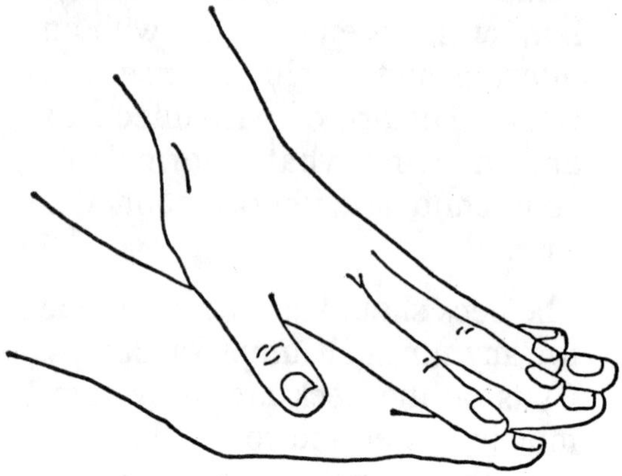

Hand Position

Inguinal hernias are those found in the groin, most frequently in males. To check for an inguinal hernia in males, look at the area just above the scrotum, and several inches to the side of the base of the penis for any soft or bulging areas. This can be seen most easily if the person is coughing, laughing, or crying. See page 159.

21. Genitals

Genital examinations are important and should be done on a regular basis.

For females, see page 138. For males, see page 154. For infants, see page 121.

22. Anus

The anus is the opening where the bowel movement or stool comes out. This area is usually darker in color than the surrounding skin and wrinkles together when closed. It stretches to let a bowel movement out and then closes again.

Check for cuts or sores near the anus. Also check for swelling. Bright red blood in the stools usually indicates small tears in the skin of the anus, hemorrhoids or, less often, other more significant problems. These should be discussed with a professional.

A black or tarry stool can be a sign of internal bleeding and should be brought to the immediate attention of your health professional. Black, but not tarry, stools can also be caused by iron supplements and Pepto-Bismol, so consider that before scheduling a visit.

You should know what the regular pattern of bowel movements is for each family member. Make a note of it on the exam record. Remember that "regular" does not mean daily. See Constipation, page 36.

23. Legs, Arms

The legs and arms should each be of equal length. Check to see if one shoulder blade is higher than the other. Many people have one limb slightly shorter than the other. It is important to know what is normal for each person.

Look for swollen joints, especially the ankles. Move the arms and legs in every possible direction to test for flexibility. Record any stiffness or pain on movement.

For walking children, check to see that the child walks normally without shuffling, staggering, or discomfort. Young children often have knock-knees, but usually outgrow this in a couple of years.

24. Hands, Nails

Examine the hands for calluses, warts, and sores. See whether both hands are about the same size and opposing fingers the same length. Nails should be clean and trimmed and not brittle or peeling.

Newborn babies have very strong grips. This is a reflex which disappears as a baby grows. You should check for a good firm grip in everyone. Also become familiar with the size and shape of fingers so any later thickening or clubbing will be recognized.

25. Feet, Toenails

Both feet should be similar in length and toes, too, should match. When the person is standing, there should be some open space between the ball of the foot and heel. This is the arch. However, little babies all have "flat feet." This is caused by a fat pad that disappears with growth. Usually even quite "flat" feet aren't a problem unless the person has discomfort when walking.

Look between the toes for any sign of infection such as athlete's foot. See page 104. Check the nails for brittleness, peeling, or infection.

Check the feet for sore spots or calluses, for unusual lumps, and for plantar warts on the sole of the foot. See Warts, page 117.

Feet, Toenails - continued

Move the legs and feet to check for flexibility or pain on movement.

26. Lung and Heart Sounds

You need a stethoscope for this exam. Place the ear pieces of the stethoscope into the ears, pointing forward. Place the diaphragm of the stethoscope on the person's back. Listen all over the back above the waistline to the right and left of the spine wherever you feel ribs. Learn what normal breathing sounds are for that person, so you can recognize when there is a change from normal. Ask the person to take a deep breath through the mouth and exhale slowly.

Repeat this process, with the stethoscope on the chest. If the person is a hairy-chested male, you will hear the hairs scratch against the stethoscope. With a fleshy or heavily-muscled person you may not be able to hear any breath sounds.

Next listen for the heartbeat. Place the stethoscope near the nipple about two inches left of the middle of the chest. You will hear a "lub-dub" sound. Count the heartbeats, which are the same as the pulse. On a weakened or severely ill person, this may be the only way to get a heart rate. If you notice a sound other than normal, it may be a possible heart murmur and should be recorded and reported to a health professional at your next visit. A heart murmur has a sssh! sound, but is really rather difficult for the layperson to recognize. Learn to distinguish normal from abnormal sounds.

Fatigue

Fatigue is a feeling of chronic tiredness. It is often caused by depression, worry, boredom, or a lack of exercise. Prevention and home treatment are the same:

- Alternate exercise and rest.
- Eat well. See page 220.
- Sleep well. See page 237.
- Learn about dealing with depression on page 236.
- Limit tranquilizers and cold/allergy medications.
- Cut back on caffeine, nicotine, alcohol, and television.

Call a health professional if you have unexplained muscle weakness or if the fatigue prevents you from doing your usual activities.

Annual Physicals: Who Needs Them?

Generally, annual physical exams are over-rated. They are expensive, time-consuming and relatively ineffective in detecting treatable illnesses. They also create many "false positives" which require still more time, money and worry to check-out.

A better approach is one that combines your own home physical exams with selected screenings and exams scheduled periodically according to age and sex. Use the "Recommended Tests for Healthy People" as a guide. See page 32.

Doctor Visits

While periodic home physicals are not a substitute for a professional examination, they can provide information which will make that professional exam more worthwhile.

By knowing what's involved in a home exam, you'll know better what's going on in an office physical exam. Children who become accustomed to pleasant home exams will be less anxious during a professional exam. You will be better able to ask good questions and to understand what your health professional tells you.

To make the most of any professional visit there are a few things to remember:

- Before a professional visit, do a home exam, so you can report any changes from normal.
- Complete "The Healthwise Approach" form on page 1 and the "Ask-The-Doctor Checklist" on page 2.
- Write down any other questions and go through them systematically. If you do not understand what your health professional is saying, ask questions.
- Get clear answers to your questions before you leave the office.
- If an illness is diagnosed, ask what, if anything, you can do to speed recovery. Is bed rest necessary? Will steam help? Many things besides a shot or a prescription can help a problem.
- If a prescription is given, be sure you understand how to use the drug. Also ask about possible side effects, and what to do if they occur. Ask if there may be a less expensive, but comparable generic substitute.
- Be sure you understand all recommended treatments and why they should help. Also, if something sounds impossible, tell the health professional. "There's no way I can stay in bed all day with three kids!" Together you can work out a suitable solution.
- Ask about restrictions on activity and how long the restrictions are necessary.
- Try to get a picture of what to expect. "Jennie should feel better in two days, but keep her in bed for three full days and on the medication for ten days."
- After the visit, call if something unexpected happens.
- If you are concerned about the accuracy of a diagnosis, talk it over with your health professional or ask for a second opinion or consultation. Most physicians will agree readily.
- If the visit is for a child's examination, you may wish to take with you:
  - immunization records
  - a urine sample in a clean container
  - any abnormal stool or vomit (if that is the reason for the visit).

By making home physical exams a routine part of your health care, you will learn a great deal about your body and get more out of every doctor visit.

RECOMMENDED TESTS for EARLY DETECTION

Test	Years Between Last Low Risk Test - By Age*							Comments
	1-5	6-17	18-39	40-49	50-59	60-69	70+	
History/physical exam, p.16	1-2	3-4	5-10	3-5	2-3	1-2	1	
Blood pressure, p.20	age 3	3-4	2-3	2-3	2-3	1-2	1	Monthly if last test was high.
Vision test	age 3	---	---	5**	5**	5	5	With glasses, every 2-3 years.
Glaucoma test	---	---	---	---	5**	5	5	
Tuberculin skin test, p.267	---	---	---	---	---	---	---	Only if exposed or high risk.
Hearing test	age 3	---	---	---	10**	5	5	At birth if high risk.
Test for blood in stool	---	---	---	---	5**	5	5	Bowel cancer
Sigmoidoscopy	---	---	---	---	10**	5	5	Bowel cancer
Urinalysis	age 4	---	P	P	10	5-10	5	Diabetes, liver, kidney, UTI P = only if pregnant.
Hematocrit	---	---	P	P	---	---	---	P = only if pregnant.
Blood glucose	---	---	P	P	---	---	---	Diabetes. P = only if pregnant.
Cholesterol, p.223	---	---	5-10	5-10	5-10	5-10	5-10	Heart disease
Women Only								
Pap smear, p.139	---	---	3	3	3	---	---	Yearly until 2 normal exams.
Breast self-exam, p.135	---	---	†	†	†	†	†	†Monthly
Breast exam, p.138	---	---	---	1-2	1-2	1-2	1-2	
Mammography, p.138	---	---	‡age 35	‡1-2	1-2	1-2	age 71,74	‡If family history of cancer.
Rubella antibody, p.134	---	---	Once	---	---	---	---	Prior to pregnancy.
Men Only								
Testicular self-exam, p.154	---	---	†	†	†	†	†	†Monthly
Prostate exam, p.160	---	---	---	5**	5**	5**	---	

*For high - risk individuals, consult your doctor. **Experts are uncertain of the effectiveness of routine testing for this age group.
Adapted from: Guide to Clinical Preventive Services, USDHHS, 1989.

A great step towards independence
is a good-humored stomach.
Seneca

Chapter 3

Abdominal Problems

Sooner or later some form of stomach pain affects us all. Although most abdominal problems are minor and require only our casual attention, other stomachaches can be caused by serious, life-threatening conditions. Between the green apple stomachache and the trauma of acute appendicitis lie a number of common stomach problems for which appropriate home care can best speed recovery.

Abdominal pain usually results from some disorder in the digestive system. When the stomach and intestines are irritated by infections, food poisons, ulcers, or obstructions, their functions of digestion, water and nutrient absorption, and waste removal are disrupted.

By closely observing these changes and by examining general symptoms such as pain, temperature, and vital signs, a person can better understand and deal with abdominal problems.

Whenever you are worried about an abdominal pain, first go through the home physical exam discussed on page 15. Remember, it is the whole person you are worried about, not just the person's stomach. The exam may uncover some important information about the problem. Next focus on the abdominal area. Use the abdominal pain history and exam questions on page 34 to find out as much as you can about the problem. Be sure to write down anything that may be helpful later in describing the problem to a health professional.

If your patient is a very small child, you may not be able to get good answers to many of the questions. In such cases, added caution is always advised. Parents who know their children and are aware of the most likely causes of bellyache will

Abdominal Pain: History and Exam

- When did the pain first appear?
  - Has it been constant, increasing, crampy, off and on?
  - What is the location of the pain? Has the location changed?
  - What is the "quality" of the pain? (sharp, burning, dull)
  - Is it painful to urinate?
- Is the patient's skin clammy or does the patient appear to be in shock?
- What are the patient's temperature and pulse as compared to her normal rates? (Retake every few hours.)
- Does the abdomen appear unusual in size, shape or rigidity? Is it tender to the touch?
- Is there any blood or unusual color in the urine? Urinating normal amounts?
- Is the patient's saliva sticky? Slippery? Dry mouth?
- Has the patient vomited? Or been nauseated? How much? How often?
- Has the patient had recent contact with anyone else with similar pain? Or similar symptoms?
- Has the patient consumed an unusual amount or type of food or drink?
- Has the patient eaten any unrefrigerated meats recently?
- Has the patient sustained any recent sharp blow or injury to the stomach?
- Has the patient been under unusually heavy stress lately?
- Has the patient appeared nervous or tense?
- Stools? Diarrhea? Constipation? Tarry?

be able to figure out what's going on.

Remember though, the cause of abdominal pain is sometimes very serious and difficult for even a health professional to diagnose. Any time abdominal pain is either severe or persistent, or increases over several hours, a health professional should be called. Cramps due to gas can be very painful. However, a doctor doesn't need to be seen unless the cramps are not diminished by the passage of gas, stools, or several hours of restful observation.

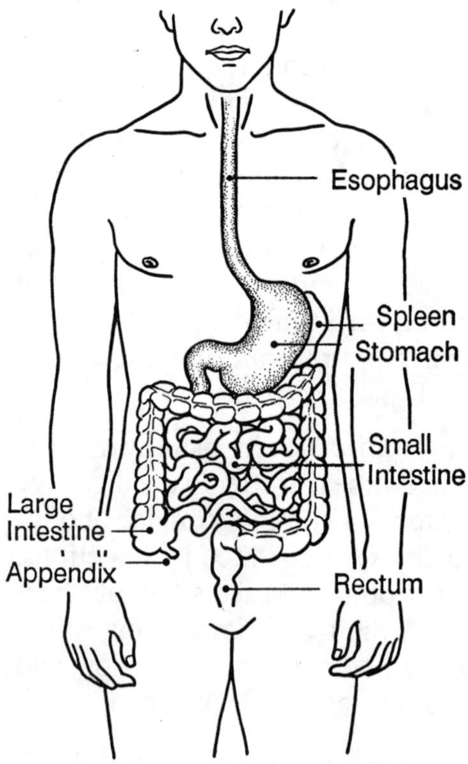

Digestive Tract

If any doubt exists regarding the cause or severity of the pain, a phone call to your health professional is strongly recommended. She can evaluate your observations and be readily available should the conditions worsen.

Many of the common causes of abdominal pain and other stomach problems are discussed throughout this section. (For Colic, see Chapter 9.) The information provided, together with some common sense and the answers to the history questions on page 34, should give you a good basis for safely handling a stomachache at home or for effectively relating the problem to a health professional.

Appendicitis

The appendix is a small, apparently useless sac extending from the large bowel. The digestive fluids circulate through it and cleanse it of any bacteria. However, if its opening becomes plugged, the bacteria can build up and cause a serious infection known as appendicitis.

Sometimes the opening is plugged by objects passing through the intestines --- pebbles, seeds, toothpicks, small bones, and clumps of hair. More often, the appendix becomes blocked by its own twisting or by small, hard bits of bowel material.

The real danger lies in the appendix bursting. That spreads the infection to other vital organs which, in turn, can cause serious problems. Fortunately, that isn't going to happen five minutes after the first pain. Usually the pain builds up for 12 hours or more before an appendix bursts. Some people have very high tolerance to pain however, and may not notice it for several hours after it begins.

Appendicitis is not common in very young children. However, since small children cannot describe their pain well, their cases often become quite serious before they are diagnosed.

Home Treatment

- Perform the basic home physical exam including vital signs. See home physical exam, page 15.
- Watch for and record any of the following symptoms:
  - Abdominal pain preceded by a period of nausea and loss of appetite. Although the pain may first be very general or seem to come from any point in the abdomen, it will usually move to the right lower quadrant as it increases.
  - Vomiting or increasing nausea.
  - Low grade fever of 100°-101°.
  - Notice any bowel movements. Diarrhea is rarely present with appendicitis and can be a good clue that the pain is due to some other cause. Good bowel movements are very common with appendicitis.
- Keep the patient quiet and in a comfortable position.

Appendicitis - continued

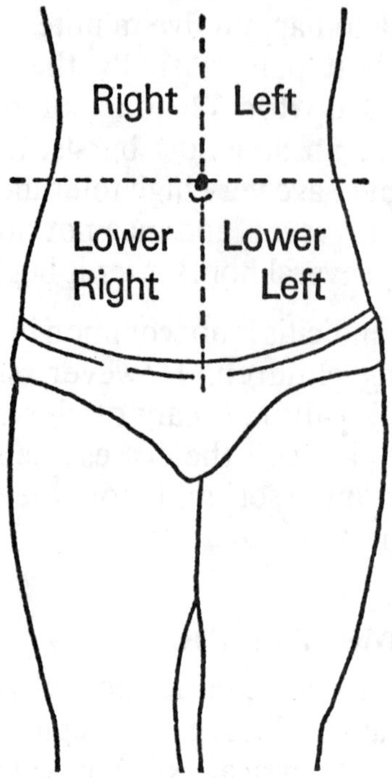

Abdominal Quadrants

- Try to identify or rule out other sources of abdominal pain such as food poisoning, page 41, gastroenteritis, page 42, or overeating.
- *DO NOT* give laxatives. They can stimulate the intestine and cause the appendix to rupture sooner.
- *DO NOT* give strong pain medication. Since the location and intensity of pain are diagnostic clues, the heavy use of aspirin or stronger pain reducers may hide important information.
- *DO NOT* apply heat to the area.

When to Call a Health Professional

- If any of the above symptoms cause you to suspect appendicitis, you should call your health professional. The call is a must if the pain is in the lower right quadrant or is increasing steadily. The call will alert your health professional to the possible problem should assistance become necessary.

Constipation

Constipation is the passage of hard, dry stools. If you pass soft stools, you are not constipated regardless of how "regularly" or "irregularly" you may pass them. The need for a bowel movement every day is a misconception. Some people pass stools every three to five days. As long as the stools are soft, such frequencies do not indicate constipation.

One of the chief causes of constipation is lack of time. The person who has had trouble with constipation should set aside a time each day, or as frequently as is normally needed, to go to the bathroom. Your bowels send you signals when there is a need to pass a movement. However, if you don't take time to heed the signal, after a while the urge will pass. Since the large intestine draws water from the stools, the stools will eventually become dry and difficult to pass. This postponing the inevitable is an all too frequent occurrence with children. Parents should be aware of their children's bowel habits, but try to relax and not make a big fuss about them. Stress can cause or add to a constipation problem. In children, stress related to toilet training may contribute to constipation problems.

Prevention

Diet is very important in constipation. Too few fruits, juices and clear liquids can create the problem. Pregnant women are especially susceptible to constipation and should pay close attention to the amount of liquids in their diets. Susceptible people should increase the fiber in their diets by eating more whole wheat bread, bran cereals, apples, and celery. Regular exercise may also help prevent constipation.

Home Treatment

Ages 0-1:

- Add water to formula or reduce breast feeding and add water.
- One teaspoon to two ounces of juice per feeding.
- Strained prunes; one and a half to three tablespoons daily.
- If constipation persists after three days of the above treatment, do home physical exam to look for other possible problems.

Ages 2-12:

- Arrange for regular, relaxed time for bowel movements.
- Add more fruits, vegetables, and liquids to the diet.
- Add lots of water --- especially in the morning.
- Avoid laxatives if possible. Very few children need them and they can cause a laxative habit if overused. See Laxatives, page 257. Never use a laxative if abdominal pain is present. See Appendicitis, page 35.
- If a very acute episode occurs with hard painful stools, a mild stool softener or laxative may be used --- but very sparingly. Ask your pharmacist to suggest one or review the examples on page 258. Discuss with the child any fears or stress related to toilet training or the passage of stools.

Adults:

- Set aside relaxed times for bowel movements.
- Add juice or fruits.
- Drink two to four extra glasses of water per day, especially in the morning.
- Avoid laxatives if possible. If necessary, use a stool softener or very mild laxative. Do not use mineral oil or any other laxative regularly. Mineral oil slows the body's absorption of vitamins. See Laxatives, page 258.

When to Call a Health Professional

- If constipation persists after the above treatment is followed for three days for babies or one week for adults.
- If dark blood is seen in stools. Small amounts of bright red blood are usually caused by slight tearing as the stool is pushed through the anus. This should stop when the constipation is controlled. More than a few streaks of bright red blood

Constipation - continued

should be discussed with a health professional.

- If constipation and major changes in bowel movement patterns occur and persist without apparent reason.

Dehydration

Dehydration is the excessive loss of water from the body. A continuous supply of water is required by all living cells in your body. When you stop drinking water or when you lose large amounts of fluids through diarrhea or sweat, body cells reabsorb fluid from the blood and other stores of water. If dehydration is allowed to continue, so much of the blood's fluids can be reabsorbed that the blood vessels collapse in vascular shock. Death then follows very quickly.

Because dehydration is extremely dangerous for infants and small children, it is important to watch closely for its early signs if vomiting, diarrhea, or both, limit fluid intake. Fortunately, there are several good ways to test for dehydration. If you try these tests when your child is normal, you will be better able to judge the test results.

Dehydration Test

- Feel the child's saliva. If it's wet and slippery, that's good. If it becomes dry and sticky, it could be an early sign of dehydration.
- A second test for the observant parent is to watch how much urine the child passes. A dehydrated baby will have darker, more concentrated urine and a diaper that is much less wet than normal.
- Look at the child. As dehydration progresses to more critical stages, the child's overall appearance will change. A dehydrated child will look sick and have "sunken eyes."
- If, when you pinch the skin on a child's stomach, it feels doughy and doesn't snap right back, dehydration may have progressed to a very serious level.
- A dehydrated child's pulse rate will be faster than normal.

Home Treatment

Treatment of mild dehydration is simple. First, stop the fluid loss. Then, restore lost fluids as soon as possible.

- If the child is nauseated or vomiting, stop all food and liquids for two to four hours to rest the stomach.
- As soon as vomiting is controlled, give clear liquids, e.g., water or bouillon, a little at a time until the stomach will accept larger amounts. You may start by giving the child one teaspoon of liquid every ten minutes for one to two hours before increasing the amount. Don't give too much at one time.
- Use Tylenol to reduce fever. Aspirin may irritate the stomach. Avoid aspirin altogether for children.

- A potassium salt electrolyte solution or a drink like Gatorade may be advantageously substituted for water since it will restore some of the salts lost with the fluids. See page 253 for directions for the solution.
- Continue to check the signs of dehydration for improvement or changes for the worse.

Since lots of fluids are needed to speed recovery from most minor illnesses, even mild dehydration can extend the length and severity of common health problems. Dehydration prevention and treatment should be considered any time anyone becomes ill.

When to Call a Health Professional

- If the child cannot hold down the small amounts of liquid given.
- If a sick, sunken eye appearance develops.
- If there has been little or no urine for 12 hours.
- If the skin is doughy.
- If you cannot stop the fluid loss, the child may have to be hospitalized and given fluids intravenously.
- If temperature of 102° develops and persists more than 24 hours.

Diarrhea

Diarrhea is the discharge of watery stools, usually repeated several times a day. The presence of mildly loose stools at regular bowel movement times is not usually considered diarrhea and is not a cause of great concern.

Diarrhea is caused when the intestines become over-stimulated to empty themselves and push the stools through before the water in them can be reabsorbed by the body. Usually the stimulation is caused by some infection or irritation in the digestive tract. Since the body can best heal the infection if the intestine is empty, the initial effect of diarrhea can aid healing.

Diarrhea in Children

Diarrhea is a frequent occurrence for infants and small children. An infant's still-developing digestive system will sometimes not tolerate excessive amounts of fruits, juice or even milk. Although food-intolerance diarrhea is upsetting and certainly messy, it usually presents no cause for concern. As long as the child appears healthy and is growing normally, no real treatment of occasional diarrhea is required.

However, when the diarrhea becomes excessive, any problem foods must be found and temporarily eliminated from the diet. Of course, food intolerance is not the only cause of diarrhea in infants. Organic disease such as gastroenteritis or flu must also be suspected.

Because of a child's small size and high need for fluids, excessive diarrhea can quickly dehydrate an infant's body. Although untreated dehydration can be very serious, careful observation of the child's appearance and fluid intake can

Diarrhea - continued

prevent possible complications. See discussion on dehydration, page 38.

Diarrhea in Adults

Diarrhea in adults is often brought on by nervousness, tension or emotional problems. It's your body's way of getting you to calm down. See page 212, for a discussion on how to cope with stress.

Acute diarrhea can be accompanied by abdominal discomfort and periodic cramping pain that is relieved by passing diarrhea. Should other pain develop or the discomfort increase, it may signal a more serious abdominal problem. In such a case, a call to your physician is advised. She can help you decide if a visit is needed.

Chronic or intermittent diarrhea lasting over weeks or months may be caused by one of many life-threatening conditions which require professional help and laboratory tests to identify. Prolonged diarrhea also leads to a secondary problem of malnutrition and fluid loss since nutrients are passed before the body can absorb them.

Home Treatment

- PUT YOUR STOMACH AT REST.
- Clear liquids only, e.g., water, bouillon, apple juice, for the first 24 hours.
- No milk products for three days.
- For small babies, temporarily substitute water for milk or formula in the diet. (An ounce of water at a time until the stomach has settled.) After several feedings, milk or diluted formula may be reintroduced. Breast milk feeding should be reduced too. A nursing mother may have to express her milk for a time.
- Bed rest if possible --- reduce activities.
- Mild foods can be added the next day.
- Spicy foods, fruit, alcohol, and coffee should be avoided until 48 hours after all symptoms have disappeared.
- Since diarrhea may sometimes speed recovery, antidiarrheal drugs should be avoided for the first six hours and then used only if cramping or discomfort continues. See discussion on antidiarrheal drugs, page 251.

When to Call a Health Professional

- If the diarrhea is tarry or bloody. If the blood is bright red and there isn't much, it probably is only a scratch in the rectal area.
- If the diarrhea does not improve after 24 hours of clear liquids only.
- If mild diarrhea continues intermittently for over one week without obvious cause.
- If symptoms of dehydration or other abdominal problems are present.
- For infants under six months old, you should discuss any diarrhea problem with your health professional.

- If abdominal pain or severe discomfort accompanies diarrhea and is not immediately relieved by the passage of gas or diarrhea.
- If accompanied by a fever over 102°.

Food Poisoning

Two million Americans per year are victims of food poisoning. Most never know it. They attribute their symptoms of nausea, vomiting, diarrhea, and severe pain to a sudden case of stomach flu.

Bacteria are always present in the air and some always get to any food we eat. Fortunately, bacteria usually present no problem in themselves. However, at temperature between 40° and 140°, the bacteria thrive and grow rapidly. They grow fastest on unrefrigerated meats and pastries (custards, whipped cream, etc.) and produce a poison or toxin which causes an acute inflammation of the intestines. The violence of the illness varies with the amount of toxin eaten and with individual susceptibility.

Most food poisoning occurs during the summer when picnickers eat unrefrigerated meats, or on special occasions when cold cuts, turkey, dressing, sauces, and other foods are not kept cold (under 40°). Other serious problems arise if foods are not prepared properly during home canning activities. If any bacteria survive the cooking, it may grow and produce toxin in the can or jar.

The symptoms of food poisoning do not begin immediately; 3-36 hours may pass before the onset of the symptoms. Illness may last from 12 hours to two days for common food poisoning.

Botulism, although rare, is fatal in 65% of cases. It is generally caused by improper home canning methods for low acid foods like beans or corn. Symptoms include blurred vision, inability to swallow, and progressive difficulty in breathing.

Prevention

- Follow the 2-40-140 Rule. Don't eat meats, dressing or sauces that have been kept between 40° and 140° for more than two hours.
- Be especially careful with large cooked meats like your holiday turkey, which require a long time to cool. Some parts of the meat may stay over 40° long enough to produce bacteria.
- Use a thermometer to check your refrigerator. It should be between 34° and 40°.
- Defrost meats in the refrigerator or with a microwave, not on the kitchen counter.
- Reheat meats to over 140° for ten minutes to destroy bacteria before serving. Even then, the toxin may not be destroyed.
- Put party foods on ice to keep them cool during a party.
- Discard any cans or jars with bulging lids or leaks.
- Wash your hands, cutting boards and counter tops frequently.

Food Poisoning - continued

- Acrylic cutting boards, not wood, are best.
- Cover meats and poultry during microwave cooking to heat the surface of the meat.
- Follow home canning and freezing instructions to the letter. Call your County Agricultural Extension office for advice.
- When you eat out, avoid rare or uncooked meats. Eat salad bar and deli items immediately.

Home Treatment

- Nothing to eat or drink until vomiting has stopped. Ice chips and small sips of water are okay.
- Clear non-carbonated liquids only for 24 hours.
- Gradual progression to easily digestible foods, such as Jell-O, applesauce and dry toast.
- No spicy foods for 48 hours after all symptoms have gone.
- Check with others who may have eaten the same thing.
- Save a sample of the suspected food for analysis in case symptoms do not improve.

When to Call a Health Professional

- If you suspect food poisoning from a canned product or have any of the symptoms of botulism poisoning, call immediately. Take suspect food with you if you still have it.
- If you cannot control vomiting after 12 hours of ice chips-only treatment.
- If vital signs are not normal (temperature over 102°, respiration rate 4 breaths per minute above or below normal).
- If the victim, especially a young child, appears very ill.

Gastroenteritis (Stomach Flu)

Gastroenteritis is usually caused by a viral infection in the digestive system. The infection brings on diarrhea to rid the intestines of irritants, and nausea or vomiting to discourage eating until the problem is cleared up. Although viral gastroenteritis (stomach flu) will usually go away on its own within 24-48 hours, your own home care may speed recovery and lessen the chance of complications.

Bacterial infections such as dysentery or salmonella food poisoning can also cause gastroenteritis. Excess alcohol or food may also be the culprit.

Symptoms of the infection include back and muscle aches, abdominal pain, headaches, and fever.

Home Treatment

- No food or drink for several hours. Ice chips and small sips of water are okay.
- Clear non-carbonated liquids only for 24 hours. Start with a few sips at a time.
- Go through the home physical exam, page 15, and read through the abdominal pain section of

this chapter, page 34. Record your observations.

- Bed rest until aches subside.
- Soups, mild foods and liquids only on second day and until all symptoms are gone for 48 hours.
- Return to regular diet several days after symptoms have stopped.

NOTE: Infants and small children can dehydrate very quickly with fluid loss from both vomiting and diarrhea. See Dehydration, page 38. Infants should be taken off all fluids until vomiting is controlled up to four hours.

When to Call a Health Professional

- If vomiting and diarrhea are violent or if patient is weakened by age (very old or very young) or by other health problems.
- If diarrhea is bloody or very black.
- If vomiting continues off and on for over 12 hours without improvement. (2 to 6 hours for small children.)
- If violent retching continues for over two hours.
- If temperature of 102° or higher persists.
- Severe, increasing, or continuing pain in abdomen for over four hours.
- Mild but continuous pain lasting over 12 hours.
- If diarrhea continues after 48 hours of liquids-only diet.
- If signs of dehydration appear. See Dehydration on page 38.

Hemorrhoids

Hemorrhoids is a term used to describe an inflammation and swelling of the veins around the anus. Straining to pass hard, compacted stools sometimes irritates these veins. The resulting tenderness or pain generally lasts several days.

Prevention

Include plenty of water and high fiber foods (fresh fruits and vegetables, whole grains, legumes) in your diet to soften the stools.

Home Treatment

- Keep the area clean. Warm baths are soothing and cleansing, especially after a bowel movement.
- Apply zinc oxide (paste or powder) or Vaseline to the painful area after drying to protect against further irritation and ease the passage of stools.
- The following over the counter medication and preparations may help: Tucks, Balneol or stool softeners. Avoid anal ointments with a local anesthetic compound. (These have the suffix "caine" in name or ingredients.)

When to Call a Health Professional

- If pain is severe or lasts longer than one week.
- If bleeding continues or is heavy or blood is dark in color.

Indigestion (Heartburn)

Heartburn is caused by stomach acids backing up into the lower esophagus, the tube which leads from the mouth to the stomach. The acids produce a burning sensation and discomfort between the ribs just below the breastbone. Heartburn can occur after overeating or sometimes in reaction to medications.

There is no need to be concerned if you experience heartburn now and then; nearly everyone does. However, repeated episodes of heartburn can lead to injury to the esophageal lining.

Prevention

- Eat sensibly.
- Avoid tight-fitting clothes, such as belts and girdles.
- Avoid constipation since it can increase pressure on the stomach. See page 36.

Home Treatment

- Discontinue alcohol, nicotine, chocolate, caffeine, and fatty foods. These weaken the valve that keeps stomach acid out of the esophagus.
- Avoid foods containing acid, such as citrus fruits, tomatoes and vinegar.
- Don't lie down too soon after eating. Try to stay upright for at least two to three hours after each meal.
- Raise the head of your bed four to six inches using wooden blocks or fat telephone books. Waterbeds are difficult to elevate; consider using extra pillows.
- Stop smoking. Nicotine weakens the opening at the top of the stomach and is directly related to heartburn.
- Take an antacid, such as Maalox, Mylanta or Gelusil.

When to Call a Health Professional

- If the problem lasts for more than three days. (See the following section on Ulcers.)
- If you suspect that a prescribed medication is causing the heartburn. Antihistamines, birth control pills or Valium sometimes cause heartburn.
- If shortness of breath or other symptoms suggest heart problems. See Chest Pain, page 64.

Ulcers

An ulcer is a break in the inside lining of the gastrointestinal tract. Ulcers are formed at the lower end of the esophagus, in the stomach, or most frequently, in the duodenum (the first part of the small intestine).

Every stomach produces strong acids and other potent gastric juices in order to digest food. Under emotional stress or tension our bodies tend to produce more acids than are needed for digestion. This excess acid may begin to burn through the protective mucus which coats the stomach or intestinal wall. Caffeine, cigarettes and aspirin increase the risk of ulcers.

Symptoms of an ulcer may include a burning pain, gas, vomiting, and belching. The burning pain is usually strongest when the stomach is empty. Ulcer patients are sometimes awakened by pain in the middle of the night. A glass of milk or a piece of bread will usually relieve that pain by neutralizing the acid for a while.

Home Treatment

- Slow down. Ulcers are difficult to heal if emotional stress and tension continue to pour more acid into the system. The suggestions on page 215 may help you deal with stress.
- Antacids are usually necessary to neutralize your gastric acids long enough for the ulcer to heal. You need frequent and large amounts of antacids to do the job. Talk to your health professional about how much to take. Nonabsorbable antacids like Maalox, Mylanta, or Gelusil are best. Most antacids have high salt content and should be used with caution by persons on low-sodium diets.
- Change your diet. Eliminate alcohol and reduce caffeine to absolute minimums. Eat more often (four to six light meals per day). Avoid foods that seem to make symptoms worse.
- Avoid aspirin and other anti-inflammatory medicine such as ibuprofen.
- When you first suspect you have an ulcer, try to heal it quickly. By taking a few days to relax and concentrate on a more soothing diet, you may avoid an expensive hospitalization.

When to Call a Health Professional

- To diagnose and evaluate a suspected ulcer. An examination, history, and tests can often determine the presence, location, and severity of an ulcer.
- For appropriate antacid dosage.
- If vomiting accompanies pain.
- If severe pain is not relieved by your treatment program.
- If patient appears unusually weak or pale.
- If black, tarry blood appears in the stools.
- A medication that reduces acid production may be prescribed by your physician. As with all drugs, become aware of possible side effects.

Vomiting

Vomiting is any rejection of stomach or intestinal contents. Although vomiting can be a symptom of a large number of moderate and serious diseases, most vomiting is due to a variety of relatively minor problems that are relatively treatable at home.

Vomiting - continued

Home Treatment

- Nothing by mouth for four hours. Small ice chips and small sips of water may be all right.
- Clear non-carbonated liquids only, for 24 hours. Start with a few sips at a time.
- Go through the home physical exam, page 15.
- Bed rest until aches subside.
- Soups, mild foods and liquids only on second day and until all symptoms are gone for 48 hours.
- Return to regular diet several days after symptoms have stopped.

When to Call a Health Professional

- If vomiting is severe or violent. (It shoots out in large quantities.)
- If vomiting does not stop after 12 hours of the suggested treatment. (2 to 6 hours for small children.)
- If there is blood in the vomit.
- If signs of dehydration appear. See discussion on dehydration, page 38.
- If abdominal pain is severe or constant and does not seem to be relieved by the passage of gas or stools. Although discomfort and cramping often accompany vomiting, other pain may signal more serious problems. Your health professional should be called if there is any doubt regarding the type, severity, or cause of pain.

Stand up straight!

Mom

Chapter 4

Back and Neck Pain

Back pain is one of the most common complaints people have about their health; it accounts for 18 million visits to doctors each year. Nearly all backaches are caused by poor posture, awkward or heavy lifting and inadequate exercise. Fortunately, the vast majority of backaches can be prevented, or kept from happening again.

Your back is made up of three elements: the spine (the vertebrae or bones), the discs which separate each bone, and the muscles and ligaments which hold everything together and allow movement.

Something can go wrong with any of these elements. The muscles can be stretched too far and strained. A sprained back happens when the ligaments have been stretched too far. Either of these conditions will cause great pain.

The third problem area, and probably the most troublesome, is the discs. Spinal discs are filled with a resilient jelly-like substance. They act like shock absorbers to protect the vertebrae from hitting each other. When discs are continually abused by physical stress, they get brittle and crack or rupture. Further abuse can squeeze the jelly-like material from the center of the disc out through the cracks. As the jelly presses on the nerves in the spinal column, it causes severe pain in the back and, frequently, down the leg. This condition is associated with the term "slipped disc." In reality, the disc has not slipped; it has flattened, bulged or ruptured, resulting in limited movement and a stiff back.

Problems with the muscles, ligaments and discs are interrelated. When the muscles and ligaments are overloaded or stretched beyond their capabilities, there is greater likelihood of injury to the disc.

There is bad news and good news with regard to back pain and back care. The bad news is that once you injure your back, you will always be susceptible to further injury. The good news is you can usually avoid future back pain if you treat your back with respect and common sense.

The remainder of this chapter is divided into two sections. The first deals with preventing back pain. Simple suggestions for exercise and posture are presented. The second section covers treating back pain.

Although 90% of all backaches can be cared for at home, they are never a welcome occurrence. If you follow the directions in the first section, you may never need to study the second.

Back Pain

There are two approaches to back pain prevention: posture and exercise. You need both. Good posture and lifting habits will reduce the abuse your back receives. The right exercises will strengthen your back and protect it against harm. With both posture and exercise on your side, most back pain can become a thing of the past for you.

Back Posture

The key to good posture is keeping the right amount of curve in your lower back. The curve, or lordosis, is meant to be a slight inward arch. Too much curve ("sway back"), or too little curve ("flat back") can, over time, place more stress on the discs and the vertebrae than they can handle. The result is muscle strains, ligament sprains or disc injuries which ultimately lead to pinched nerves.

In general, good posture is obtained when you can draw a straight line through the ear, shoulder, hip, knee and ankle. Here are some simple tips to help you with your everyday posture:

Sitting

- Maintain a slight arch in the lower back.
- Avoid slouching or extreme arching in either direction.
- Keep your knees even with or lower than your hips.
- Use chairs that allow for support in your lower back or use a lumbar support to assist you in maintaining a slight curve.

Standing

- Stand tall, avoid slouching or extreme arching in either direction.

Driving

- Use many of the same ideas described above in "sitting."
- On long drives, stop periodically to stretch and walk around.

Sleeping

- Sleep in a posture which allows you to maintain a slight arch in your back. Using a towel roll may be helpful.
- A firm bed is best. Placing a sheet of plywood under the mattress may help.

Lifting

- Improper lifting places a tremendous compressive force on the discs of the lower back. Discs cannot hold up forever under such abuse and their weakening will eventually cause low back pain.
- Keep the back as straight as possible with a slight low back curve.
- Bend your knees and lift with your legs.
- Keep the load as close to your body as possible.
- Avoid lifting heavy loads above the waist.
- Use mechanical devices to help you whenever possible.

Daily activities

- Maintain good posture as much as possible. If you are engaged in activities which require prolonged postures in awkward positions, make sure you take a periodic break to restore the normal curve in your lower back.

Proper Lifting Posture

Back Posture - continued

The key to preventing increased back pain if you experience back pain is to maintain a slight arch in your back at all times.

Exercises To Save Your Back

There are two basic types of exercises that can help your back: flexion and extension. Which type is best for your back depends on your back pain symptoms. People with healthy backs would do well to practice both in equal balance.

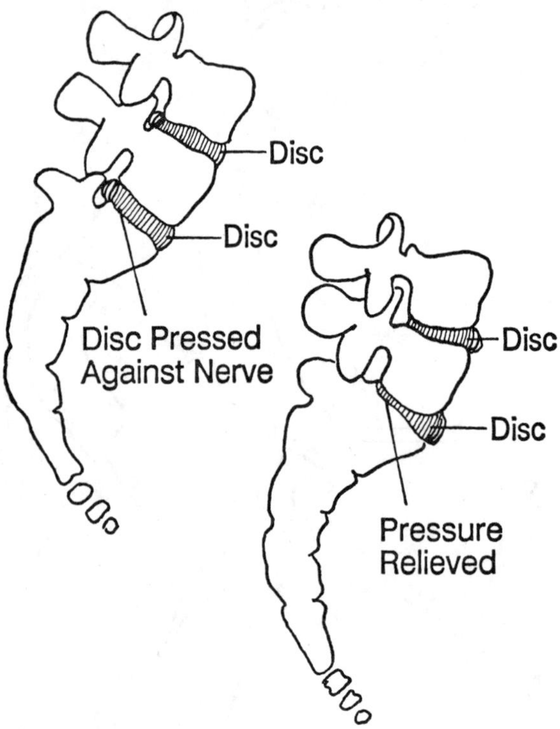

Extension exercises are designed to strengthen the muscles in your lower back and to stretch the muscles and ligaments on the stomach side of your back. Extension exercises are particularly helpful when your pain is related to a disc problem.

Flexion exercises are designed to strengthen your stomach muscles and stretch the muscles of the low back. They are particularly helpful if your back pain comes from muscle strain, arthritis or inflammations of the facets between the vertebrae. (See illustration.)

Because the two types of exercises do opposite things to alleviate different problems, it is often confusing to the back pain sufferer. The following questions may help you determine which type of exercise to emphasize in your exercise program.

1. Does your back hurt more after sitting or after standing for long periods?
   a. Sitting --- extension exercises may help most.
   b. Standing --- flexion exercises may help most.
2. Does your back hurt more in the evening before you go to bed or in the morning after a night's sleep?
   a. Morning --- extension exercises may help most.
   b. Before bed --- flexion exercises may help most.
3. Are you generally worse after long periods of bending or stooping or after long periods of reaching up or stretching?
   a. Bending or stooping-extension.
   b. Reaching up or stretching-flexion.
4. Are you generally worse when inactive or on the move?
   a. Inactive-extension

b. On the move-flexion.

5. Do you have weakness in either your abdominal or low back muscles?
   a. Low back weakness-extension.
   b. Abdominal weakness-flexion.

If your answers to the five questions are mostly "a's" your exercise program should highlight the extension exercises below. If your answers were mostly "b's", focus on the flexion exercises. If your answers were both a's and b's, try a balanced mix of the exercises.

Caution: Let Your Pain Be Your Guide.

A good motto for all the following exercises is "Strain, not Pain": Strain - continue; Pain - stop.

Flexion exercises can aggravate acute episodes of disc problems and extension exercises can aggravate acute episodes of facet inflammation and pain. If you have back pain before exercising and continuing the exercise makes it worse, stop. Sometimes, however, you may have to work through some mild, increased discomfort for a few minutes before beginning to feel the relief. (This is particularly true of extension exercises).

Basic Extension Exercises

1. Press-ups

Press-ups can become your basic tool for pain prevention if you have disc-related back pain. It is often recommended that you begin and end every set of exercises with a few press-ups.

- Lie face down with hands at shoulders, palms flat.
- Press up upper half of body with lower half relaxed.
- Keep hips down and feel a stretch in the lower back.
- Lower to starting position.
- Repeat 3-10 times, slowly.

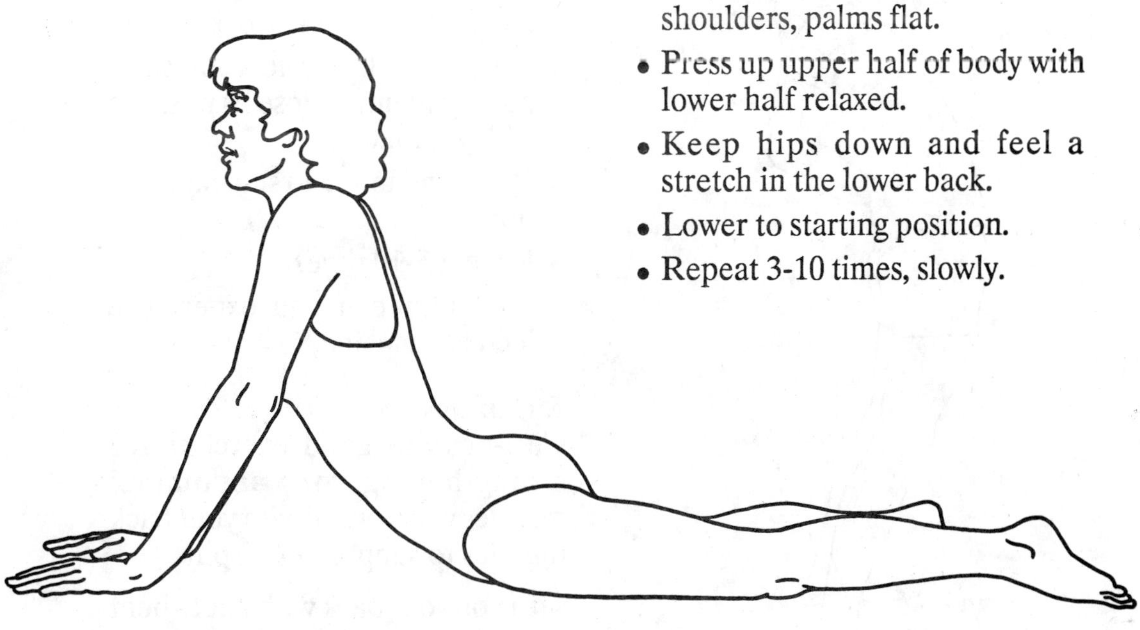

Press-Ups

Back Exercises - continued

2. Backward Bending

For people needing extension exercises, the backward bend can be helpful. Practice it at least once a day and anytime you find yourself working in a forward bent position.

- Stand upright with your feet slightly apart.
- Keep your knees straight and bend only at the waist.
- Back up to a counter top for greater support and stability.
- Place your hands in the small of your back and gently bend backward.
- Hold the backward stretch for 1-2 seconds.
- Repeat 5 times, bending a little further each time.

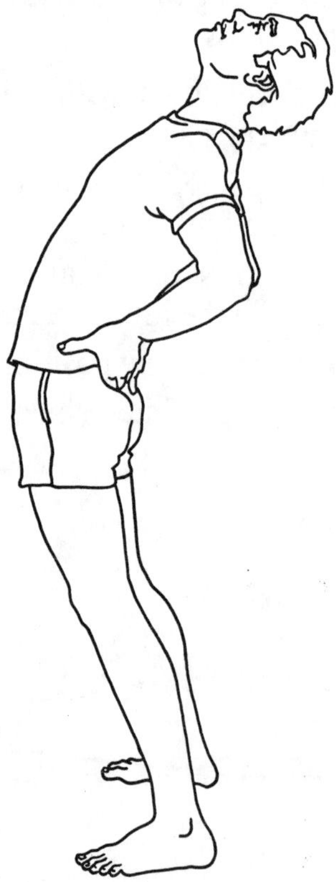

2. Backward Bending

3. Shoulder Lifts

Shoulder lifts will strengthen the back muscles which support the spine.

- Lie face down with your arms beside your body.
- Lift your head and shoulders straight up from the floor as high as your pain allows.
- Start with 5 repetitions, increasing one per day until you can comfortably do 25-30 without problem.
- Stop if you experience increasing pain.

Basic Flexion Exercises

4. Knee to Chest

The knee to chest exercise stretches the low back muscles and relieves pressure on the vertebrae facets.

- Lie on your back with knees bent and feet close to buttocks.
- Bring your knees to your chest pulling them as close as possible with your hands.
- Relax and lower to starting position.
- Repeat 5-10 times.
- Discontinue if you experience increasing pain.

5. Curl-ups

Curl-ups are good exercises for strengthening your abdominal muscles which work with your back muscles to support your spine.

- Lie on your back with knees bent (60 degree angle) and feet flat on floor.

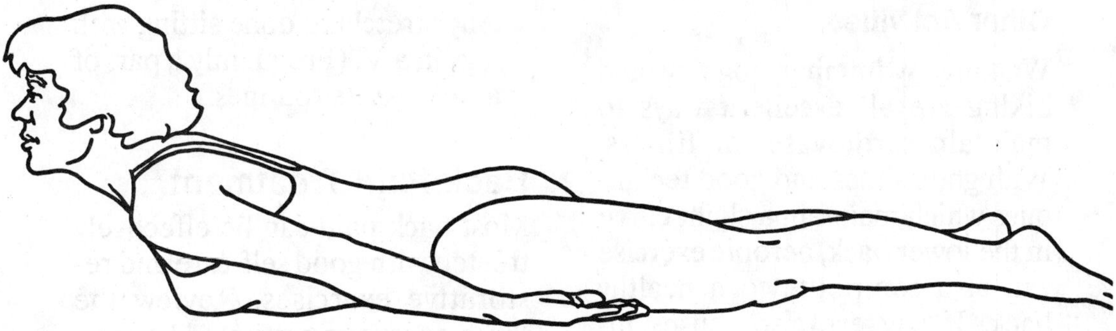

3. Shoulder Lifts

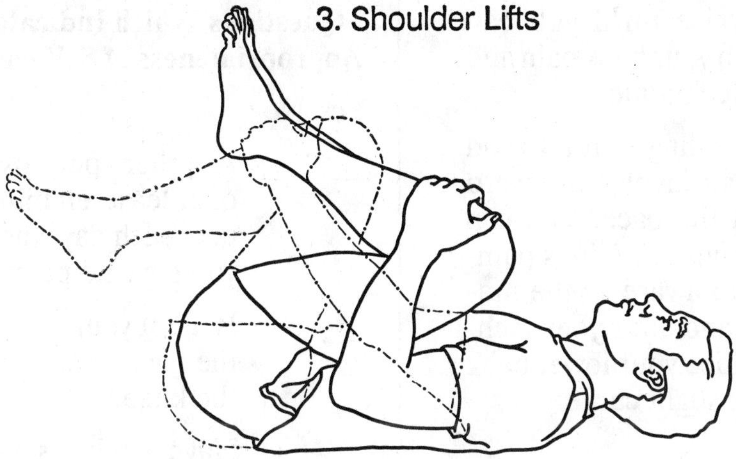

4. Knee to Chest Exercise

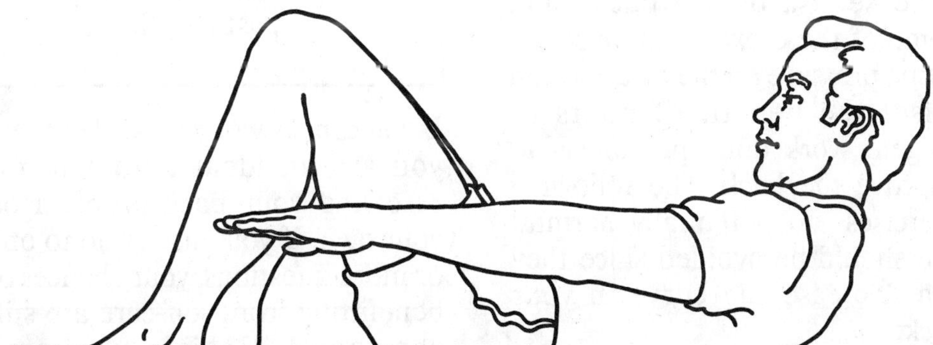

5. Curl-Ups

- Reach for your knees with your hands while tucking your chin and lifting your shoulders up. Remember to lift your shoulders and not force your head up and forward to avoid neck problems.
- Curl up and uncurl down slowly.
- DO NOT HOOK YOUR FEET UNDER ANYTHING.
- Start with 5 repetitions, increasing one per day until you can comfortably do 25-30.
- Discontinue if you experience increasing pain.

Other Activities

Walking, swimming, jogging and biking are all excellent ways to maintain cardiovascular fitness. With good shoes and good techniques which maintain a slight curve in the lower back, aerobic exercise will also contribute to a healthy back. If any exercise causes increasing or continuing back pain, stop the exercise until you can reevaluate both your back pain and your exercise technique.

Golf, tennis, bowling, aerobics and weight lifting all involve awkward movements of the back. You can participate in these activities painlessly if you are aware of the motions to avoid and alter your techniques to stabilize your lower back and maintain a slight curve.

Exercises to Avoid

Many common exercises actually increase risk of low back pain. Some of these exercises place extreme pressure on the disc and can offset the benefit of hours of diligent work done previously to improve the back. The following exercises are potentially harmful and should be avoided since they can decrease the curve in your back:

- Legs up (lifting both legs in an extended position while lying on your back).
- Heavy weight lifting above the waist.
- Straight leg sit-ups.
- Knees to chest and/or bent knee sit-ups during acute disc pain.
- Any stretching done sitting with legs in a V. (Frequently a part of aerobic class routines.)

Back Pain Treatment

Most back pain can be effectively treated with good self-care and restorative exercises. Review the three questions presented below.

Questions Which Indicate Appropriateness of Self-care

Yes	No	
___	___	Are there periods of at least ten minutes each day when you have no pain?
___	___	Is all of your pain in the back or above the knee?
___	___	Have you had several episodes of low back pain over the past months or years?

If you can answer yes to all of them you are an ideal candidate for resolving your back problem on your own. If you answer no to one or more questions, your chances of benefitting from self-care are still very good. Begin your home program immediately but also consider seeing a doctor or physical therapist who is skilled in back care. Even then, a self-care program will become an important part of your recovery as you start to progress.

Also see "When to Call a Health Professional" on page 56.

First Aid for Back Pain

When you first feel a catch or slip in your back there are four things you can do to avoid or reduce the expected pain.

First Aid #2

First Aid #1
Stand with hands on hips and stretch backwards. See the illustration on page 52.

First Aid # 2
Go into a flat-footed squat. Hold the squat for 20 to 40 seconds. Just try to relax. Don't bounce. This will be particularly helpful for muscle strains.

Do not stand up from the squat as it could aggravate a disc pain problem. Instead, go right to first aid #3.

First Aid #3
Lie flat on your stomach with your arms beside your body and your head to one side. Relax as much as possible.

First Aid #4
After one or two minutes prop yourself up on your elbows with

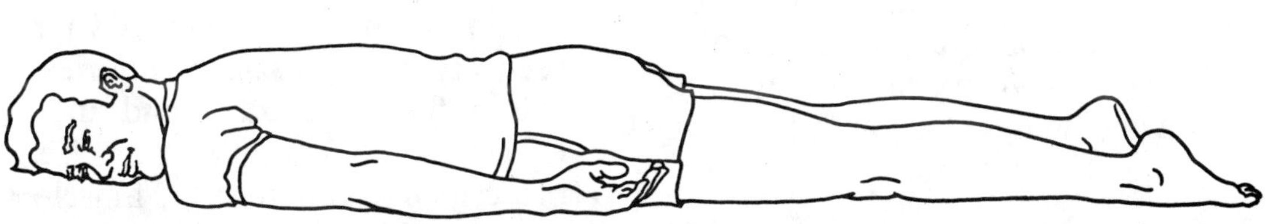

First Aid #3

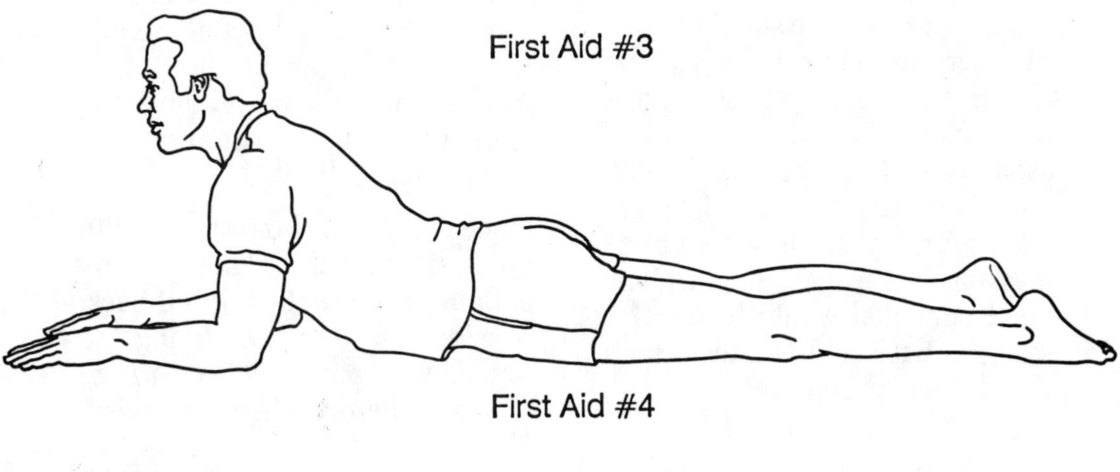

First Aid #4

First Aid for Back Pain - cont.

your forearms out in front and partially arch your back. Hold the arch for two to five minutes unless there is severe or increasing pain.

If you can successfully complete all four first aid exercises, you are safe to get up. However, avoid any awkward movements and maintain as perfect posture as possible. You would do well to repeat the exercises every two to three hours throughout the day.

Drop any of the exercises that increases your pain. The squat can sometimes aggravate disc injuries. If it makes your back hurt more, concentrate on the other exercises.

Ice, Not Heat

If because of past experiences you are still worried that the "catch" in your back will bring more pain later, put a cold pack or ice bag on the lower back. There is growing evidence that heat is not good for a strained or sprained back. Cold is useful in limiting the swelling, avoiding later pain and shortening the healing period.

Based on the severity of the back pain, use your common sense to judge how often you should repeat the exercises and cold packs over the next few days. Use pain relievers sensibly. Moderate use of aspirin combined with cold packs and good posture can reduce the discomfort significantly. Complete masking of the pain might allow movement that would further injure the back and greatly extend the recovery period.

Restoration Exercises

A week or two after the pain has subsided, you may resume the basic prevention exercises on page 51.

When to Call a Health Professional

- If you have severe pain in the leg that extends below the knee or experience a sense of weakness, numbness, or tingling in the foot and toes.
- If the low back pain followed a recent traumatic accident.
- If an episode of back pain is followed by bladder problems.
- If you feel ill in conjunction with this episode of back pain.

Who To See And What to Expect

Except for determining the cause of the pain and ruling out serious illnesses, there is little that a physician can do to help speed your recovery from most back injuries. While muscle relaxants and anti-inflammatory drugs can be prescribed to eliminate the muscle spasm and reduce the inflammation, ice, aspirin and careful posture can do an equally effective job. If muscle relaxants are used, take special care not to reinjure the back through improper movements.

Since the trip to and from a health professional's office can be very painful to a recently injured back, consider the merits of trying the first aid exercises and ice for at least a day before scheduling a visit.

One important way a physician can help is by referring you to a physical therapist with training in orthopedic treatments. (The physician referral is usually necessary for insurance coverage.) A physical therapist can help you determine if extension or flexion exercises are best for you. He will then help you design a self-care plan of exercise and posture improvements that will give you long-term relief from back pain.

Short-term relief from back pain is available from many sources. Physical therapists can also provide ultrasound, electrical stimulation or other therapies to reduce back pain. Chiropractors can provide temporary pain relief through spinal manipulations and other treatments. Acupuncturists can also be effective in reducing back pain over limited periods. Massage therapists may be very helpful, too. While your pain can justifiably take you to any of these professionals, it is almost always advisable to try the self-care exercises and posture changes first and to combine a continued self-care plan with whatever other treatments you may choose to receive.

Back Surgery

Back surgery, once a common operation, is now being done much less frequently. Unless there is substantial nerve damage and continuing pain that cannot be relieved by rest, posture, exercise and the use of ice, the costs of surgery are not usually justified by the possible benefits. Overall, only one to two percent of back pain sufferers should need to resort to surgery.

Recommended Reading for Back Care

See Resource #F1-2 on page 269.

Neck Pain

Neck pain and stiffness are usually caused by strained or cramped neck muscles. Your neck movements may be limited, usually more to one side than the other. Headaches are often associated with neck pain. Causes of neck pain can range from sleeping on too high a pillow (or too soft a bed) to poor posture, or by extended periods of "the thinker's" pose (resting your forehead on your upright fist or arm). Postural causes are the most common and are typically associated with poor sitting postures at work or home.

Neck pain can also be caused by a traumatic blow or snapping action as in an automobile accident, ski fall or any sudden twist. This can result in a strain in the muscles and ligaments which support the head and neck. Such an injury may involve a pinched nerve.

Some illnesses can be the cause of neck pain. Meningitis, a life-threatening condition, is known for its severe stiff neck together with headache and fever. If these three symptoms come together without a clear cause, you should see a doctor promptly.

Neck Pain - continued

Home Treatment

- If the stiffness is worse in the morning, improve your sleeping support.
- A hard mattress or a special neck support pillow will solve the problem. A towel folded lengthwise into a four inch pad can be wrapped around the neck and pinned or placed inside the pillow to provide support.

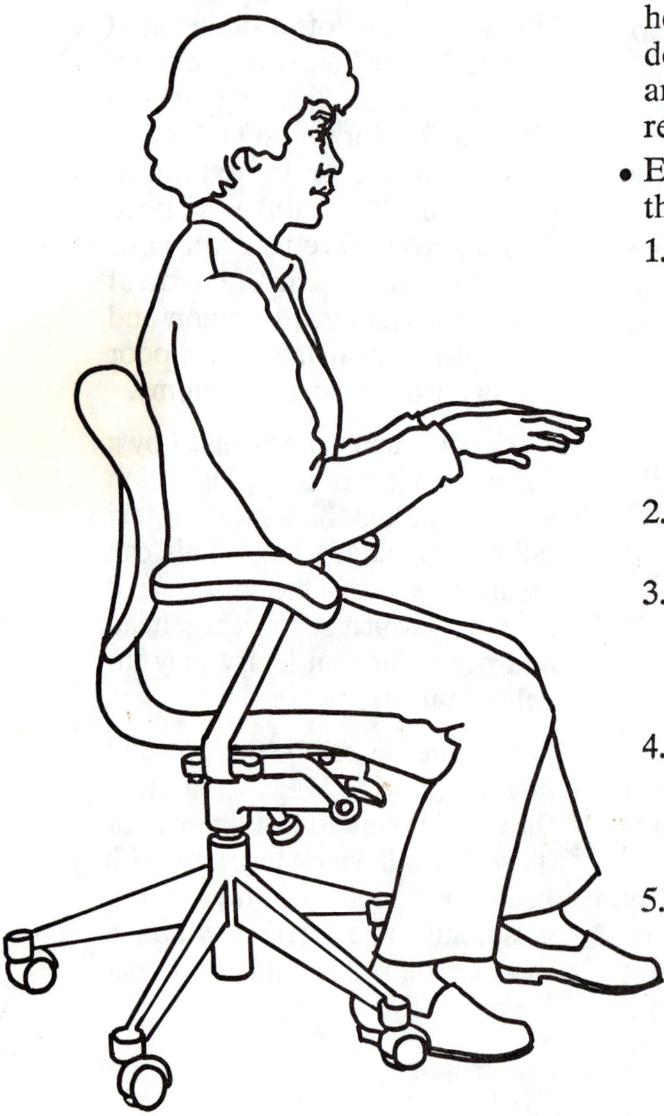

- If neck pain is worse at the end of the day, review your posture and body mechanics at work. Desk workers should try to adjust their chairs and work stations to allow for proper posture of the entire spine. This will decrease the stresses on the neck. Keep a straight line through the ear, shoulder and hips. Keep your elbows at a 90 degree angle for typing.
- Place a cold pack over the painful muscles for 10-15 minutes at a time. You can do this every hour if you need to. This will help decrease the muscle pain, spasm and any swelling that may be the result of an injury.
- Exercises can be very helpful. Do these every 2-3 hours.
  1. Try to sit or stand with a "Buckingham palace guard" posture. This is an extremely erect posture which results in stretching of the muscles in the back of the neck. Do it gently and repeat 6 times.
  2. Squeeze your shoulder blades together gently 6 times.
  3. Starting from the "palace guard" posture, gently drop your head backward and repeat 6 times.
  4. Gently drop your head backward, forward and side-to-side with gentle pressure from your hands. Repeat 6 times.
  5. Practice the shoulder lifts described on page 53.

- Aspirin can help to relieve the pain. Anti-inflammatories may be helpful in reducing swelling in the damaged tissue.

When to Call a Health Professional

- If you can't touch your chin to your chest or if stiffness, headaches and fever are present. A spinal tap may be required to rule out meningitis. The more severe the symptoms, the faster you should act.
- If the pain extends or shoots down one arm or you have numbness or tingling in your hands. An x-ray or other special tests may be needed to rule out a pinched nerve. Muscle relaxants may be prescribed. See page 7 for questions to ask about x-rays.
- If the pain is becoming chronic (two weeks or more) and the home care does not seem to be working. A physician or physical therapist with orthopedic training can help you develop a treatment program.

When dealing with neck pain, it is often helpful to utilize the services of a physical therapist skilled in these problems. In the United States, such a physical therapist is known as an orthopedic or manual physical therapist.

Recommended Reading for Neck Care

For a self-help guide in treating neck pain, see Resource #O1 on page 269.

Keep breathing.

Sophie Tucker

Chapter 5

Chest and Lungs

Life is a lot more than breathing and keeping your heart beating, but it's impossible to live long without both your heart and lungs working well. If either stops, you have only a few minutes to restore the flow of blood and oxygen throughout the body. Rescue breathing and cardiopulmonary resuscitation are discussed in detail on pages 183-186.

But, problems in the chest and lungs are not all life-threatening. Whether the concern is a minor cough following a cold, a chronic case of emphysema or the possibility of a heart attack, the quality of the self-care you provide at home will be important to your health and recovery.

This chapter will help you to better understand the symptoms of chest and lung problems and to develop plans for both self-care and professional assessment when needed. The next time you hear a cough, a wheeze or a gurgle, look for help here.

Asthma

Asthma is a chronic condition of recurrent, reversible obstruction of the airways. The bronchial tubes go into spasm and the mucous lining swells, resulting in obstructed breathing. Asthma is the Greek word for panting. The person with an asthmatic attack is literally panting for breath. The person usually coughs a lot and spits up mucus. The wheeze, a noisy breathing, can be heard some distance away. The person may perspire heavily and the lips and nails may turn blue. Some people with asthma have attacks when exposed to an allergen, or simply from a change in weather or exertion.

Chest and Lung Symptom Guide

See page 21 for how to count respiration.

Wheezing, difficulty in breathing:
- Stop smoking.
- See Pneumonia, page 68.
- See Allergy, page 72.
- See Asthma, page 61.

Fast, shallow breathing or difficulty in breathing:
- Accompanied by loud cough, see Croup, page 127.
- Check for object in mouth, throat.
- If severe or prolonged unexplained difficulty in breathing, call health professional.

No respiration:
- Perform cardiopulmonary resuscitation (CPR). Get someone else to call health professional. See page 183 for how to perform CPR.

Coughing:
- See Coughs, page 65.

Chest pain:
- See page 64.

Asthma - continued

Despite these frightening symptoms, asthma is not often fatal. It can often be prevented using drugs and other methods of treatment. A severe attack is a serious condition. However, it may be effectively treated by inhaled medications and, at times, injections.

An asthma attack is a traumatic event. Anxiety is a normal response to breathing difficulties. To avoid panic, family members need to remain calm and provide a supportive influence.

Prevention

The prevention of asthma is based on two principles:

1. Find out what causes the attacks.
2. Avoid the irritant.

Keep records of the time, place and circumstances of each asthma attack. Careful observation combined with allergy testing can help identify the irritants. Often more than one substance is the problem.

A calm, stress-free environment can help prevent or reduce the severity of asthma attacks. The person who feels some control over the attack will cope better with the problem.

Frequent asthma attacks, over a long period of time, may lead to serious complications. Good medical treatment and home care can help avoid complications.

Home Treatment

- Remain calm.
- Follow the home treatment plan you develop with your doctor. This could include use of a medication inhaler.

- Look for ways to reduce exposure to irritants which may induce an attack.
- Keep your bedroom and living area as dust free as possible.
- Get plenty of rest and exercise.
- Drink extra fluids to thin bronchial mucus.
- DO NOT SMOKE. Avoid people who smoke.

When to Call a Health Professional

- To develop an asthma attack response plan. Discuss exactly what to do in case of an attack. With a good response plan and confidence in asthma medication, most attacks can be handled without immediate professional help.
- If an acute asthma attack does not respond promptly to home treatment.
- If sputum becomes discolored (green, yellow or bloody). This may be a sign of a secondary bacterial infection. Antibiotic treatment may be required.
- To discuss allergy skin testing to better identify the causes of asthma attacks.
- To discuss allergy hyposensitization shots which may be useful in preventing severe and recurring asthma.
- For information on support groups. Talking with others can be an effective way to gain confidence in dealing with prevention and treatment.

Bronchitis

Bronchitis is an inflammation of the lower windpipe and the bronchial tubes which carry air to and from the lungs. In bronchitis, the bronchial tubes are injured by the infection and secrete a sticky mucus. It becomes increasingly difficult for the cilia or hairs on the bronchi to clean out this mucus.

Bronchitis often occurs after a cold or upper respiratory infection which doesn't heal completely. It may be caused by a virus or a bacterium and is much more common among smokers and those who work in polluted air. *Seventy-five percent of patients with chronic bronchitis have a history of heavy smoking.*

The body attempts to clear out the sticky mucus through the cough, the most significant symptom of bronchitis. Other symptoms are tiredness, low fever, sore throat, runny nose, and sometimes, wheezing. The treatment for bronchitis is basically to help the cough clear out the mucus.

Untreated bronchitis can lead to pneumonia. Chronic bronchitis can be a part of chronic obstructive pulmonary disease (emphysema), a very serious, incurable ailment. See page 67.

Bronchitis - continued

Prevention

Give proper home care to minor respiratory problems such as colds. Stopping smoking may help prevent the irritation to the cilia and decrease the chance of complications.

Home Treatment

- Drink a large amount of fluids -- as much as a gallon a day. Liquids help thin the mucus in the lungs, making it easier to clean out. This is the most important part of treatment.
- Rest in bed. The lungs need lots of rest to cure themselves.
- Stop smoking. The smoke irritates the tissue and slows healing.
- Inhale steam frequently from a vaporizer or over the bathroom sink. Steam inhalation will dilute mucus and help the cough bring it up.
- Take expectorant cough medicines to help bring up the mucus. See page 256 for examples of cough medicines.
- Twice daily, lie on your stomach and hang your head and chest over the side of the bed for one minute. This procedure, called postural drainage, helps drain the mucus. Any posture which gets the head lower than the chest will work.
- Massage the chest and back muscles. Use Vicks VapoRub, Ben-Gay, or a similar over-the-counter preparation, if desired. The massaging increases blood flow to the chest and aids relaxation.

When to Call a Health Professional

- If sputum, usually clear or white, is green, brown, or yellow. This can indicate bacterial infection and requires antibiotic treatment.
- If the mucus coughed up becomes thick and rusty colored.
- If there is a history of frequent bronchitis.
- If breathing difficulty is present when not coughing.
- If there is wheezing.
- If there is increasing chest pain.
- If mucus continues to thicken.
- If patient is an infant, elderly, or chronically ill.

Chest Pain

To most people, chest pain signifies a heart attack. Although chest pain is the best warning of a heart attack, there are different types of pain that may indicate other problems.

If you have chest pain that increases when you press your finger on the pain, you probably have chest-wall pain. This pain can be caused by muscles, ligaments, or bones in the chest wall.

A shooting pain that lasts only a few seconds is common and there is no need for concern. Also, a quick pain that occurs at the end of a deep breath is usually trivial.

Chest pains can be associated with other disorders. The pain from pleurisy gets worse with a deep breath or cough; heart pain doesn't get worse. An ulcer can cause chest pain and is worse on an empty stomach. Gallbladder pain often becomes worse *after a meal.*

When to Call a Health Professional

- Call 911 or other emergency services immediately for severe chest pain or chest pain associated with:
  - Sweating
  - Difficulty in breathing or shortness of breath
  - Nausea or vomiting
  - Dizziness
  - Pulse irregularity
  - Pain radiating to the arm, neck or jaw
  - Persistency or increasing intensity
- Any chest pain in someone who has a previous history of a disease associated with chest pain, such as a heart attack or a blood clot in the lung.
- Any chest pain that is constant and nagging and is not relieved by a change in position.
- Chest pain that lasts longer than two days.

Cost Management Tips

Checking out chest pain, while important, can be very expensive and is not without risk. Tests can run from electrocardiograms and angiography to radioactive imaging. These tests can build up several thousands of dollars in expenses over a few hours. Your job at such times is to stay calm. You have a need for your regular physician or someone else you trust to give you sensible advice. You should always understand the costs, benefits and risks before agreeing to such diagnostic tests.
See Resource #A3 on page 268.

Coughs

Coughing is the way the body expels foreign bodies and mucus from the lower respiratory tract. While a cough's loudness only shows the degree of effort put into the cough, all coughs have distinct characteristics you can learn to recognize. A dry, hacking cough indicates something is irritating the respiratory tract. Loose and juicy coughs indicate mucus is being produced. This mucus often flips into the esophagus and gets swallowed, and then appears in vomit or the stool.

Coughs - continued

There are three types of coughs. The productive cough is one that produces phlegm or mucus which comes up with coughing. The non-productive cough is a very dry cough, producing no mucus. A reflex cough is one that is a result of a disturbance or irritation which may or may not be associated with the respiratory tract. The irritation may originate in the vocal cords, the ear, or even the stomach.

In general, the simplest cure for any cough is water. Water helps to loosen phlegm and soothe an irritated throat. Dry, hacking coughs often respond to honey in hot water, tea or lemon juice. Suppressants to control the cough and expectorants which liquify the mucus and make it easier to bring up are two drugs that may help. Detailed descriptions of these drugs can be found on page 256.

DESCRIPTION and TREATMENT of COUGHS

Description	Possible Cause	Home Treatment
Seal-like bark	Croup	See page 127.
Wheezing, noisy breathing out	Allergy Asthma	See page 72. See page 61.
Dry coughs that occur only in the morning and seem better after breakfast	Dry air Cigarettes	Increase fluids. Use a humidifier in the bedroom. See page 247.
Hacking, dry, non-productive coughs	Post nasal drip Cigarettes	Increase fluids. Decongestants are helpful.
A dry, sudden-onset cough that appears immediately following a choking episode, most often in an older infant or toddler	Foreign object	See page 190 for how to remove the object.
Dry coughs intermittently day and night, especially with a fever	Respiratory infection	Increase fluids. Use a suppressant at night and expectorants during the day.
Chronic cough following a cold	Bronchitis	See page 63.

Cough drops can soothe the irritated parts of your mouth and accessible parts of your throat. They have no effect on the cough-producing mechanism. Expensive, medicine-flavored cough drops are not any better than inexpensive candy-flavored ones or hard candy.

When to Call a Health Professional

- If a non-productive cough suddenly becomes productive.
- If mucus becomes thick or green.
- If there is blood in the sputum on several occasions.
- If the cough lasts more than five days without improvement.
- If the cough suddenly gets worse.
- If the cough is accompanied by a fever of 103°.

Emphysema (Chronic Obstructive Pulmonary Disease)

Emphysema is a chronic lung condition caused by repeated irritation or infection of the tissues of the lungs. Over the years, repeated irritation by cigarette smoke, pollution, or infection stretches the elastic lung tissue so it cannot expand and contract properly. Emphysema is much more likely to occur in the person who has been a heavy cigarette smoker for a long time. The lungs lose their ability to add oxygen to the blood and the person is susceptible to frequent attacks of bronchitis. Symptoms of emphysema are shortness of breath on exertion, frequent respiratory infections and bronchitis, wheezing, and chronic cough.

Prevention

Emphysema is caused by irritants to the lungs. Therefore, elimination of as many of those irritants as possible can help to prevent emphysema. Avoid pollution, and if you work where the air is polluted, do what you can to filter the air and control dust and irritants. You should also know that cigarette smoking is a known contributor to emphysema.

Home Treatment

Emphysema must be diagnosed by a health professional. Once diagnosed, a detailed routine will be prescribed. There is no cure for emphysema, but proper treatment can help you lead a more normal life. Be sure you understand all instructions for the control of your disease.

When to Call a Health Professional

- If you have shortness of breath on exertion.
- If you have frequent respiratory infections, especially bronchitis.
- If you have chronic cough.
- If you have persistent wheezing.
- If you are a smoker and want help quitting.

Pneumonia

Pneumonia is an infection of the smallest air passages (the alveoli) in your lungs. It can be caused by a variety of bacteria or viruses. Pneumonia often follows a bout of upper respiratory illness, especially in older adults or in people whose resistance is poor due to inadequate diet, overexposure to the cold, or fatigue. While cold air cannot of itself cause illness, it can lower your body's resistance. Improper home treatment of a minor upper respiratory illness may lead to pneumonia.

Usually, the person with pneumonia will appear very ill. The first signal of the disease, especially in a child, is very rapid breathing. An older person may have pain in the chest, especially when coughing or taking a deep breath, and may cough up green or brown sputum. This is mucus from deep in the lung. Each breath is labored. Shaking, chills and fever are other symptoms.

Prevention

To prevent pneumonia, take adequate care of minor illnesses. Keeping up the body's normal resistance with adequate diet, rest, and exercise may help prevent pneumonia from developing.

Home Treatment

- A health professional must be called if you suspect pneumonia. After a diagnosis of pneumonia, follow the home treatment below.
  - Pneumonia requires lots of rest for the lungs to clear themselves.
  - Extra fluids are necessary to help thin mucus. Give adults and children at least an eight ounce glass of water or juice every hour.

When to Call a Health Professional

- If during any respiratory illness, there is rapid or labored breathing.
- If a cough following a cold lasts longer than five days without improving.
- If an unexplained cough appears a few weeks after a cold.

A mighty creature is the germ,
Tho' smaller than the pachyderm ...
His childish pride he often pleases,
By giving people strange diseases.
Ogden Nash

Chapter 6

Eyes, Ears, Nose, and Throat

Is it possible to get through an entire year without suffering from a cold, the flu, springtime hay fever or a painful earache? Some families do. But for most of us, a few germs always seem to slip by. Fortunately, there is a great deal we can do to relieve the discomfort of upper respiratory problems and hasten a cure.

Adenoids

The adenoids are lymph tissue located behind the nose. The adenoids become inflamed and swell in upper respiratory infections and may block the eustachian tube, which can lead to middle-ear infections.

The surgical removal of adenoids is called an adenoidectomy. Previously, many children had tonsils and adenoids removed in one operation as a matter of course. Now it is thought that lymph tissue may be helpful in filtering infection and should not be removed without due consideration. It is important to remember that the two operations are separate, and each should be considered as a distinct operation.

Home Treatment

Home treatment of adenoid problems should be merely to relieve symptoms before seeing a health professional. Your treatment could include:

- Decongestants which may help nasal stuffiness.
- Small amounts of aspirin, or for children, acetaminophen (Tylenol or Datril) for accompanying fever.

EYES

Symptoms	What To Do
Red, itchy eyes Matter in eyes Pussy discharge	• Think about: Enough sleep? Crying? Windy day? See Allergy, Hay Fever, page 72. • If accompanied by other symptoms, see Colds, page 76. • If unaccompanied by other symptoms, see Conjunctivitis, page 78. • If minor, wash with appropriate eye wash.
Runny, tearing eyes	• Note for next health professional visit. • Check for object in eye, see page 174 for removal of object.
Red, burning eyes	• Chance of any chemical in eye? If so, see Chemically Burned Eye, page 168.

EARS

Symptoms	What To Do
	• See Ear Problems Symptom Guide, page 80.

NOSE

Symptoms	What To Do
Stuffy nose	• See page 255.
Nasal discharge-clear (runny nose)	• See Colds, page 76; look for other signs of a cold. • See Allergy, page 72; look for other signs of allergy.
Nasal discharge-green or yellow, thicker discharge	• If unaccompanied by other symptoms, see Object in the Nose, page 130.
Foul nasal odor	• If unaccompanied by other symptoms, see Object in the Nose, page 130.
Swollen, inflamed nasal tissue	• See Object in the Nose, page 130. Look for other signs of object in nose.
Pale, bluish nasal tissue	• See Allergy, page 72.

FACE

Symptoms	What To Do
Pain in face, especially around sinuses	• See Sinusitis, page 86. Look for other symptoms of sinusitis. • See Allergy, page 72. (Sinusitis may occur with allergy.)

MOUTH AND THROAT

Symptoms	What To Do
White spots in mouth or throat	• If unaccompanied by other symptoms, see Canker Sores, page 75. • Also, observe, and if still there in ten days, call a health professional.
Sores, bleeding in mouth or throat	• If unaccompanied by other symptoms, see Canker Sores, page 72. • May be a sign of dental problems. (Frequent in those with orthodontic appliances.) • If unexplained sores or bleeding continue for more than five days, see a health professional.
Bright red patches in throat	• If sore throat is very bright red, see Strep Throat, page 88. • Bright red patches in the throat may be caused by some viral infections, but you should always read the section on Strep Throat when such patches are observed. A throat culture is needed to distinguish viral from bacterial infections.

MOUTH AND THROAT

Symptoms	What To Do
Bad breath	• If accompanied by other symptoms, such as sore throat, see Strep Throat, page 88. • May be a sign of dental problems. • May be a symptom of indigestion. See Indigestion, page 44.
Sore throat	• See Sore Throat, page 87. • See Strep Throat, page 88.
Postnasal drip (mucus on back of throat)	• See Postnasal Drip information under Colds on page 78.
Swollen lymph glands or other lumps on neck	• See Swollen Glands, page 90. • If in adult or child with no recent disease history, see Mumps, page 129 and Strep Throat, page 88. • If unexplained lumps are seen in throat or mouth or on neck for more than two weeks, see a health professional.

Adenoids - continued

When to Call a Health Professional

- When a child breathes through the mouth rather than the nose. Discuss this on your next visit to your health professional.
- If there is fever, obstructed nasal breathing, or the nasal and postnasal drainage contains pus.

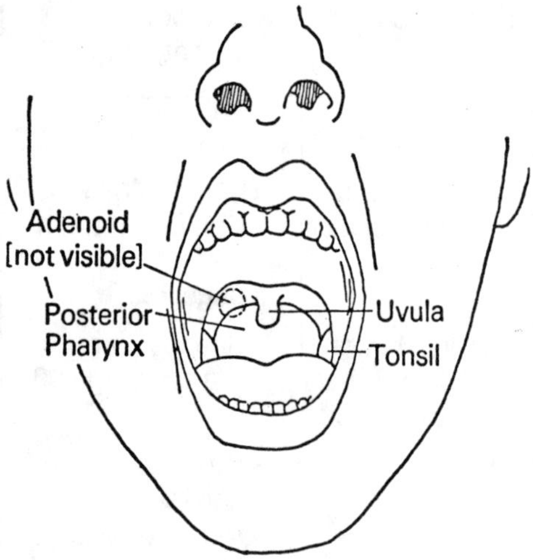

Adenoids

Allergy (Allergic Rhinitis, Hay Fever)

Allergy is the abnormal reaction some people's bodies have to certain substances with which they come in contact.

A person may be allergic to foods or other substances taken by mouth, or things inhaled such as plant pollen or dust. Some people's bodies react to something on the skin or to something injected such as a bee sting or a shot. Allergic reactions range from very mild (itching eyes, sneezing, or runny noses) to very severe (difficulty in breathing, shock, or even circulatory collapse). About twenty percent of the entire United States population has some kind of allergy at some time during the year. Allergies appear to be hereditary. Parents with allergies are somewhat more likely to have allergic children. In childhood, allergies differ according to age groups: infants are more likely to be allergic to foods; older children to what they breathe.

The infant who has food allergies is more likely to be allergic to things in the air when older. Suspect allergies if your child has a cold all winter long or has a constant runny nose and itchy eyes. The child may rub or pick an itchy nose. The child with allergies may be a mouth-breather, snore and wake with a scratchy sore throat.

Sometimes, allergy symptoms will be mistaken for something else. The child may simply be listless and have dark circles under the eyes, or the allergic reaction may be a stomachache or a headache. You need to be a good detective to discover an allergy and its cause. Skin rashes and redness are often allergic reactions.

Allergy to substances in the air such as plant pollen can usually be discovered with the use of skin tests. Skin tests are most reliable for inhaled allergens. Blood tests for allergies are less sensitive and more costly. Diagnosis for food allergies must be made by trial diets, eliminating and gradually reintroducing suspect foods.

A health professional will usually prescribe antihistamines to relieve the symptoms of allergy while trying to discover the cause.

Cost Management Tips

Successful allergy treatment is based on three principles:

1. Identify a few irritants that cause most of the problems. The more allergies you have, the less likely treatment will help.
2. Avoid the irritants.
3. Save immunotherapy for selective, unavoidable irritants that contribute to severe allergy symptoms.

The best results come from working with physicians who have special training in allergy treatment. Beware of treatments prescribed without both a careful history and adequate allergy testing.

Prevention

If you or your spouse has a history of allergies, consider breast feeding your child. Allergy to breast milk is very rare. There is some evidence that keeping a child solely on breast milk for six months may increase the child's resistance to food allergies later. At any rate, by introducing simple solid foods gradually into a diet, any allergy will be more easily found. Milk, wheat, eggs, chocolate, corn, and citrus foods are foods most likely to cause allergic reactions in children. Rice cereal is a good introduction to solid foods for most children.

Once the cause of an allergic reaction is found (which may not be at all easy), the best prevention is to avoid that irritant as much as possible.

Children often outgrow allergies. Thus, you may wish to try to reintroduce foods which caused an infant problems when the child is older.

Home Treatment

- Keep air, especially in sleeping rooms, humidified.
- Keep a diary of all contacts --- foods, flowers, weeds, trees, grasses --- and relate these to the symptoms.
- Avoid whatever causes allergies. Wear a mask while sweeping a dusty place or cutting grass.
- Keep the home, especially bedrooms, as dust-free as possible. If the allergy is severe, you may wish to look into air filters, either portable or those for the whole heating system. However, the effectiveness of filters has not been confirmed.
- In the bedroom, use synthetic pillows and plastic covers on mattresses and pillows. Take out carpets and rugs, if they harbor a lot of dust.
- Get extra rest during an allergy attack.

Allergy - continued

- Oral nasal decongestants or antihistamines may relieve symptoms.
- Blow nose gently to prevent forcing mucus into the eustachian tube leading from the ear to the throat.
- Stop smoking. These tissues are already irritated.
- House pets should not sleep in or enter the bedroom of the allergic person. In severe cases, the pet may have to stay out of the house completely.

When to Call a Health Professional

- If the allergy causes severe breathing difficulty or wheezing.
- If nasal discharge turns green or yellow.
- If symptoms seem worse over time or the inconvenience is too much, you and your physician can consider desensitizing shots. These allergy shots may help to gradually build immunity to the allergy-causing substance. However, the things you are allergic to may change, or you may move to an area with different irritants.

Bacterial Infections

Bacteria-caused upper respiratory infections are often hard to distinguish from those which are caused by a virus. Often, the only way they can be discovered is by culturing them in a laboratory. A tissue scraping or a bit of exudate (mucus, pus, or phlegm) is placed on a growth plate and "grown out." The growth can then be analyzed and identified if it is a bacteria. This process takes about 24-48 hours.

Often bacteria will attack the already weakened system of a person with a viral infection. Thus bacterial infections sometimes follow viral infections, particularly if the viral infection is not given proper home treatment.

The most common bacterial complications of viral upper respiratory infections are ear infections and strep throat (streptococcus bacteria). Impetigo is another strep infection and it will need professional help if at all extensive.

You **cannot** *prevent complications of a viral infection by starting antibiotic therapy.* Once a bacterial infection is suspected, there is usually time to verify it and treat it without endangering the patient.

Use of Antibiotics

It is important to remember that only one-tenth of all infections will respond to antibiotic treatment. *You should not expect your health professional to prescribe an antibiotic treatment before seeing the patient,* and if necessary, taking a culture to verify presence of a bacterial infection.

Most bacteria-caused infections are cured fairly easily with antibiotic drugs. However, it is important that not all infections be treated as bacterial infections. Antibiotics destroy both "good" and "bad" bacteria and thus should be used only when necessary. Sometimes, women who have been treated for a bacterial infection come down with a vaginal infection. That's because the "good" bacteria in the vagina were eliminated by the antibiotic treatment. The organisms (often yeast) which those bacteria controlled could then grow quickly.

Another reason to use antibiotics only when necessary is that bacteria subjected to antibiotics can build resistant strains. The strong bacteria survive, making later treatment more difficult. It's possible for a person to develop an allergy to an antibiotic so that it cannot be used when really needed.

When to Call a Health Professional

- If there is a high fever (over 103°) accompanying any illness.
- If the person is not starting to improve after four days. If the symptoms are clearly viral, you may wait ten days.
- If sputum or nasal discharge turns from white or clear to yellow or green or is bloody.
- If a cough lingers after a cold for more than five days without improvement. You may have a nonproductive cough seven to nine days after a cold. If other symptoms are clearing, there's no need to see a health professional.

Canker Sores

Canker sores are little blisters on the membranes of the mouth and cheek which break and leave open sores. These sores usually heal by themselves in about ten days, but they can be very painful.

VIRAL OR BACTERIAL?

Viral Infections	Bacterial Infections
Usually involve different parts of the body: sore throat, runny nose, headaches, muscle aches. In the abdominal area, viruses cause nausea, diarrhea.	Usually localized at a single point in the body: very sore throat with strep throat, ear infections.
Typical viral infections: cold, flu, stomach flu.	Typical bacterial infections: strep throat, ear infections.
Antibiotics **do not help.**	Antibiotics **do help.**
Bacterial infections may follow a viral infection if proper home care is not applied.	

Canker Sores - continued

No one knows for sure what causes canker sores, but some people are more susceptible than others.

Home Treatment

- Avoid eating spicy or salty foods, or citrus fruits when you have a canker sore.
- Apply an oral paste, like Orabase, to the canker sore. It sticks to the sore and protects it, eases the pain and speeds healing.
- Baking soda and water mixed to a thin paste may bring relief.

When to Call a Health Professional

- If mouth sores began after starting a medication, call your doctor.
- If a canker sore, or any sore, does not heal within 10-14 days.
- If a sore is very painful or comes back frequently.
- If white spots that are not canker sores appear in the mouth and do not heal within ten days.

Cold Sores (Fever Blisters)

Cold sores or fever blisters, caused by a herpes virus, are small red blisters which often weep and scab and have a dry ring around a moist center. Canker sores appear inside the mouth, while cold sores are outside the mouth. Cold sores are sometimes confused with impetigo. Impetigo is usually located between the nose and upper lip, and the fluid from it is pussy. Cold sores usually appear on the lower lip or the outer edge of the mouth and the fluids in them are clear. Cold sores may appear after colds, fevers, or exposure to the sun. They may come with menstruation or for no apparent reason at all. Cold sores are contagious; don't expose others.

Home Treatment

- Be patient. Cold sores usually go away within seven to ten days.
- Blistex or Campho-Phenique may ease the pain. Don't share with others.
- Cornstarch may be soothing. Apply in a paste made with a little water.

When to Call a Health Professional

- If sores last longer than two weeks.

Colds (Viral Rhinitis, Pharyngitis)

The common cold is an inflammation of the membranes of the nose, throat, pharynx, or tonsils. Infection can spread to the bronchi and middle ear. A cold is always virus-caused and there is no immunization. A cold cannot be cured by antibiotics, but occasionally the complications of a cold may be treated with an antibiotic. Antibiotics do not prevent complications.

Colds occur throughout the year, but are most common in late winter and early spring. The average child has six colds a year, adults much fewer.

The symptoms of a cold are runny nose, red itchy eyes, sneezing, sore throat, coughing, headache, and general body aches. As a cold progresses, nasal mucus may become superficially contaminated with bacteria and become pussy and thick. This is the stage just before a cold dries up. Children often have a fever with a cold, but fever in adults with a cold is less common. A cold usually lasts two weeks in a child and should be gone in a week in an adult. There is a gradual one or two day onset.

Frequently, a cold will lead to more serious complications. These are sometimes caused by improper or no home treatment; some people, especially children, are more susceptible to complications. Ear infections, tonsillitis and strep throat are three such complications. You should be able to recognize symptoms that warn of these.

You should suspect strep throat and go to your health professional for a culture if, during a cold: the throat becomes very sore and/or bright red or spotty, the clear nasal discharge turns green or yellow, there is an overall foul odor from the mouth or throat, or a fever of 103° is present. An earache, which is more than just a feeling of fullness in the ear following a cold, should also be investigated by your health professional.

If it seems you or your child has a cold all the time, or if cold symptoms last three weeks or more, suspect allergy. See page 72 for symptoms of allergy.

Prevention

Colds are almost an inevitable fact of life, but there are some hints which might help you prevent a cold, especially during the "cold" months of late winter and early spring.

- Eat and sleep properly and get plenty of exercise to keep up your resistance.
- Wash your hands frequently, particularly when you're around people with colds.
- Keep your hands away from your nose, eyes, and mouth.
- Use disposable tissues, not handkerchiefs, to reduce the spread of the virus to others.
- Humidify the bedroom.
- Using a mouthwash won't prevent a cold.

Home Treatment

- Get extra rest after work or school. It is not necessary to stay home from work or school if you feel well enough to accomplish something, providing you don't needlessly expose others.
- Drink hot liquids. Eight ounces of hot water or herbal tea every two hours will help relieve congestion; cold drinks, such as fruit

Colds - continued

juices or soft drinks, are not as helpful.
- Take aspirin or acetaminophen (Tylenol, Datril) to reduce fever and relieve aches and pain. Aspirin should be avoided for children. See dosage chart, page 253.
- Humidify the bedroom and take hot showers to relieve the congestion.
- Watch the back of your throat for postnasal drip. If streaks of mucus appear, gargle them away to prevent a sore throat or chest cold.
- Some over-the-counter preparations may relieve cold symptoms, making the patient more comfortable. Decongestants, cough syrups, cough drops, or nose drops may be helpful. See page 255 for their purpose and use. Sometimes use of decongestants at the first sign of a cold may prevent onset of an ear infection.
- Antibiotics will not help a cold.
- Antihistamines, although effective against allergies, will not help with colds.
- Vitamin C? If you think it will help, take it. Studies have not yet confirmed its value.

When to Call a Health Professional

- Fever over 103° with other symptoms of a cold. (104° if under age 12, 102° if over age 60.)
- Wheezing or breathing difficulty.
- A very sore, bright red, or spotty throat.
- An overall foul odor from the throat, nose, or ears.
- A yellow or green nasal discharge rather than clear.
- Cough which persists more than five days after a cold without improving.
- Earaches lasting more than an hour, more than just "stuffy."
- If the patient does not seem to be improving or if you are quite concerned.

Conjunctivitis

Conjunctivitis, or "pink eye," can be caused by bacteria, a virus, or by irritation from polluted air. It usually will clear by itself, or your health professional can prescribe some antibiotic eye drops. The symptoms of pink eye are redness in the whites of the eyes or excess matter in the eyes, without other upper respiratory symptoms. Some redness or swelling of the eyes is quite common with many respiratory infections and allergies and is not serious. With conjunctivitis, the lower lid will be red and swollen on the inside. The person may complain of a sandy, scratchy feeling in the eyes.

Prevention

Because conjunctivitis is very contagious, it is important for you to wash your hands thoroughly after treating a person with pink eye.

Just by rubbing the eyes, a child can transfer the condition from one eye to the other, so try to keep your child from eye-rubbing. Hands should be washed often. Conjunctivitis can spread to the whole family quite quickly.

Home Treatment

- Prevent spreading of the disease.
- Sometimes pus or matter in the eye will cake and dry during the night and on waking the person is unable to open the eyes. Lightly wipe the eyes with moist cotton or a clean washcloth and water.
- Do not cover the eye with a patch.

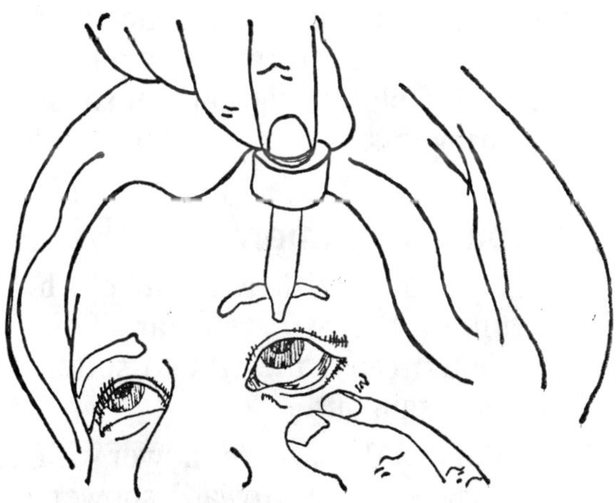

Inserting Eye Drops

- If eye drops are prescribed, insert in the following manner: pull the lower lid down with two fingers making a little pouch and put the drops in there. Close the eye to let the drops move around. Be sure the dropper is clean and does not touch any surface. Eye drops are washed out by normal tearing in about 20 minutes, so they should be replaced about once an hour.

When to Call a Health Professional

- If eye is red with thick, pussy discharge.
- If the problem is very bothersome or recurring.
- If there is distinct pain in the eye rather than irritation.
- If there is an abnormal difference in size of pupils. A constricted pupil may indicate iritis, which needs professional treatment.

EAR	
Symptoms	**/ What To Do**
Pain in ear	• See Middle Ear Infections, page 81.
Outer ear tender, painful when wiggled	• If preceded by a cold, see Middle Ear Infections, page 81. • See Swimmer's Ear, page 83.
Crusty, pussy discharge	• See Swimmer's Ear, page 83. • If preceded by earache and then pain subsides after a discharge, see Middle Ear Infection, page 81.
Fullness, feeling of something in ear	• If accompanied by other symptoms, see Colds, page 76. • See Swimmer's Ear, page 83. • Using penlight, inspect ear for object in ear. If object is in ear, call a health professional. • Using penlight, inspect for insect in ear. See Insect in Ear, page 173. • Using penlight, inspect ear for ear wax. See Ear Wax, page 80.
Itching, burning in ear	• See Swimmer's Ear, page 83.
Hearing loss, nonattentiveness	• See Ear Wax, page 80. • If continues over 10 days, see a health professional.
Pulling at ears by infants, small children	• See Middle Ear Infections, page 81.

Ear Wax

Ear wax is a protective secretion, similar to mucus or tears, which filters dust and keeps the ear clean. Normally, ear wax is liquid, self-draining, and not a cause for concern. Occasionally, the wax will build up, become crusty, turn black, and cause some hearing loss. Poking at the wax with cotton swabs, fingers, or other devices will only further compact the wax against the eardrum. Professional help is needed to remove tightly packed wax. You can handle most ear wax problems by avoiding cotton swabs and following the home treatment tips below.

Children have a lot of ear wax. It seems to taper off as they grow older. You should be concerned only if the ear wax causes ringing or a "full" feeling in the ears, or some hearing loss.

Home Treatment

- Lie down with a warm cloth under the affected ear. This should cause the wax to soften and drain out.
- Stand under a warm shower with waxy ear tilted toward showerhead or gently wash wax out with ear syringe and warm water. The warm water should help loosen the wax.
- If the warm cloth and shower do not work, apply Debrox, or some other over-the-counter wax softener each night for three to four days. Put in 5 drops at bedtime and apply a hot water bottle or heating pad set at medium heat

to the ear for 15 minutes. Tilt the head so the ear is over a handkerchief or tissue and gently remove excess solution.

When to Call a Health Professional

- If above procedures do not work. If wax build-up is hard, dry, and compacted, it may take up to three visits to remove it.

Middle Ear Infections (Otitis Media)

When an ear infection sets in, professional help is needed.

Middle ear infections are almost always bacterially caused. The viral infection of a cold causes tissue in the eustachian tube to swell. The eustachian tube carries air from ear to throat, and equalizes pressure between the middle ear and the outside world. As the tube is gradually closed off, a vacuum is created and fluids seep in, providing an excellent breeding ground for bacteria. White cells and body fluids come to fight the infection, causing pressure on the eardrum and pain. Sometimes the pressure builds to a point where the eardrum ruptures and the fluid leaks out, thus equalizing the pressure. While this is nature's way of healing and it is not necessarily harmful, repeated ruptures of the ear drum can cause scarring and possible hearing loss.

Left untreated, the bacteria can spread to the skull bones or brain. Fortunately, antibiotics will control the growth of bacteria and prevent complications.

Ear infections are more common in young children because their eustachian tubes are narrow and block more easily. Children also have more colds. Parents who had frequent childhood earaches often have children with earaches, indicating that anatomy apparently plays a role. Ear infections can also be caused by hard blowing of the nose or by excessive sniffing which send bacteria up the eustachian tube.

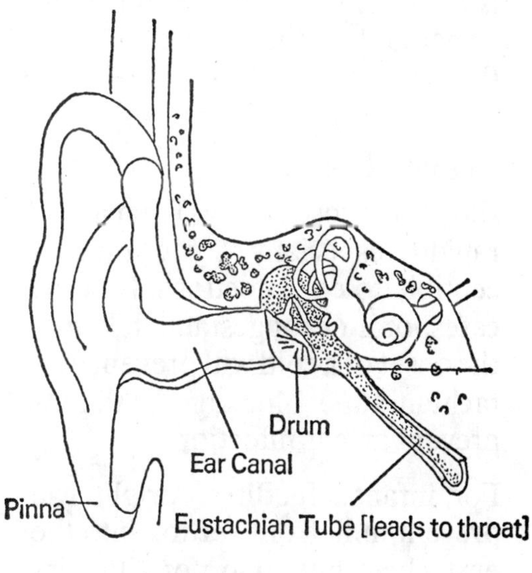

Ear

Middle Ear Infection - cont.

Because very young children cannot describe ear pain, the first sign of an earache might be a pulling or tugging on the ears. It is important to notice; untreated ear infection can readily cause hearing loss in children under age three.

Symptoms of a bacterial ear infection or earache will be pain, dizziness, ringing or fullness in ears, hearing loss, fever, headache, and runny nose.

Serous otitis media is a collection of fluid in the ear without infection. Usually, the only symptoms are temporary hearing loss or temporary fullness in the ear. If only these symptoms are present, there is no need to see a health professional, unless they continue more than ten days.

Prevention

Blow your nose gently. Treat a cold rapidly, especially if you are susceptible to ear infections. In some cases, oral decongestants taken at the onset of a cold will prevent eustachian tube blockage and thus prevent an ear infection.

For infants, feeding upright can prevent milk from getting into the eustachian tube. Do not allow infants to fall asleep with a bottle.

Home Treatment

After calling a health professional, the following may help relieve pain:

- Heat applied to the ear will ease the pain. Use a warm washcloth or a heating pad.
- Rest. Let your energy go to fighting the infection.
- Increase clear liquids.
- Aspirin or acetaminophen will help relieve the pain of earache. Aspirin should be avoided for children unless recommended by a physician. See dosage chart, page 253.
- Oral nasal decongestants may help relieve earache.

When to Call a Health Professional

- Any earache that lasts over one hour and is accompanied by acute pain should be checked by a health professional within 24 hours of the first pain. If the pain is severe at night, call the next morning *even if the pain has stopped.* The infection may still be present even if pain has subsided and should at least be discussed with a health professional.
- If home otoscope exam shows redness in a small child who can not describe ear pain. See page 248.
- Take the full course of antibiotics, if prescribed, but call if there is any adverse reaction to the antibiotic and stop taking it.
- If pain increases despite treatment.
- If there is no improvement after two to three days of antibiotics.
- If temperature is over 102°.

- If a headache, fever and stiff neck are also present. This may be a sign of meningitis.
- If an eardrum rupture is suspected.

Swimmer's Ear (Otitis Externa)

Swimmer's ear is an infection of the external ear canal. It is called swimmer's ear because it often appears after one has been swimming or otherwise has gotten the ear filled with water.

The first symptom of swimmer's ear is a feeling of tenderness or fullness in the ear, as if water were in it. The person may complain of itching and burning in the ears, and wiggling the outer ear will cause pain.

More acute swimmer's ear will cause redness of the ear canal and a crusty, pussy discharge. These symptoms indicate a secondary bacterial infection has set in, and this more acute secondary infection must be treated.

Prevention

- After swimming, shake your head to remove trapped water. Drying the ear carefully immediately after swimming may control swimmer's ear. One simple, safe method: twist each of the four corners of a facial tissue into a tip. With head tipped to the left, gently place the tissue tip into the left ear canal. Each of the four corners should be held in place for a count of ten. Dry the right ear with the four corners of a second facial tissue.
- Swim teams have found that recurring swimmer's ear can also be prevented by using prescription ear drops which change the acid/alkali level in the ear canal.
- Swim-Ear, a preparation made of boric acid and alcohol, is available over-the-counter at your local pharmacy.

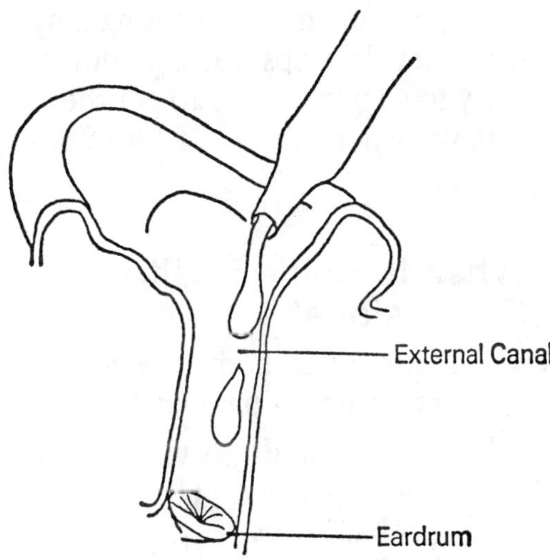

Ear Canal and Drum

Home Treatment

- Look in the ear with a penlight to be sure there is not an object or an insect in the ear. See Insect in the Ear, page 173.
- Soak a piece of cotton in alcohol or Burrow's Solution and place it in the ear over night. Then rinse the ear with three percent hydrogen peroxide and warm water in the morning.

Swimmer's Ear - continued

- If drops are prescribed, you need to know how to insert them. Have the person lie down, ear facing up. You may find it easier to insert ear drops in a small child in the following manner: Hold the child on your lap with legs around your waist and head down between your legs. Place drops on the canal wall in small quantities, so air can escape up the other side. If air gets trapped under the drops, it will keep the solution from penetrating any further. If drops don't go down, try to wiggle the ear to get them down where they will be effective.

When to Call a Health Professional

- If five days of home treatment has not reduced pain or itching.
- For antifungal drops which may cure swimmer's ear. However, it will probably recur.
- If there is a bloody or pussy discharge.
- If the earache follows a cold.

Encephalitis

Encephalitis is an inflammation of the brain, generally caused by a viral or bacterial infection. Mild encephalitis may occur with many diseases, even mumps or chicken pox.

The most common symptoms of encephalitis are high fever, headache, nausea, vomiting, and excessive sleepiness.

When to Call a Health Professional

- If any of these symptoms --- high fever (103°), severe headache, nausea, vomiting, or excessive sleepiness --- accompany or follow a viral or bacterial illness.
- If any of the above symptoms occur following a mosquito bite. In some areas, equine encephalitis is transmitted by mosquitoes.

Influenza (Flu)

Influenza, often called flu, is a viral illness which commonly occurs in the winter. It usually appears in epidemic form and affects many people at once. Influenza has symptoms similar to a cold, but they are usually more severe and come on quite suddenly.

The most characteristic symptoms of influenza are weakness and fatigue. Others are muscle aches, headaches, fever (101°-102°), sneezes, and a runny nose.

Although a person with influenza feels very sick, it rarely leads to more serious complications. The disease is usually dangerous only for infants, the elderly, or the chronically ill.

Flu-like symptoms can also be caused by Lyme disease which is spread by deer ticks. See Ticks page 116.

Prevention

Immunization against influenza provides fair protection, or may lessen symptoms if the disease is contracted. Older adults or chronically ill individuals should be immunized. The immunization is given each fall in anticipation of the coming flu season. You must be immunized within one week to four months prior to exposure for the shots to be effective.

Home Treatment

- Bed rest will be needed.
- Drink extra fluids, at least one full glass of water or juice every hour.
- Acetaminophen (Tylenol) can relieve head and muscle aches. See dosage chart, page 253. Aspirin should be avoided for children.
- Antihistamines may help dry up mucus and help the patient breathe more easily.

When to Call a Health Professional

- If cough brings up heavy mucus.
- After three days of fever over 102°.
- If there is increasing difficulty in breathing.
- When a patient seemingly gets better, then gets worse again.
- If flu-like symptoms occur ten days to three weeks after a possible tick bite. See Lyme disease discussion on page 117.

Laryngitis and Hoarseness

Laryngitis is a viral or bacterial infection of the voice box or larynx. The most common cause is a cold, but it can also be produced by allergy. Hoarseness can be caused by yelling or cigarette smoke and displays similar symptoms. Symptoms of laryngitis are an urge to clear your throat, fever, tiredness, pain in throat, coughing, and loss of voice.

Prevention

If you have a respiratory infection, take time to treat it so that the infection won't spread to your voice box.

To prevent hoarseness, stop shouting as soon as you feel minor pain. Give your vocal cords a rest.

Home Treatment

- It will usually heal itself in five to ten days and medication will do little to speed recovery.
- If it is caused by a cold, treat the cold. See page 76.
- Rest your voice by not shouting and by talking as little as possible.
- Stop smoking and avoid other people's smoke.
- Humidify the air.
- Drink lots of liquids.
- To soothe the throat, gargle with warm salt water (one teaspoon. in eight oz. of water) or drink honey in hot water, lemon juice, or weak tea.

Laryngitis - continued

When to Call a Health Professional

- If you suspect a bacterial infection. See page 74.
- If hoarseness isn't associated with a viral infection or smoking, and persists for one month.

Sinusitis

Sinusitis is an inflammation of the sinuses. The sinuses are cavities lined with mucous membranes, which drain easily unless there is an infection. There are two categories of sinus infections: acute, lasting less than three weeks, and chronic, lasting longer. Because the sinus cavities are not completely developed until late adolescence, sinus infections are seldom found in young children.

The key symptom to sinus infection is pain in the face under the eyes and opposite the bridge of the nose. There may also be headache, fever, runny nose, postnasal drip (mucus running down the throat), sore throat, and toothaches. Headaches may occur on rising and get worse in the afternoon.

To distinguish sinus pain from toothache, jump up and down on your heels. If the pain is from a sinus infection, it will be felt above the teeth. If a toothache is causing the pain, it will center on the tooth.

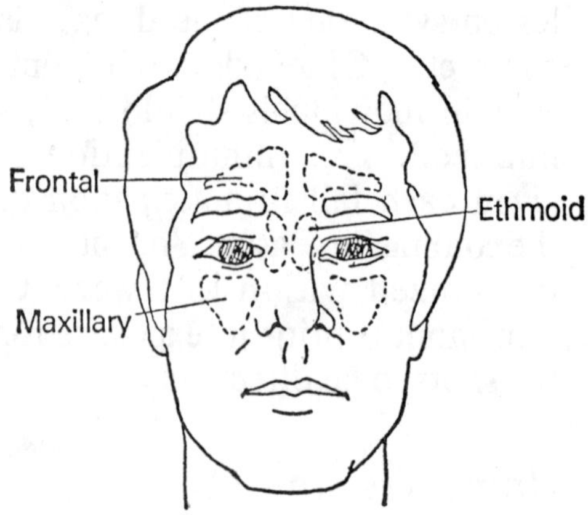

Sinus Cavities

Prevention

Blowing of the nose can cause sinus infections by forcing mucus up into a sinus and blocking it. Prompt, correct treatment of a cold may prevent a sinus infection.

Home Treatment

- When you first notice sinus pain, lie down on your back and apply alternating hot and cold compresses to your forehead and cheeks, about one minute each, for ten minutes. If needed, repeat four times daily, giving the last treatment at bedtime. This treatment seems to stimulate the flow of mucus.
- Apply decongestant nose drops to each nostril while lying down. See page 255 for types of decongestants. Do not use decongestant nose drops for more than three days.

- Try repeating the letter K (kay-kay-kay) for 30 seconds. This can help open the sinuses.
- Gargle with warm water to clear the throat of draining mucus.
- Increase home humidity, especially in bedrooms.
- Drink extra fluids to keep mucus thin. Drink eight ounces of water or juice every hour.
- Breathe steam from a vaporizer or over a sink filled with hot water.
- You may take aspirin or acetaminophen for headache. See page 253 for dosage.

When to Call a Health Professional

- If you feel pain along the ridge between the nose and lower eyelid. This could indicate infection of the ethmoid sinus, which is quite serious. Before the era of antibiotics, this complication often led to meningitis and death.
- Fever over 101°.
- Increased swelling of the face.
- Severe headache not eased by aspirin or acetaminophen.
- Bleeding from the nose.
- Increased thick yellow or green nasal discharge.
- Changes or blurring in vision.
- No improvement after two days of home treatment.

Sore Throats

You should usually be able to trace the cause of a mild sore throat. Often a mild sore throat is due to low humidity, smoking, air pollution, perhaps yelling. People with allergies and stuffy noses may breathe through their mouths while sleeping, thus causing a mild sore throat on rising. Sometimes a mild sore throat accompanies a cold.

If you can not determine the cause of a sore throat, or if you have been exposed to strep throat infections, you should get a throat culture. See Strep Throat on the next page.

Sore throats that are particularly bad in spite of a negative strep culture could be a symptom of mononucleosis. Mononucleosis, or mono, is caused by the Epstein-Barr virus and primarily affects young adults between 17 and 30. In addition to a severe sore throat, mono symptoms often include weakness, aches, dizziness, swollen lymph nodes in the neck, and an enlarged spleen. Since antibiotics will not affect the Epstein-Barr virus (nor any other virus), the home treatment is much the same as for mild sore throats. Add a large dose of bed rest to avoid relapse. Because mono is spread through saliva, infected individuals should refrain from sharing drinking utensils and kissing.

Sore Throats - continued

Mono is usually self-limiting within a week or two. A more chronic form of Epstein-Barr virus is thought to cause fatigue in some people for months or even years. While conventional medications and treatments can do little to combat the problem, efforts to boost the immune system may be effective. See page 242.

Prevention

An irritated throat may be prevented by avoiding the irritant. For example, try increasing the humidity of your living and working environments.

Home Treatment

- Humidify the home, especially the bedroom.
- A mild sore throat can be eased by gargling with hot salt water (one teaspoon in eight oz. water), or with Cepacol or another commercial mouthwash.
- If postnasal drip is present, gargle frequently to prevent chest colds and further throat irritation.
- Sucking cough drops or hard candy may soothe irritated tissue.
- Honey and lemon or weak tea may help.
- Drinking more fluids will soothe a sore throat.
- Stop smoking.

When to Call a Health Professional

- If you cannot trace the cause of the sore throat, such as postnasal drip, low humidity, excessive yelling, etc.
- If someone in the family has recently had strep throat.
- If you have a history of frequent strep throats.
- If sore throat is accompanied by a fever of 103°.
- If mild sore throat lasts more than two weeks (becomes chronic).
- If, on examination with a penlight, the throat is very bright red, or has white spots or pus on it.
- If there is a foul odor from the mouth.

Strep Throat

Strep throat is an infection caused by a streptoccal bacterium which can lead to rheumatic fever and possible rheumatic heart disease in three percent (3%) of children and young adults who get it. Strep is a serious infection which must be diagnosed and treated by a health professional. It is usually accompanied by a moderately high (103°) fever, bright red throat, pus or white spots on tonsils or throat, swollen glands and severe pain, and sometimes by a foul odor from the mouth. In an adult, there may be only a low fever (99°).

Strep is very difficult to recognize without a culture. Sometimes the person has no symptoms other than a mild sore throat. Even an experienced physician trained in diagnosis cannot be sure whether or not a sore throat is caused by strep bacteria without a throat culture.

If you have a sore throat you cannot trace to a specific cause such as low humidity or too much yelling or smoking, or if a sore throat with a cold is more than minor, you should get a culture.

With just a little practice, almost anyone can learn to take a proper throat culture, which could save you time and money. If strep throats are a frequent occurrence in your family or if you face the need of having the whole family cultured, investigate the possibility of throat culture kits. You swab the throat at home, place the swab in a test tube, and cork the tube. It is then cultured at your physician's office or a laboratory. See Throat Culture Kits, page 263.

Home Treatment

- You must see a health professional whenever any bacterial illness such as strep throat is suspected. An antibiotic, given either by injection or orally, is the usual treatment if the diagnosis is positive.
- Continue taking prescribed medication for the length of the time prescribed (usually ten days). *Do not stop* even if you feel completely recovered. The full ten days are needed to kill the bacteria and to prevent a quick recurrence of the infection.

Styes

A stye is an infection of the eyelash follicle that appears as a small, red bump, much like a pimple. It usually comes to a head and breaks after a few days. Most styes respond to home treatment.

Prevention

Styes are easily passed among family members. If you have a stye, keep your hands washed so you don't spread the infection.

Home Treatment

- Do not rub the eye.
- Apply warm, moist compresses for 10 minutes, 3 times a day until the stye comes to a point and drains.

When to Call a Health Professional

- If the stye persists for more than two days after home treatment has been applied.
- If it interferes with vision.
- If many styes appear at once or in quick succession.

Swollen Glands (Lymph Nodes)

The lymph nodes are small glands that swell and harden when infection occurs in the body. The most noticeable nodes are those in the neck. For location of lymph nodes, see page 26. The lymph nodes swell as the body fights minor infections from colds, insect bites, or small cuts. More serious bacterial infections may cause the glands to greatly enlarge and become very firm and tender.

Once lymph nodes harden, they may remain hard long after the initial infection is gone. This is especially true in children whose nodes can remain hard and visible for several weeks after a bad cold.

Home Treatment

- There is no specific home treatment for swollen lymph glands. Continue treating the cold or other infection which is causing the lymph nodes to swell.

When to Call a Health Professional

- If the nodes are large, very firm, and very tender.
- If enlarged lymph nodes are associated with other significant symptoms of infection.
- If enlarged nodes appear without apparent cause and persist for two weeks or more.
- Small hardened nodes that follow a child's cold or minor infection and are not tender can be observed without professional help. Report swollen glands at your next regular visit to a health professional.

Tonsillitis

Tonsillitis is an inflammation of the tonsils. Tonsils are lymph tissue located at the back of the mouth on each side.

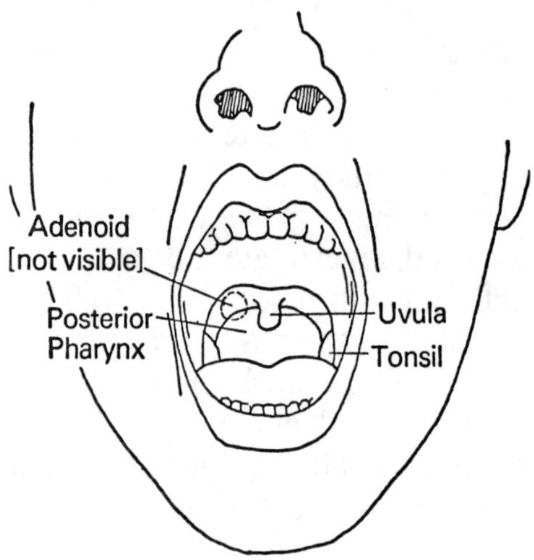

Location of Tonsils

Since lymph tissue filter infections, the tonsils are affected by any throat infection.

Symptoms of tonsillitis are tiredness, fever, and sore throat. The tonsils will be very dark and swollen and perhaps pussy or spotted. The person sometimes vomits and may have a coated tongue.

A tonsillectomy (surgical removal of the tonsils) will only cure recurrent tonsillitis; it will not prevent colds or other infections. The infection will merely settle elsewhere. There are two main reasons to remove tonsils:

- At least four recorded strep-tonsillitis infections in a year.
- Abscess on the tonsils.

A tonsillectomy, like any surgery, is serious and carries some danger. The surgery should only be done for valid reasons after discussion with your physician.

Home Treatment

- Tonsillitis requires the care of a health professional, who will probably take a culture to see if the infection is strep.
- Gargling with salt water may ease the pain of tonsillitis.
- Extra fluids will help dissolve the bacterial secretions and bring more healing blood to the area. Children and adults should drink a full eight ounce glass of water or juice every hour or so.
- Bed rest will help the body fight infection. Energy can then go to the healing.

When to Call a Health Professional

- If there is a history of tonsillitis, especially several bouts per year.
- If a sore throat involves the tonsils and they are red, swollen, or pussy.
- If a fever over 103° accompanies a child's sore throat (101°-102° for an adult.)

I don't deserve this award, but I have arthritis and I don't deserve that either.

Jack Benny

Chapter 7

Headaches and Other Pains

Nobody said that life would always be easy. Our aches and pains remind us that it is often not. But like everything else in life, our pain can be much better borne if we know how to manage it. This chapter covers pains from arthritis to headaches. The focus is less on reducing the pain than on limiting its impact on our enjoyment of life. As with most chapters in this book, we hope you have little need to refer to these pages. But when you do, we hope you will find that the guidelines here make your life a little more bearable.

Arthritis

Arthritis refers to inflamed joints. It generally brings pain when the inflamed joint is used. Arthritis can occur at any age, but since most cases are related to wear and tear, it affects older people the most.

The causes of arthritis are diverse and not fully understood. Genetics play a part in that some types of arthritis (gout, osteoarthritis and rheumatoid arthritis), seem to run in families. But, even then, it seems to take something else to bring it on. Joint abuse, body chemistry imbalances, hormonal changes and breakdowns in the immune system can all trigger a problem.

There are over one hundred separately identified types of arthritis, each with its own specific mix of symptoms. The chart on page 94 describes the four most common kinds.

Prevention

Wear and tear is the most frequent cause of arthritis. Heavy and extended use of a joint can wear it down. Even a single injury or period of joint abuse can trigger long-lasting inflammation. You

Arthritis - continued

can prevent a lot of pain by being kind to your joints. Avoid repeated jarring activities, particularly if any pain or fatigue starts to develop.

Wear and tear is bad but regular exercise can be terrific! Stretching exercises can help maintain a full range of motion in the muscles and joints. Because joint cartilage requires regular movement to get nourishment and rid itself of waste, some motion exercise is essential to healthy joints. Strengthening exercises protect against the muscle decline that leads to loss of function. Isometric exercises are particularly good at building muscle strength without putting a lot of stress on the joint.

Weight management is also an important part of a prevention plan.

Home Treatment

- Temporarily resting a sore joint and applying heat packs will speed healing and relieve the pain. Extreme cold seems to increase the pain. (Although cold packs can help after an acute traumatic injury or over- use of a joint.) Apply moist heat two to three times per day for 20-30 minutes. Massage sore spots after heat treatment.

TYPES OF ARTHRITIS

	Osteo-Arthritis	Rheumatoid Arthritis	Gout	Ankylosing Spondylitis
Cause	Breakdown of cartilage in joint	Inflammation of the membrane in joint	Build-up of uric acid crystals in the joint fluid	Inflammation of ligament at a joint of the spine
Symptoms	Pain, stiffness and swelling of joint	Pain, stiffness and swelling of joint, fever	Pain, stiffness and swelling, commonly of the big toe	Pain and stiffness of the spine
Comments	Most common type for both women and men between the ages of 45-90	Occurs most often in middle age; more common in women	Condition may be aggravated by foods high in purines, such as organ meats, or by alcoholic beverages	Most common in young men but results of the illness (stiff back) can last a lifetime

- Aspirin helps to reduce the swelling and ease the pain. Be aware of the symptoms of aspirin overdose on page 254.
- For long-term treatment, read the recommended reading, develop an exercise plan and find ways to avoid unnecessary abuse to your joints. See Resource #E1 on page 269.

When to Call a Health Professional

- If the pain is associated with a fever.
- If the pain is severe to the point that you can not use the joint.
- If the problem continues for over six weeks and the home treatments are not working.
- If there is sudden, unexplained swelling, redness or pain in any joint.

Bursitis

A bursa is a small sac of fluid which normally helps the muscles to slide easily over other muscles or bones. Injury or extended use and abuse of the bursa results in localized pain, redness, heat and inflammation, a condition know as bursitis. Bursitis usually develops quickly, over no more than a few days, often as a result of a specific injury. Tennis elbow, frozen shoulder, housemaid's knee and similar local soreness problems often involve some form of bursitis.

Prevention

The first case of bursitis may be difficult to prevent. Knee pads, good tennis instruction (two-handed backhand stroke) and sensible activities will certainly help. Once you have experienced a case of bursitis, future episodes can be prevented by avoiding the specific actions that lead to the problem.

Home Treatment

- Bursitis, if left alone, will usually go away or at least subside in a few days or weeks.
- Rest the inflamed part. Avoid the original cause of the injury as long as possible even after the pain subsides. Use a sling to support an elbow or shoulder for a day or two.
- Heating pads and hot baths will feel good, but ice or cold packs will speed healing.
- Apply cold for 15 minute periods, twice an hour for 6 to 12 hours. Begin the treatment as soon as you notice the problem.
- Aspirin may help, but don't overdo it. See page 253.
- Gently move the part through its full range of motion several times a day to prevent stiffness. Gradually increase the exercise to rebuild the strength of the affected muscles.

When to Call a Health Professional

- If there is fever and redness or an inability to use the joint.

Bursitis - continued

- If the problem is severe and you can think of no injury or activity that might have caused it.
- If the pain persists for a month or longer. Your physician can help you develop a new home treatment plan. Cortico-steroid drugs can be injected for severe cases. Be sure to ask about the risks and alternatives before agreeing to such treatment.

Headaches

Most headaches occur when the muscles of the head or neck become tense and contract. Both the muscle contraction and its effect on blood flow can cause headache pain. Headaches caused by tension or stress are the most easily controlled.

Home Treatment

- See the home treatment sections on page 97-99.
- Aspirin is not a cure-all for headaches. Occasionally, aspirin masks symptoms that might aid in diagnosis. Also, continued overuse of aspirin may lead to aspirin poisoning. See page 253.

When to Call a Health Professional

- If you are bothered by persistent severe headaches which have no cause you can discover.
- Sudden onset of pain without a specific cause. If pain wakes you in the middle of the night, or you know exactly what you were doing when the pain struck, that is a sudden pain.
- High fever of 103° and headache with no other symptoms.
- A stiff neck, fever and headache are danger signals of meningitis. Test to see if the person can touch chin to chest, mouth shut, without pain.
- Headache and confusion *not* following an injury. Confusion is common following an injury. (See Head Injuries, page 172.)
- Headache accompanied by loss of coordination, double vision, or other neurological symptoms.
- Recurring headaches in children.
- Headaches of increasing frequency and severity.

Otherwise, you can usually discover the cause of a headache and ease the pain simply, at home.

Headaches in Children

Headaches in children are quite rare. They are more frequent in children whose parents complain often about headaches. This is not so much because of inherited physical tendencies, but because children are mimics. Therefore, it is wise for parents to mention headaches as infrequently as possible.

Children are susceptible to tension headaches and it is up to a parent

Clues to Potential Headache Causes

- Does the headache occur on rising? Teeth grinding, and jaw clenching lead to morning headaches. Check with your dentist. The culprit may also be sinus or allergy trouble. Humidifying the bedroom may ease this problem. Sinus headaches can worsen in the afternoon.
- Does the headache precede the menstrual period each month? It may be caused by premenstrual tension.
- Does the headache occur each afternoon or evening? This may be a sign of eyestrain. Rest your eyes and have your vision checked.
- Do you sit at a desk all day? Poor posture can cause neck strain and headaches.
- Does the headache occur an hour or so before mealtime? Hunger is a frequent cause of headache.
- Is there a sharp pain directly behind the eye? This can be a sign of glaucoma, a serious eye disease, and should be checked by a health professional.
- Is the headache just on one side? This is a clue to migraine, discussed on page 98.
- Does the headache regularly follow any activity or event? It may be a tension headache. These headaches are described on page 99.

Headache Causes - Continued

- Did you over-indulge in alcohol the night before a headache? Hangovers are unpleasant. Coffee may help by constricting dilated blood vessels in the head. Prevent the next one!
- Are you taking any new medication? Some medications cause severe headaches in susceptible people.
- Smoking, pollution, hay fever and allergies can cause headaches.
- Headaches also accompany other illnesses,such as colds and flu.

to try to discover the cause. Often, just talking about a problem may help a child. Some children try to do too much, or are pushed by family or school to do too much. Even fun activities can be overdone and the child may be exhausted. Some methods for talking about problems with your children are on page 240.

Hunger can also cause headaches in children. A daily breakfast and a nutritious after-school snack may prevent them. Eyestrain may also cause headaches.

Home Treatment

- Talk to your child and try to discover the source of the headache and deal with it.
- Play quietly with the child.

Headaches in Children - cont.

- If the headache is still present, have the child lie down in a darkened room with a cool cloth on the forehead.
- Let the child know you care. "Tension" headaches are sometimes "attention" headaches.
- Acetaminophen is rarely needed, but if used, give the correct dose. See page 253 for the proper dosage. Do not give aspirin to children.

When to Call a Health Professional

- If a child's headaches occur two to three times a week or more.
- If a headache is severe and is not relieved by relaxation or acetaminophen.
- If you cannot discover a reasonable cause. Sometimes just talking to a different adult will allow a child to share problems.
- If you suspect eyestrain.
- If you are using pain relievers to control headaches at least once a week.

Migraine Headaches

Migraine headaches are a specific kind of headache with specific symptoms. The pain of a migraine headache is caused by the increased dilation or widening of the blood vessels in the head.

Migraine headaches come on quite suddenly and recur every few weeks or months. There is almost always pain on only one side of the head, often at the temple. The pain may switch sides. The person becomes sensitive to light. Because the victim is nauseated, migraines are sometimes called sick headaches.

Sometimes, the person who has a migraine will see spots before the eyes just before it occurs, and some people experience great bursts of energy and activity just prior to the onset of a migraine.

Prevention

If you know your migraine headache comes at a certain time each month, experiment and try to relax and eliminate tension from your life at these times.

Make an effort to become aware of any substances that bring on attacks, e.g., certain foods, alcohol, hormone pills.

Home Treatment

- A mild migraine headache may pass if you go immediately to a darkened room and lie down. Relax the entire body, concentrating on the eyes, the forehead, the jaw and neck muscles, and working down to the toes. See page 216.
- Most migraine headaches will require professional diagnosis and treatment.

When to Call a Health Professional

- If you suspect your headaches are migraine headaches --- one-sided, very severe, "sick" headaches. You will need professional diagnosis and evaluation.
- A health professional can provide drugs for treating migraine headaches.
- Discuss with your health professional relaxation and biofeedback techniques which may prevent migraines.

Tension Headaches

About 90% of all headaches are caused by tension. Tension headaches are often caused by the tightening of the muscles of the back and shoulders either from emotional stress or from physical stress such as sitting at a computer too long.

A tension headache may occur as pain all over the head, as a feeling of pressure, or as a band around the head. Some people feel a dull, pressing, burning feeling above the eyes. Rarely can you pinpoint the center or source of pain.

Prevention

For tension headaches particularly, the best cure is prevention. Often you can relate your headache to a recent activity which caused tension: grocery shopping, a meeting, sitting in one position for too long, or paying bills. The elimination of the cause is the best prevention, but that is often impossible. In those cases, just knowing some event makes you tense and taking time before and after the event to relax may help.

Home Treatment

- Aspirin or acetaminophen may relieve a tension headache. Avoid frequent use.
- Try to stop whatever you are doing and just close your eyes and sit. Exhale and inhale slowly and deeply.
- Lie down in a darkened room with a cool cloth on your forehead.
- Try to relax the head and neck muscles.
- Apply heat with a heating pad or hot water bottle or take a hot shower.
- Massage the neck muscles. Massage gently, firmly, toward the heart.
- Try a relaxation exercise:
  - Imagine that your neck muscles are loose, that your head is balanced at the end of your spine, and if you tip your head just slightly, it will fall in that direction. Let your mouth fall open, jaw relaxed.
  - Close your eyes. Relax the forehead muscles.
  - Now imagine a hole in your head, and inhale and exhale slowly. As you exhale imagine that the pain is flowing out of that hole. This will take some time and concentration. It is

Tension Headaches - cont.

not an instant cure, but a good one.

- Evaluate your usual neck and shoulder posture at work and make adjustments if needed.
- Either vigorous or isometric exercise helps relieve tension for some people. See page 58 for neck exercises.
- Good ways to cope with stress begin on page 215.

When to Call a Health Professional

- If unexplained headaches continue to occur more than three times a week.
- If a headache is of very sudden onset.
- If a headache is very severe and cannot be relieved with the above measures.
- If you are using pain relievers for headaches at least once a week for several weeks.
- If you need help discovering or eliminating the source of your tension headaches. Often talking it over with a health professional is helpful.

I have a simple philosophy... scratch where it itches.

Alice Roosevelt Longworth

Chapter 8

Skin Ailments

Skin problems affect most people. Although they are rarely life-threatening, they can be a nuisance. Diagnosing skin problems may require the help of a health professional or a dermatologist (a physician specializing in skin problems), especially the first time you have a particular ailment. The second time it appears you may be able to recognize it and use treatment previously prescribed or a home remedy. After diagnosis or recognition, refer to your individual problem listed alphabetically in this chapter.

First, try some general treatments for skin rashes to determine if the problem will clear up by itself. If practical, leave it exposed to the air. Observe it and if it seems to get worse or spread within 24 hours, call your health professional. Do not apply salves or ointments if the cause of the rash is not known. The ointment itself might cause a reaction and perhaps make it more difficult to diagnose.

Any time a rash looks infected, call your health professional. An infection will be very bright red or pussy and you may have a mild fever. Streaks of red leading away from the rash or from any skin problem are a more serious sign of infection.

If you have decided to call a health professional, first do a home physical exam. Then go through the questions on page 102 and answer those which pertain to your problem. Your answers will help you and your health professional in the diagnosis. You may even discover what is wrong by calling.

A rash may sometimes be caused by emotional stress, tension, or nervousness. If stress appears to be a possible cause, review the relaxation techniques suggested on page 215, and try to reduce the tension-causing events in your daily routine.

Skin Rashes: History and Exam

- Have you come into contact with something which irritates your skin? For a list of possible skin irritants, read about contact dermatitis on page 106.
- Where and when did the rash first appear?
- Does this rash appear anywhere else on the body?
- Is there a fever accompanying the rash? Record your temperature taken in the morning and at night.
- Does the rash appear to have spread?
- Does the rash itch? (Surprisingly, many do not).
- Does it hurt?
- Does anyone else in the family have a similar rash?
- What immunizations have you had?
- Are you taking any new medication, either prescribed or over-the-counter?
- Is there a sore throat with the rash?
- Have you been under unusually heavy stress recently?
- Have you been unusually nervous or tense?

General Prevention of Skin Problems

One of the most important keys to good healthy skin is cleanliness. However, the skin can be washed too often. The body secretes natural oils to lubricate it. Soap and water wash these oils off; this is useful when there is excess oil, but harmful if the skin is dry. Too much soap and water can remove the protective lubrication causing dry, flaking, itching skin.

If you have dry skin, give some thought to whether you really need a shower twice a day or even daily, particularly in the winter months. Try bathing about three times a week with daily washing of the underarms, feet, and genitals. By eliminating a daily shower, you may be able to break the habit of washing off the skin's protective covering, then putting on creams and lotions to replace it. If you really feel you need a daily shower but have dry skin, try a soap substitute which contains no detergent, or a mild soap without built-in deodorants. Your pharmacy will have many brands. Read the labels. It will be stated that it is a soap substitute.

Too many Americans have been convinced that human odor should be completely masked. The creams, lotions, sprays, and powders applied daily to the body can harm your skin. They can be a source of an allergic reaction, causing itching, rashes, or infections. Soap and water are more effective than perfumed cover-ups.

Acne

Acne is the term for inflamed spots appearing over the face, back, and shoulders. It occurs most often in adolescence. Acne is caused by a number of things. Apparently, hormonal balance affects acne, and adolescence is the time when hormones are adjusting. Small hair follicles become plugged with dead skin cells. Secretions accumulate and bacteria grows, causing pimples, cysts or blackheads

Prevention

- Cleanliness is essential. Clean, but don't scrub your skin.
- Stress or anxiety seem to aggravate acne in some people, so worrying over acne probably only makes it worse.
- For years it was believed that diet played an important role in causing acne flare-ups. Teenagers were discouraged from eating nuts, chocolate, and other forbidden foods. Most doctors now feel that diet is not a significant cause of acne. If acne seems to occur after eating a particular food, avoid that food.

Home Treatment

- Again, cleanliness is essential. Wash your face, shoulders and back with soapy water. If your regular soap doesn't seem to help, try an over-the-counter soap manufactured for acne. Always rinse very thoroughly.
- Long hair brushing against the face seems to make acne worse. Consider keeping your hair shorter and off the forehead.
- Steam or warm wet towels placed on the skin for 10-15 minutes two or three times a day, will often help open the glands and allow for deeper cleaning.
- Benzoyl peroxide gel or cream, an over-the-counter preparation, may be helpful in treating acne. Start with the lowest strength and apply once a day after washing. You may experience mild redness and dryness as a side effect; it may take several weeks to work.
- If you wear make-up, use only water-based cosmetics and only if they don't aggravate the acne.
- Try to eliminate some of the tension in your life. See page 215 for ways to cope with tension.

When to Call a Health Professional

- Cases that cannot be controlled with the above suggestions should be seen by a physician.
- Some doctors prescribe oral antibiotics which have been known to control acne. However, do not over-use antibiotics. You must decide whether or not controlling your acne is worth the risk of antibiotic treatment. See the discussion of the appropriate use and dangers of antibiotics on page 261.
- Your health professional may also prescribe medication that is applied directly to the skin.

Acne - continued

- If your acne continues to be a real problem, don't hesitate to see your doctor to discuss further therapeutic measures that may help.

Athlete's Foot

Athlete's foot is a fungal infection which is not restricted to athletes. Fungus is present everywhere, but grows best in warm, moist, dark places. Bare feet come in contact with wet surfaces where the fungus is present, such as in community showers. The fungus then thrives on the skin or anywhere we perspire a lot and where air cannot circulate.

Symptoms include cracked and peeling areas between the toes, redness and scaling on the soles, and intense itching. If symptoms don't subside with the use of antifungals, then you may have other skin problems such as eczema, contact dermatitis or psoriasis.

Prevention

Keep your feet clean and dry. If members of your family are susceptible to athlete's foot, use an antibacterial agent such as Lysol or Pinesol when cleaning showers. Wear thongs in community showers or public swimming pools.

Home Treatment

- Wear cotton socks to absorb perspiration.
- Consider changing your socks during the day to keep your feet dry.
- Alternate your pairs of shoes from day to day. This will allow your shoes to dry out completely between use so that they are less likely to harbor the fungus.
- Tinactin and Desenex are good antifungals available over-the-counter. They come in powder, cream, or spray form.

When to Call a Health Professional

- If you are a diabetic or have poor blood circulation in your legs, you should not try self-treatment. See a health professional. It is particularly important to avoid inflammation or infection if you have either condition.
- If the skin appears to get worse after you apply the antifungal, discontinue using it and see your health professional.
- If the infection continues and does not seem to be getting better. You may need a more powerful antifungal prescription.

Bald Spots

Bald spots should be distinguished from baldness. The natural tendency of some people toward baldness poses no major health risk (other than sunburn-related problems). Bald spots may be caused by repeated stress to the hair such as tight braids or habitual unconscious pulling. Bald spots that occur on a normal scalp may not be natural occurrences and may perhaps indicate a more serious problem.

When to Call a Health Professional

- Bald spots with a gray-green scale are often ringworm. Ringworm of the scalp can be very difficult to cure. Seek your health professional's help.
- If you have bald spots, it is a good idea to call your health professional as this may be a signal of a variety of problems.

Bee Stings

Some people are more sensitive to bee stings than others. Most bee stings cause localized reaction; the area stung will swell, redden, and itch. Sometimes this localized reaction will be quite severe and persist over a length of time, but it is not an allergy as long as it is still localized. An allergy to a bee sting is a reaction that is generalized throughout the body. There can be hives all over the body, shortness of breath, tightening of the throat muscles, or difficulty in swallowing. A very severe reaction can cause death. In fact, more people die annually as a result of bee stings than from snake bites.

Prevention

Anyone who has had a generalized reaction to a bee sting should carry a bee sting kit which contains adrenalin (Epinephrine). It can be obtained with a prescription and contains immediate treatment for bee sting reactions. Ask your doctor or pharmacist for instructions on how to use the kit.

If you have had a generalized reaction, desensitization shots can be a good idea. Talk with your physician or allergy specialist.

Home Treatment

- For a localized reaction, use cool cloths or ice to relieve the pain. Antihistamines may be used if the itching is severe. See page 255 for antihistamines.
- Bees leave stingers imbedded in the skin. Remove the stinger by flicking it out. Be careful not to squeeze more venom into the skin. The localized symptoms should then decrease.

When to Call a Health Professional

- If a person has a generalized reaction, *IMMEDIATE* professional help is needed. These signs are:
  - Hives all over the body.
  - Shortness of breath/wheezing.
  - Difficulty in swallowing.
- To discuss bee sting kits (with adrenalin) or desensitization shots for a person who has had a generalized reaction.

Boils

A boil is a red, swollen, painful area on the skin similar to an overgrown pimple. Boils occur most often in areas where there is hair and irritation, such as on the neck, armpits, genitals, breasts, face, and buttocks. A boil occurs when a hair follicle gets plugged and doesn't drain. This becomes a perfect place for bacteria to grow because the body fluids are trapped in that one place. The pus inside a boil is white blood cells that came to clear the infection away. Pain is caused by pressure on the nerve endings due to the swelling.

Prevention

Do not scratch a boil that you already have. You might carry the bacteria to healthy areas of the skin and cause more skin infections.

Home Treatment

- Bring moist heat to the area as often as possible. Soak a washcloth in very warm water and place it directly on the boil for 15 minutes. Keep the cloth warm by replacing it in the warm water whenever it gets cool. This moisture will keep the surface soft and free from scabs that might close the skin and trap the infection. The heat increases the blood flow to the area which promotes the healing process and brings the boil to a head. This treatment is most effective when you first notice a boil.
- Do not squeeze, scratch, drain or lance the boil.

When to Call a Health Professional

Your health professional can surgically drain the boil or treat it with antibiotic drugs. See the discussion of the appropriate use of antibiotics on page 261. You should call a health professional if:

- The pain stops you from normal activities.
- You have a fever over 100°.
- No progress has been made in two to three days of good soaking treatment.

Contact Dermatitis

Contact dermatitis is a rash that occurs when the skin has an allergic reaction to a substance.

Any rash that appears only on a specific localized part of the body is likely to be contact dermatitis. Poison ivy, laundry soaps, and jewelry are all common sources of contact dermatitis although hundreds of other items may cause irritations in certain individuals.

If you have a localized rash, try to discover the possible source of irritation. Ask yourself the questions in the Contact Dermatitis History listing. The list is a starting point for your history-taking process. Your list of questions should start with the location of the rash. A foot rash, for example, would probably relate more to new shoes or socks that it would to your new shampoo.

Contact Dermatitis History

- Where did the rash appear?
- When did the rash first appear?
- Does the rash appear anywhere else on the body?
- Have you changed shampoos or hair dyes lately?
- Does the rash involve any part of your body where clothes are worn?
- Have you changed detergents lately?
- Any new jewelry?
- Have you been near plants such as poison oak, poison sumac or poison ivy?
- Any new hand cream or nail polish?
- Any new medications taken recently?

Home Treatment

- If you do discover the cause of the rash, remove the irritant.
- Avoid using soap on a rash.
- If practical, leave the rash exposed to the air.
- For itching relief treatments, see page 109.

When to Call a Health Professional

- If the rash becomes infected. This means that it is very bright red or there is pus.
- When fever is 101° or more.
- If there are red streaks leading away from the rash.
- If after five days it has not improved.
- If after two weeks the rash continues to bother you.
- Answer the Contact Dermatitis History questions on this page before calling your doctor.

Dandruff

Dandruff occurs when the skin cells of the scalp flake off. This flaking is natural and occurs all over your body. On the scalp, however, flaking can cause problems by mixing with oil and dust to form dandruff. Although dandruff cannot be cured, it is often necessary to control it.

Home Treatment

- Try frequent and energetic shampooing with any shampoo. Hair can be shampooed daily and should be if this controls your dandruff.
- If the dandruff is excessive and itchy, you might try a dandruff shampoo. Experiment, then use the one that works best for you. Some brands to try include Selsun Blue, Sebulex, and Tegrin.

When to Call a Health Professional

- If shampooing frequently doesn't seem to control dandruff. Your health professional might prescribe a dandruff shampoo.

Impetigo

Impetigo is a bacterial infection which often starts when a small cut or scratch becomes infected. Symptoms are oozing, scabbed, honey-colored, crusty sores. These sores usually appear on the face between the upper lip and the nose. However, impetigo spreads easily so it may appear anywhere on the body. Bacteria get under the fingernails and are spread by scratching.

Prevention

Washing all scratches with soap and water is one of the best ways to prevent impetigo. If your child has a runny nose, keep the area between the upper lip and nose clean to prevent the start of infection. In the summer, children often go swimming as a substitute for a bath, but baths and shampoos are still necessary. Fingernails should be kept short and clean.

Home Treatment

- If one honey-colored crusty sore appears, try scrubbing it with soap and water. Bacteria grows under the scabs, so scabs must be removed. Twenty minutes of soaking every two hours followed by gentle soapy scrubbings should remove the scabs. You can give warm soaks on the face by using a warm washcloth. When the washcloth becomes cool, rinse it in warm water.
- Dry the skin without rubbing the sores. Try using a hand-held hair dryer after light towel drying.
- Follow the soapy scrubs with application of an over-the-counter ointment such as Bacitracin.
- If one person in the house has impetigo, the other members are susceptible to the infection because it spreads easily. Try to insure against this spreading by:
  - Having each member of the household use separate washcloths and towels.
  - Not having anyone share the same bath water.
- Men should not shave over the sores but around them. Use a new razor blade daily and do not use a shaving brush.
- DO NOT put adhesive bandages on the sores. The adhesive applied to the skin provides a warm shelter for the bacteria to multiply. Also, when the adhesive is pulled off, it pulls dead skin with it. This creates new entry points for the bacteria to invade. If you must cover the infection, use gauze and keep the adhesive as far away from the infection as possible.

When to Call a Health Professional

- If you cannot seem to make any progress in controlling impetigo and any new crop appears. Your health professional will be able to prescribe an antibiotic to clear it up.
- If the area around the nostrils, face, and/or lips swells and becomes tender.
- If there is red streaking leading away from the infected area or

there is pain in a nearby lymph gland.

- If the infected person gets sick and has a fever over 101°.

Ingrown Toenails

Ingrown toenails most often occur on the big toe. The nail gouges into soft skin tissue causing pain, inflammation, and infection. This usually results from trimming the nails too short, especially at the corners. Shoes which are too tight or an injury to the toe might be other causes of ingrown nails.

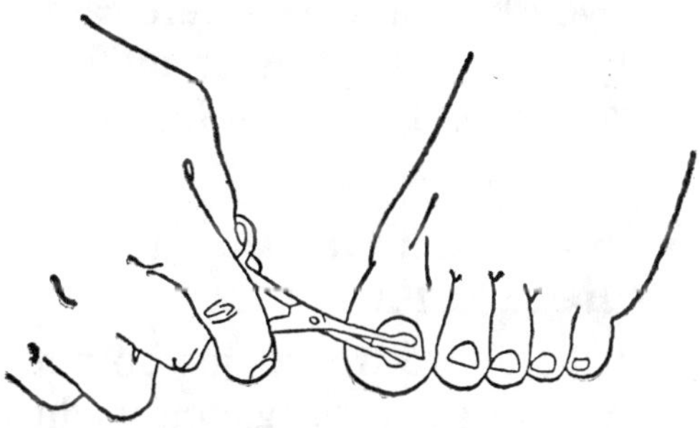

Cutting Toenails

Prevention

- Cut your toenails straight across rather than rounding them. Be sure to leave the corners of the nails long enough to prevent gouging.
- Buy roomier shoes if yours are too tight.

Home Treatment

- Soak your foot in warm water. You should then be able to draw the nail away from the toe far enough to place a wisp of cotton between the nail and the toe. This will cushion the area where the nail is gouging. This procedure should be done daily until the corner of the nail has grown beyond the point where it cuts into the flesh. It is not necessary to replace the cotton daily; leave the first one in place throughout all soakings, checking to make sure it's there daily.

When to Call a Health Professional

- If the toe is very infected, your health professional may have to remove a portion of the nail. If it is infected, the toe will be painful, swollen, red, and may ooze pus.

Itching

Itching accompanies many skin rashes. Since for most rashes it is advisable not to scratch the skin, you need to know how to relieve itching.

Home Treatment

- Keep the area cool and wet. Try cool compresses or a compress soaked in Burrow's solution, which is available at the drugstore.

Itching - continued

- Apply cornstarch or baking powder paste to the skin.
- Try to forget about the itching by putting your mind on other things. Games may keep a child's mind off the itching.
- Aspirin can help relieve itching. Use acetaminophen for children.
- Alpha-Keri and Syntex are bath oils which are excellent for dry, itching skin, but use them very sparingly.
- Also, over-the-counter hydrocortisone can be tried for a contact dermatitis or any local small areas of itching.
- Try an over-the-counter antihistamine such as Chlor-Trimeton or Benadryl.

When to Call a Health Professional

- If itching is very severe, a stronger antihistamine may be prescribed for relief.

Jock Itch (Tinea Cruris)

Jock itch is a fungal infection that occurs in the groin area of males and females. This fungus grows best in warm, moist places.

Symptoms include severe itching and moistness in the genital area and thighs. There are red, raised areas on the skin which may also weep or ooze pus or liquid.

Prevention

People who perspire a lot are susceptible to jock itch, especially if they do not bathe often enough to wash away the perspiration. You should wear cotton underpants to absorb perspiration, bathe often, and keep your clothes clean.

Home Treatment

- Rub cornstarch over the genital area after bathing. This will dry the infection and prevent friction.
- Wear cotton underpants.
- Avoid pants that are too tight and cause friction.
- Avoid pantyhose.
- Bathe often.
- If you have a more severe case, try an over-the-counter antifungal such as Tinactin or Desenex.

When to Call a Health Professional

- If the above treatments do not seem to be working, you might need an antifungal prescription.

Lice

Lice are small, white, wingless insects about the size of tiny ants that live on the human body. The adult is called a louse and its eggs are called nits. Nit-picking, then, is the removal of the louse eggs, a tedious task since the nits are so small.

There are three types of lice: head, body, and crab. Head lice appear on the hairs of the head, behind the ears, and on the back of the neck. To check for head lice, look through the hairs; lice or nits should be seen along the hair shafts. Body lice are rarely seen as they inhabit the seams and lining of clothing and move to the body only when feeding. Crab lice infest the groin and pubic area.

Lice suck blood. However, it is their saliva and excretions which cause you to itch. Lice are spread by close contact with such things as car seats, coat racks, theatre seats, combs, sexual contact, and bedding. Head lice are very common in school children since they are in such close contact.

The main symptom of lice is itching. You should also be able to see the nits, which adhere to a hair shaft.

Home Treatment

- Kwell, a prescription shampoo, is highly effective in getting rid of lice. Cuprex, RID and A-200 Pyrinate are over-the-counter remedies that will usually do the job. Shampoo the entire family and thoroughly clean the clothing, bedding, rugs, and furniture in your home. You may need to boil things to sterilize them or iron those things you cannot boil. Repeat this treatment in 48 hours to kill the lice that hatch from eggs already laid.
- Use a fine-toothed comb to remove all eggs (nits) from the hair. Ask your pharmacist or public health department for more information.

When to Call a Health Professional

- If you tried over-the-counter remedies and were not successful, you can discuss whether a prescription for Kwell is needed.
- Call your public health department and they will assist you both in treating the problem and in preventing reinfestation.

Moles

Pigment gives skin its color. When the pigment is close together, it is called a mole. Moles are sometimes raised and hairy and appear more on some people than others. Heredity may play a part in the number of moles you have, as parents with moles tend to have children with moles. They appear throughout a person's life, and during pregnancy and adolescence may tend to darken and enlarge.

Moles are rarely precancerous. Actually, a mole has about the same chance of becoming cancerous as any other part of your skin.

If there is a family history of melanoma (highly malignant mole), you should periodically check your moles (or have family members help) for any changes. Look for any unusual colors (black, red or blue), irregular borders, bleeding or itching. Let your health professional know of this family history.

Moles - continued

Home Treatment

- Become familiar with your own moles. Know their normal color, shape, and size so that you will be aware if they change.
- It is okay to pluck offensive hairs from a mole.

When to Call a Health Professional

- If a mole changes in size or color by darkening or lightening.
- If a mole bleeds or itches.
- Moles should only be removed by a qualified health professional.

Mosquito Bites

A mosquito bite appears as a red, raised bump. While not dangerous, itchy mosquito bites can be a real nuisance.

Prevention

Good insect repellents are very effective in preventing mosquito bites. Apply them to all exposed areas of the skin and thin clothing whenever a lot of mosquitoes are around. Reapplication every few hours may be needed. Be sure to protect your infant by applying a repellent or by keeping the child covered when you are in an area that has many mosquitoes. Your pharmacist can recommend a good repellent. Prevention is especially important if there are reported cases of mosquito bite-caused encephalitis in your area.

Home Treatment

- To relieve itching, see page 109.
- If the bite is bothersome because of swelling, apply a cool compress.
- Trim the fingernails of children to prevent them from scratching and infecting the bites.

Psoriasis

Psoriasis is a chronic skin disease. It appears as silvery skin patches which are often on the knees, elbows and scalp. Fingernails, palms and soles can also be involved. With normal skin, the outer layer of skin cells is replaced every 30 days. In a psoriatic, the outer layer is replaced every three or four days. The silvery patches, called plaques, are composed of dead skin cells which accumulate in thick, scaly layers.

Prevention

Psoriasis seems to be partly hereditary. It is *not* contagious so there is no fear of catching it.

Home Treatment

- There is no known cure for psoriasis although many treatments can help to control it. Spontaneous remissions may occur. Very rarely, the condition may disappear completely.

- Sunlight exposure seems to be one of the most effective treatments. Sunbathe often, but avoid sunburn.
- The therapeutic value of sunlight can be increased by the use of tar products (bath emulsions, shampoos, creams, gels, and oils) available in most pharmacies. Be careful; these products greatly increase the risk of sunburn.
- For moderate scalp scaling, try tar shampoos such as Sebutone, Zetar, or Polytar shampoos.
- Try to reduce some anxiety and tension in your life. These can cause outbreaks or increase severity of outbreaks. See page 215 for ideas on how to relieve stress.

When to Call a Health Professional

- See your health professional for a diagnosis if you suspect psoriasis. Your health profcssional may prescribe topical steroids, tars, anthralin or other forms of therapy. Systemic medications are usually avoided, except in severe cases, because of undesirable side effects.
- If it is generalized, that is, covers much of your body.
- If you experience joint pain.
- If the psoriasis gets worse despite home treatment.

Ringworm

Ringworm is a fungal infection of the skin. It develops into a red, scaly, itching ring which can appear anywhere on the body. Ringworm of the scalp may appear as areas of hair loss in children.

Prevention

Ringworm is frequently transmitted to people by cats and dogs which carry the fungus. If your family adopts a cat or dog, have it checked for ringworm by your veterinarian. Teaching your children not to snuggle with stray cats and dogs with bald patches is wise, but they may still contract the disease from cats and dogs which have ringworm buried beneath their fur.

Home Treatment

- Try Tolnaftate, Desenex, or Tinactin, over-the-counter drugs, on small spots.

When to Call a Health Professional

- If ringworm is severe and spreading, a prescription is probably needed.
- If there are spots on the scalp, especially if the hair is missing.

Scabies

Scabies is caused by tiny mites which burrow into the skin. They cause severe itching which starts about a month after being infested. The mites are seldom seen for they live in the burrows they make under the skin. You can acquire scabies by direct contact with an infected person.

The key symptom of scabies is severe itching. Your skin will have tiny bumps, burrows, and tunnels that look like exclamation marks. These can be found on the genitals, breasts, in the armpits, along the belt line, or between the fingers.

Prevention

- Promptly treat any symptoms of scabies with Kwell lotion to prevent spreading.
- General cleanliness will prevent scabies.
- Since scabies infestations are highly contagious, wash more thoroughly and more frequently, especially if you have had recent contact with an infected person.

Home Treatment

- Wash all bedding and all clothing articles and iron the mattress to kill the eggs of mites. It is important to kill not only the mites but eggs to prevent further infestation. The entire household must be treated at the same time or else eggs will be left in clothing or bedding to start the cycle again.
- Kwell lotion, a prescription, must be applied to all household members.

When to Call a Health Professional

- To discuss whether a prescription for Kwell is needed.

Scarlet Fever

Scarlet fever is a strep throat with a rash. It is not as prevalent today as it once was and, once contracted, can be treated with antibiotics.

Symptoms of scarlet fever include a high fever and a rash formed with pinhead-sized dots which are prominent over the cheeks, chest, abdomen, and groin. The skin appears "sandpapery." The little bumps on the tongue get bigger and redder, making the tongue appear to have a strawberry or raspberry texture. In many cases, about ten days to three weeks after the illness, the skin peels.

Prevention

Scarlet fever is spread through contact with an infected person. Avoid people with a known case of the fever.

When to Call a Health Professional

- If a rash accompanies a sore throat.
- If a rash peels and the child has had a sore throat in the recent past, see a health professional.

Even if the child seems well and is peeling, it is worth having a throat culture taken. If the culture indicates strep, antibiotics will be prescribed to cure the strep throat infection.

- Antibiotics are especially important to prevent rheumatic heart disease which is caused by a toxin made by the strep bacteria.

Skin Cancer

Skin cancer is the most common of all cancers. Fortunately, it is also the form of cancer we know most about. Most skin cancer is caused by prolonged and frequent exposure to the sun. In fact, 90% of all skin cancer occurs on the face, neck, and arms where exposure to the sun is most frequent. Fishermen, farmers, construction workers, and others who spend much time out-of-doors are very likely to develop skin cancers along with a very leathery complexion. Lighter skinned, blue-eyed people are also more likely to develop skin cancer than those who normally tan easily. Black people run little risk of skin cancer.

Skin cancer doesn't usually develop until middle age or later. Even so, solar damage to the skin in early life will greatly contribute to skin cancer later.

Fortunately, most skin cancers are slow-growing and are easy to recognize and treat long before they reach a serious state. Virtually all of these slow-growing cancers can be completely cured by simple, inexpensive removal in a physician's office.

A small percentage of skin cancers are much more serious. Such cancers, called malignant melanomas, can quickly invade the body and spread to other body tissue. Melanomas, unless treated quickly, may be fatal.

Prevention

- Use a sunscreen with at least a sun protective factor (SPF) of 15. SPF factors of 20 or 25 are even better. Apply 15 minutes before exposure and reapply every hour or two. Sunscreens are now recommended for children as well as adults. Protective clothing, rather than sunscreen, is best for infants. Although sunscreens allow a person to get a light tan, they prevent the burning and dark tanning that lead to premature aging and skin cancer.
- Wear loose-fitting, light-colored clothing and a hat.

Home Treatment

- Once skin cancer has developed, nothing can be done at home to treat it. Home emphasis should be placed on preventing further cancers by using sunscreens and other protective measures.

When to Call a Health Professional

- If a pigmented mark or elevation appears or changes size or color.

Skin Cancer - continued

- If a scaly blemish persists, bleeds, or changes in character.
- If a sore persists without healing for four to six weeks.
- If a wart or mole changes in size or color.

Sunburn

A sunburn is usually a first-degree burn which involves just the outer surface of the skin. Sunburns are uncomfortable, but usually not dangerous unless they are extensive. They are, however, quite dangerous if extensive in infants or small children.

Prevention

There is really no good excuse for getting a sunburn. There are excellent creams available which screen out the sun's burning rays but still allow a tan. Over-the-counter products containing PABA are good unless you have a PABA allergy. Examples are Sundown, Presun, or Sure Tan sunscreen. Non-PABA lotions are available. Sunscreens should be reapplied periodically, especially after swimming.

Home Treatment

- Watch sunburned children or infants for signs of dehydration. See page 38 for dehydration symptoms.
- Cool baths can be very soothing.
- A low-grade fever and a headache can accompany a sunburn. Lie down in a cool, quiet room to alleviate the headache.
- Drink lots of water and eat some salty crackers to replace fluid and salt loss.
- Sucking on ice chips will help control nausea.
- There is nothing you can do to prevent peeling; it is part of the healing process.
- Watch for signs of heat exhaustion. See symptoms on page 190.

When to Call a Health Professional

- If there is severe blistering.
- If there is a fever of 102° or more.

Ticks

A tick is a small pest that fastens itself to the body. A tick should be removed as soon as you discover it.

Lyme disease is a bacterial infection spread by deer ticks. Early symptoms include a bright red rash that forms around the bite ten days to three weeks after being bitten. Flu-like symptoms of fatigue, chills, headache, muscle ache, and low fever may also appear. Months later, temporary heartbeat irregularities and loss of muscle coordination may develop, as well as recurring arthritis.

Prevention

Wear light-colored clothing and tuck pant legs into socks.

Home Treatment

- Check regularly for ticks when you are out in the woods and thoroughly examine your skin and scalp when you return home.
- Remove any tick by gently pulling with tweezers, as close to the skin as possible. Pull straight out and try not to squeeze the body.
- Wash the area and apply an antiseptic. See page 250.
- Save the tick in a closed jar for tests by your doctor or health department if symptoms develop.

When to Call a Health Professional

- If a fever, infection or red rash develops up to three weeks after a tick has been removed. Lyme disease can be effectively treated with antibiotics.
- If you are unable to remove the entire tick.

Warts

Warts are growths on the skin that are caused by a virus. They can appear anywhere on the body but usually on hands and the backs of fingers. Warts are not dangerous, but can be very bothersome.

Little is known about warts. Most are only slightly contagious. They can spread to other areas on the same person but rarely to others. Genital and anal warts are an exception. Genital warts are sexually transmitted and must be treated. They have the potential to promote cancer of the cervix. See page 149. Because warts seem to come and go for little reason, it's possible that they are sensitive to slight changes in the immune system. In some cases, your thoughts and attitudes can help them go away.

When necessary, your health professional can remove warts by freezing them, by cautery, with chemicals, or by cutting them off. Unfortunately, they often come back or leave a scar.

Home Treatment

- Warts appear and disappear spontaneously. They can last a week, a month, or even years. To get rid of your warts, it helps to believe in the treatment. Faith and incantations seem to work just as well as over-the-counter preparations.
- If the wart bleeds a little, stop the bleeding with a little pressure.
- If the wart is in the way, use a pumice stone or a mild ointment containing 5% salicylic acid. Both of these are over-the-counter products.
- Plantar warts appear on the feet and can be painful. You can buy doughnut-shaped pads made of foam rubber which alleviate the pressure on the wart when you walk. If a pad does relieve the pain and the wart doesn't increase in size, use it. Otherwise, see your health professional.

Warts - continued

- Try the least expensive method of treating warts that you can think of. You may save a trip to your health professional.
- Don't attempt to cut or burn off a wart yourself.
- Warts often go away if you leave them alone.

When to Call a Health Professional

- If the wart has been irritated or knocked off. It could then become infected.
- If a plantar wart is painful when you walk and is not relieved by the foam pads.
- If you have warts in the anal or genital area. See page 149.
- If the wart causes continued discomfort.
- If the wart hasn't disappeared from the feet or hands in two months (to confirm that it is a wart).
- If warts are present on the face or are of cosmetic concern.

My mother had a great deal of trouble with me, but I think she enjoyed it.

Mark Twain

Chapter 9

Infant and Child Health

When your child gets sick or hurt, you are usually the first person around to provide care. Your calmness, confidence and competence in caring for the health problems of your children will help them enjoy healthy childhoods, and learn the importance of self-care for their own use as they mature.

Virtually every health problem in this book may be of concern to children. However, there are a few which are almost exclusively childhood concerns. For convenience, we have grouped these problems into this chapter.

If the problem you are looking for is not included in this chapter, please look for it in the index.

Facts About Infants

The following brief notes are of particular concern to parents of infants (birth to one year). They may dispel some unnecessary parental fears.

Umbilical Cords and Belly Buttons

The umbilical cord will drop off and the navel will usually heal in one to three weeks. At the time the cord comes off, there may be a moist or bloody oozing for a few days. This does not need special treatment. After leaving the hospital, clean the navel daily with a bit of cotton wet with rubbing alcohol. Discontinue this when the navel is healed. Do not give a pan or tub bath until the navel is healed. The appearance of the navel is not affected by the way the cord is tied off. Bellybands will not prevent an umbilical hernia (bulging out). Hernias usually go away within a year, although sometimes it will take several years.

Skin

Newborns frequently have rashes or white "pimples" scattered over their bodies which usually clear without treatment. Often the skin will peel or flake off during the first two to three weeks after birth. This is normal and requires no treatment.

Eyes and Ears

Many babies have no tear ducts for the first few months of life. In some babies, tears will spill out. These tears are not a problem and need no treatment.

The eyes may cross. This should be discussed with your doctor at your next scheduled well baby checkup.

Ears on newborns may be soft and floppy. The cartilage has not yet hardened but it will become firm as the baby grows.

The Head

Often there is hair on the face or body of a newborn. This will go away in a few months. The head may be misshapen but will round out in a few days.

An infant may commonly snort and sneeze during the first few weeks of life. This rarely indicates a cold. Hiccups and spitting are also common.

Breasts

Newborns, male and female, often have some swelling in one or both breasts and sometimes there will be a secretion from the nipples. This is perfectly normal and it should go away in a few weeks. If not, see a health professional.

Hips

You should check infants for hip dislocation (the hip bone is not in its socket):

1. Check the thigh folds. If the hip is dislocated, one thigh fold will be higher than the other.

2. When the child is lying face up with thighs and knees bent, as in Position 1, legs should be the same length. If one leg appears shorter than the other, there is a possibility of hip dislocation.

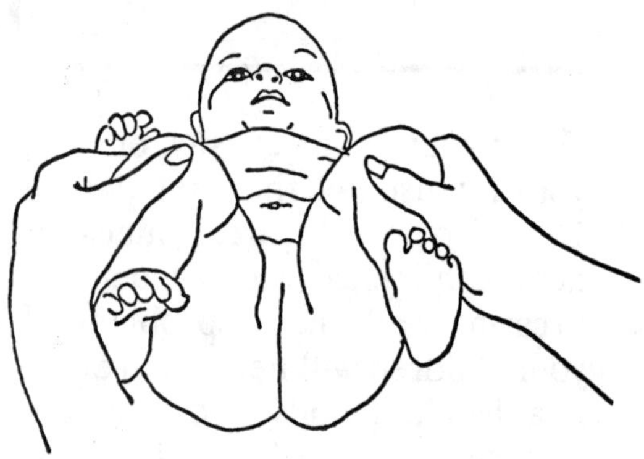

Position 1

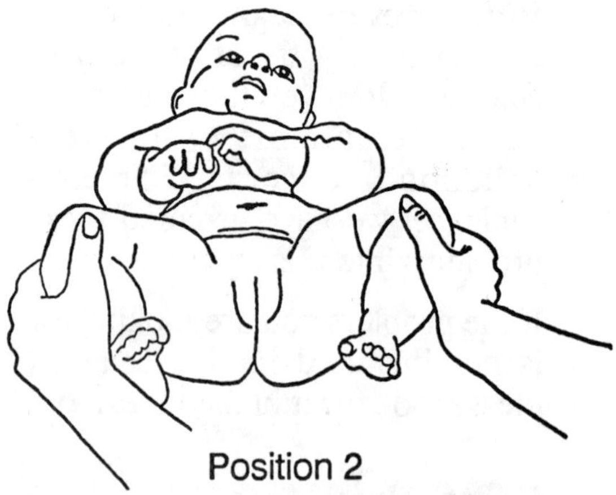

Position 2

3. In the same position, when legs are bent outward as in Position 2, legs should bend outward to the same distance.

Any abnormalities should be reported to a health professional. When discovered early, hip dislocation is easily corrected. Late correction is difficult and time-consuming.

Bowel Movements

The baby's first bowel movement will be black, tarry and sticky. This is from meconium which was in the baby's intestines before birth. Over the first week, the stools will change in color and consistency. If your baby is breastfed, the stool will eventually become a yellow, seedy paste. Bottlefed babies' stools are brown and more formed.

The number of bowel movements will vary with each baby: anywhere from several times a day to once a week. This range is normal. Your baby has diarrhea if the stools are watery, mucusy, green and foul-smelling. Loose stools, which a breastfed baby will have, is not a sign of diarrhea unless other signs are present. Since diarrhea can lead to dehydration, your health professional will need to be notified. Be prepared to tell your doctor the color, consistency and number of bowel movements. See page 39 for more information about diarrhea.

Your baby is constipated if the stools are hard, dry and difficult to pass. Constipation is not related to the frequency of bowel movements. See page 36 for more information.

Genitals

Female: Frequently, newborn baby girls have swollen genitals and a vaginal discharge is present for the first two weeks of life. A girl's genitals include two sets of lips called the inner (labia minora) and the outer (labia majora), which form around the urinary opening and the vaginal opening. In babies, the inside lips and the clitoris (the front part where the two lips come together) stick out much more than when the girl is older. The outside lips look like a red cuff around the vaginal opening. The redness fades as the baby grows. The lips are sometimes stuck together but generally separate as the baby grows.

Later sexual development in girls usually begins between the ages of 9 and 11 with a widening of the hips, hair growing under the arms and in the pubic area, and enlarging of the breasts. These changes usually take place before menstruation begins.

Examine the entire genital area for any sores, red swollen areas, or discharge. The area inside the two lips should be pink and moist.

There should be no pain or straining on urination and the urine should come out in a fairly steady stream. The color should be pale yellow and there should be no strong ammonia odor.

Male: In baby boys, the size of the penis and scrotum will vary. Normally, the testes are in the scrotum

Genitals - continued

at birth and will descend in a short time. You and your health professional should watch for undescended testes. Occasional hardening (erection) of the penis is normal in babies and small boys.

To examine a male baby's genitals, look at the penis for sores, red spots or "pimples." Now check the glans (the head of the penis covered by the foreskin) to see that the urinary opening (urethra) is at the tip of the glans. Sores are common in circumcised babies, so check carefully. In uncircumcised babies, do not force the foreskin back. A waxy substance is a normal lubricant.

Also check the scrotum, the sac which holds the testes. Note any sores or red areas. Notice in a baby whether the testes have come down into the scrotum. Gently squeeze. You should feel two, one in each side of the scrotum, about the size of a kidney bean. The testes and scrotum enlarge when a boy is about 10 to 13 years old.

There should be no pain or discomfort on urination. Urine should come out in a fairly steady stream, without straining. Urine should be pale yellow and there should not be a strong ammonia odor, which is a sign the urine is too concentrated (a clue to possible dehydration).

Strain, pain, or dribbling on urination are symptoms which should be discussed with a health professional. Also swelling, bluish discoloration, pain, or tenderness of the scrotum require medical attention.

About Circumcision

Circumcision is the most common surgery performed. It may also be one of the most unnecessary. Although the surgical removal of the foreskin of a newborn boy's penis is a simple procedure with few complications, it does cause pain for the new baby and provides little benefit.

Circumcision was once advocated as a way to prevent infection under the foreskin and penile cancer. It is now known that regular bathing and cleaning under the foreskin does just as well. If you teach your son to wash under the foreskin, there is no reason to accept the costs and risks of circumcision. The American Academy of Pediatrics states flatly that there is "no absolute medical indication for routine circumcision of the newborn." Some insurers will no longer pay for it. Only in the United States is circumcision for non-religious reasons so common.

Some parents worry that uncircumcised boys will wonder why they look different. Tell them that you did not want to hurt them and that most boys all over the world look just like they do.

On the other hand, circumcision is nothing to get too worked up over. The risks are low and if you feel a strong traditional need to have it done, no one will blame you.

Birthmarks

Birthmarks, which come in all sizes, shapes, and colors, usually disappear by themselves. The flat purple ones on the upper eyelids, lower forehead, and back of the neck and large, flat, bluish ones on the lower back will go away eventually. Brown, flat, oval birthmarks are there to stay and will do no harm. You can watch this type during regular home physicals and report to your health professional if they grow or otherwise differ from their normal appearance.

Strawberry birthmarks are lumps that can appear anywhere on the body. They usually appear after birth and enlarge during the first year of life. They become raised, red, and soft but most of them will disappear if they are left alone; 70% are gone by age seven. They will start to recede after a year but will leave an area of skin that does not tan well. It is best not to have these removed as the treatment is unnecessary. They need to be removed only if they interfere with vision or breathing or if they are distorting the face. If surgery is necessary for cosmetic reasons, it is better to wait until the child is older.

When to Call a Health Professional

- For surgery if a birthmark is unacceptable.

Chicken Pox (Varicella)

Chicken pox is highly contagious and almost all children will get it. It is a relatively minor disease, however, and children do not usually become very sick. Chicken pox can occasionally lead to encephalitis, an inflammation of the brain. See page 84. However, encephalitis usually subsides without complications.

Symptoms of chicken pox include a rash or red, pimple-like spots that turn into clear blisters. The rash can cover the entire body including the throat, mouth, ears, genitals, and scalp. A child might also have just one or two spots. If anyone in the neighborhood or classroom has chicken pox, start looking for symptoms in your child in about two weeks. Chicken pox is contagious one day before the rash appears until all the pox are scabbed and dry. In the first couple of days, your child will be in generally ill health, and have a fever and abdominal pain. Then the blisters on the skin appear.

Prevention

There is no useful prevention. In fact, the disease is less bothersome for a young child than an adult so some parents willingly expose their children. However, the severity of the disease has no relation to how close to an infected person a child is when exposed.

Chicken Pox - continued

Home Treatment

- No aspirin! Aspirin should not be used for children who may have chicken pox because of its connection to Reye's Syndrome. Use acetaminophen (Tylenol) instead.
- Try to make the child comfortable.
- Control the itching because if scabs are scratched off too early, they may become infected. For itching relief treatments, see page 109.
- Cut the child's fingernails.

When to Call a Health Professional

- If there is fever over 102° that lasts for more than two days.
- If severe itching cannot be controlled by acetaminophen (Tylenol) and warm baths.
- If bruising appears without injury.
- If sores are in the eyes.
- If you notice signs of encephalitis that can occur after any viral infection. These signs are:
    - Severe headache
    - Unusual sleepiness
    - Continued vomiting

Colic

Parents of young babies are often painfully aware of colic. Colic is not really a disease. Rather, it is a name we give to a whole assortment of problems that can cause babies to draw up their legs, tighten their abdomens and holler. First determine if the child is hungry. If the baby has just eaten and is still upset, it's a good chance colic is the problem.

Colic may often be caused because the child's digestive tract has not completely developed for handling milk. Also, any abnormality in feeding may bring on the problem. The most common include:

- Swallowing air because of feeding too fast, too slow, or while lying down.
- Taking overheated milk.
- Using nipple holes that are too small.
- Nervous tension in the family during feeding.
- Intolerance to sugar in the formula.
- Allergy to cow's milk.

The same symptoms could also be caused by a tight rectal muscle or by pain elsewhere in the body (earache, hernia, or urinary infection).

The nice thing about colic is that it goes away as the baby's system matures, almost always by the end of the third month. Of course, it's over sooner for many babies and may never appear in many others. Although no one method always works to relieve colicky babies, there are a number of possible remedies you can try.

Home Treatment

- Most important --- stay calm and try to relax.
- Make sure the child is getting enough to eat --- the problem may be hunger, not colic.
- Prop the baby up during and for 15 minutes after feeding. Burp the baby after each ounce.
- Don't overheat the formula but heat to body temperature.
- Make sure manufactured nipple holes aren't too small. To test the size of the hole, put cold formula in the bottle and turn it upside down. Without shaking, the milk should drip out at a rate of about one drop per second. If it doesn't, enlarge the hole by making a cross cut over the hole with a knife. Babies can swallow more air if the nipple holes are too small because they suck air around the nipple.
- Try a different cow's milk preparation, or use a milk substitute.
- Use a pacifier, and try rocking or walking the baby. Putting the baby stomach-down over your knee may be helpful.
- Don't worry about spoiling a baby the first three months; comforting babies makes them and you feel better.
- Get a friend or neighbor to baby-sit some evening while you go to dinner and a movie!
- If nothing else works, colic medicines are available to help relax the baby's stomach and intestinal muscles. They require a prescription. Be sure to ask your pharmacist to explain the correct dosage and any possible side effects the drug might cause.
- Don't feel guilty about shutting the bedroom door and turning up the stereo once in a while; if it will help you to relax, it will help the baby.

When to Call a Health Professional

- Colic normally does not require professional treatment unless it is accompanied by vomiting and /or diarrhea or other signs of more serious illness. If the child looks healthy between episodes and if your emotions can stand the noise for the first three months, you have little cause for worry.

Convulsions-Febrile (with fever)

Convulsions or fits are involuntary spasms of muscles which may involve the whole body or only part of it. Although frightening, convulsions with fever in children between six months and four years of age usually do not indicate any serious ailment.

Convulsions are more likely to occur when children have a rapid elevation to a high temperature. Some young children's temperature-regulating mechanisms are not completely developed, and their bodies can't perspire enough to cool the body quickly.

Convulsion-Febrile - cont.

For general information on fever, see page 19.

The child with a convulsion stiffens up, clenching fists and teeth. The eyes will roll back and the child will hold his or her breath, salivate a lot and maybe turn a little blue. The child may urinate or pass stools.

Prevention

- Dress a child with a fever loosely to prevent overheating.
- If your child has a tendency to convulsions, discuss with your health professional the possibility of fever-reducing suppositories which prevent convulsions if given at the onset of a fever.
- Much depends on how sick the child appears. A fever is a sign that the body is fighting infections. There is usually no need to reduce fever under 101° (102° rectally).
- As fever climbs, observe the child. A fever of 103° in a child who otherwise looks okay need not be reduced. But if the fever goes over 103°, to 104° or higher, it should be reduced. Reduce the fever with the help of a tepid bath and/or acetaminophen.
- Children run much higher fevers than adults. A fever of 103°-104° is considered quite high in an adult.

Home Treatment

- Protect the child from falling against a table edge or some other sharp object.
- Time the length of the convulsion, if possible.
- Roll the child to the side to drain saliva from the mouth. Clear mouth of any vomit or saliva so the child can breathe.
- Do not put a blunt object between the teeth; either you'll break the stick or a few teeth.
- To reduce fever, sponge the child with cool (not cold) cloths or immerse in lukewarm water. Some shivering indicates the child is cooling rapidly.
- Do not use ice packs. That is too sudden a reduction.
- Check for injuries.
- Dress the child lightly, and put her or him to sleep in a cool room.
- Try to stay calm. This will greatly help the child.
- After the convulsion is over extra fluids can be helpful. Wait until the child is alert to avoid choking. Drowsiness often persists after a convulsion.

When to Call a Health Professional

- If the convulsion is not accompanied by fever.
- If it is the child's first convulsion.

- If the child is under six months old or is five years or older or if convulsion is in adult.
- If the convulsion lasts longer than one minute.
- If you are unable to successfully reduce the fever after a convulsion. You should reduce it to 101° to be sure it is well below the seizure-producing level.

Cradle Cap

Cradle cap is a thick scaling or greasy crusting, like dandruff, common to many babies. It is often caused by not washing an infant's head well enough for fear of damaging the skull during a bath. A baby's skull is not that delicate and can be regularly and thoroughly washed to prevent cradle cap. If you see some crusting or discoloration of the scalp, you are probably not washing vigorously enough.

Home Treatment

- Give the baby's head a good scrubbing with a washcloth or soft brush and your regular baby shampoo. Scrub hard. You can also try loosening the scales with baby's comb before shampooing.
- If scrubbing with regular shampoo doesn't work, try using Ionil•T, Sebulex, or Selsun Blue shampoos. Use caution when applying these as they are not baby shampoos and will irritate your baby's eyes.

Croup

Croup is a respiratory problem most common of children two to four years of age. It usually occurs at night. A child with croup has a hacking cough, seal-like bark, and has trouble breathing. The child is terrified and fighting for breath with a low-grade fever of 100°-101°.

Home Treatment

- Stay calm. The child is already terrified and needs you to be calm.
- Get moisture into the air to make it easier for the child to breathe. The simplest method is to take the child into the bathroom, turn on all the hot water faucets, then both of you sit on the floor and read a story in the steamy room.
- Set up a vaporizer or croup tent in the child's bedroom. Another person could do this while you are still in the bathroom with the child. To make a croup tent, put a humidifier under the crib and drape a blanket over the head of the crib to trap the moisture near the child's head. If the child is older and no longer in a crib, you can drape the blanket over an umbrella or card table. With a cold mist humidifier, the air will be quite cold but you need not worry about your child getting too chilled. The humidity is the important part.
- If the child starts crying, the worst is over. Someone who can cry can breathe.

Croup - continued

When to Call a Health Professional

- If the child drools or is breathing with the chin jutting out and the mouth open.
- If the child is gasping and can't breath.
- If croup lasts longer than three nights.
- If 20 minutes of steam inhalation does not relax the child enough to allow sleep.
- If there is a "sucking-in" or retraction between the ribs as the child breathes in.
- If the child has a high fever of 102°-103°.
- If you or your child becomes hysterical and cannot seem to calm down.
- If it is the first case of croup in your family.
- A very late sign to call your health professional is if the child's skin turns bluish or dusky. This is a sign that the child is not getting enough oxygen.

Diaper Rash

Diaper rash is a reaction to the ammonia in babies' urine, to their stools, or to the soap used to wash diapers. While it is uncomfortable, diaper rash is usually not dangerous.

Symptoms of the rash are a red bottom and thighs. It will be easier for you to recognize this after you have seen it the first time.

Prevention

- Try to change the diapers as soon as possible after they have been soiled or wet.
- Leave the skin open to the air as often as possible.
- Don't wash the diapers in too much soap.
- Make sure the diapers are rinsed well after they are washed thoroughly.
- Avoid using disposable diapers or plastic pants for a while, if your baby has frequent problems. These trap the moisture against the baby's skin.

Home Treatment

- Every baby is unique, so try a few different methods to find out what is best for your baby.
- Wash your baby's skin around the diaper area thoroughly with plain soap and water and then dry the skin well.
- Don't use excessively bulky or multilayered diapers.
- Add one ounce of vinegar to one gallon of rinse water when washing diapers.
- You can try protecting the skin with Desitin, Diaparene, zinc oxide, or Vaseline, but discontinue if a rash develops as the creams slow healing.
- Change diapers frequently.
- Sometimes cornstarch or baby powder on the diaper area will be more comfortable. If you do use

powder, be sure to put it in your hand first as shown, rather than sprinkling it right on your baby. You and your baby will inhale less powder this way.

- Stop using plastic pants when the rash appears.
- Try changing detergents if the rash does not clear.

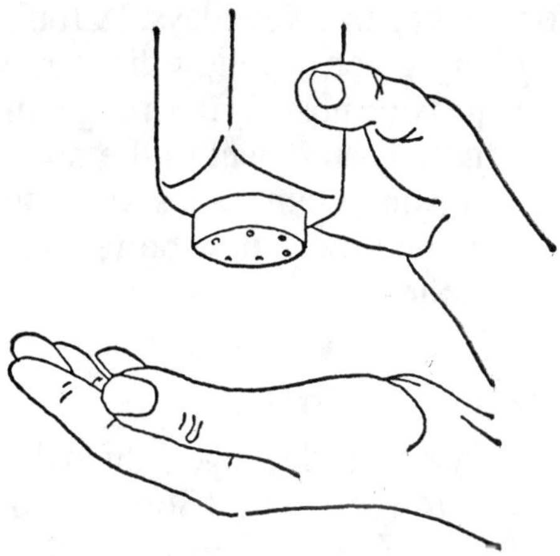

Applying Powder

When to Call a Health Professional

- If the diaper rash becomes very bright red.
- If the rash becomes raw or sore looking.
- If the rash has blisters or crusty patches.
- If the problem is caused by frequent diarrhea, see dehydration, page 38.

Measles

There are two types of measles: rubeola (called red, regular, two-week, or hard measles), see page 133; and rubella (called German, three-day, or soft measles), see page 133. The symptoms of these two diseases are quite different so they will be discussed separately. However, prevention for both is the same.

Prevention

Every child should be immunized against both types of measles. The MMR (measles, mumps, rubella,) immunization is available and effective. In the 1940's, an immunization for measles was made from a dead virus. It has long since been discovered that this type will not provide lifelong immunity. Anyone given this type of vaccine was also given an additional shot of gamma globulin at the same time. If you or a family member were given this type of vaccine, you should be revaccinated with the live virus.

Mumps

Mumps, once a common childhood illness, is another disease being conquered through immunization. When a person gets mumps, the parotid gland, located in front of and below the earlobe, swells on one or both sides. To help determine if it is mumps, run your finger down the jawline. If it is mumps, the jawbone will not be felt. If it is swollen lymph glands the jawbone can still be felt. This swelling may be accompanied by fever and vomiting. The person is contagious from one day before the swelling

Mumps - continued

begins until the swelling has gone down, at least seven days.

Mumps can *occasionally* lead to encephalitis, an inflammation of the brain, to deafness, or to sterility in males after puberty.

Prevention

Your child should be immunized after 12 months of age. There is now a convenient measles-mumps-rubella shot for children which can be given all at once. Only one shot is necessary for life-long immunity. Adults who have never had mumps should be immunized against them. Males, after puberty, can become sterile if they get the mumps. Females won't become sterile, but mumps can go to the ovaries which can be very painful.

Home Treatment

- Give extra fluids. It may be more comfortable for the patient to sip through a straw.
- Isolate the patient until the swelling subsides.
- Sucking ice may ease vomiting.

When to Call a Health Professional

- If the fever goes over 103°.
- If the patient has a severe headache.

Object in the Nose

Quite often curious children will put something such as a bead or a piece of popcorn up their noses. With a little patience, you often can save a physician visit by removing a foreign object yourself.

If the child does not tell you right away what has happened, you'll get some clues in a few days. A foul-smelling, green or yellow discharge from just one nostril is a strong hint that there is an object in the nose. The mucous membranes are also swollen and there may be tenderness in the nose.

Home Treatment

- Spray a nasal decongestant in the affected nostril. (See "Your Home Health Center," page 256). This will reduce the swelling of the membranes, and sometimes the object will drop out.
- Using a good light and holding the child quiet, try to remove the foreign object with blunt-nose tweezers. If you do not succeed after two tries, call a health professional.
- The nostril may bleed a little. This is not serious.

Pinworms

Pinworms are small, thin parasites that commonly infect the digestive tracts of young children. Pinworms are most common in four to six year-olds although children of any age may be infected. The worms live in the upper end of the large intestine, near the appendix, and must travel to the outside of the anus to lay their eggs. The egg-laying almost always occurs at night and usually causes the child to scratch the anal area. Then, when the child later sucks a thumb or licks a finger, the eggs are ingested and the cycle begins again.

The symptoms of pinworms vary with the degree of infection. Severe cases can cause acute abdominal pain. More common symptoms include the loss of appetite and occasional diarrhea. Signs of itching in the anal area are the surest clues.

If you suspect pinworm, it's easy to find out for sure in your own home and at no cost. Go into your child's darkened bedroom several hours after bedtime. Shine a flashlight on the anus. The light will cause the tiny thread-like worms to start back into the anus. If you don't see the worms after checks on two or three nights, it is unlikely that the child is infected.

Remember, pinworms will hit most American families at one time or another. Most never realize it. Alert parents can watch for signs of pinworms and limit their effect on the health of their growing children.

Home Treatment

- Ask your pharmacist for a nonprescription drug effective against pinworm.
- Treat every child in the house between the ages of two and ten. If infection recurs, you may wish to treat the entire family.
- Check the infected child several nights after the treatment using the flashlight. If worms are still present, a more powerful prescription drug be may needed. Improve all cleanliness practices in the household.
- Trim and keep short all fingernails.
- Require frequent hand washing.
- Sanitize toilet area with a strong disinfectant cleaner.
- Wash all bedding and sanitize bed area.
- Require morning shower, daily change of pajamas and underwear.

When to Call a Health Professional

- If use of any drug produces adverse reactions such as vomiting or increased pain.
- If you suspect pinworm but the nighttime checks find nothing. A health professional can do a number of lab tests to diagnose pinworm. These tests are not highly reliable, however, and may require several return visits.
- If you are not able to eliminate the pinworm with the nonprescription drug, a health professional can prescribe a stronger, more effective drug.

Prickly Heat (Sweat Rash)

Prickly heat, also called miliaria or sweat rash, is a rash consisting of single or multiple red dots that appear over an infant's head, neck, and shoulders. These dots look like tiny, white-headed pimples.

Prickly heat is often caused by well-meaning parents who dress their baby too warmly, but it can happen to any baby in really hot weather. An infant should be dressed just as lightly as an adult and will be comfortable at the same temperature. Babies' hands and feet feel cold to your touch because most of their blood is near the stomach helping digestion.

Prevention

Do not over-dress your baby. You can tell if a baby is too warm by placing your hand between the shoulder blades. If the skin is hot or moist, the baby is too warm.

Home Treatment

- Dress the baby lightly.
- Cornstarch or powder will make the baby more comfortable.

When to Call a Health Professional

- If the rash seems infected.
- If the infant has a sick appearance.
- If the rash persists over three to four days.
- If sweat rash is accompanied by a fever of 101° that doesn't come down after you remove warm clothing.

Roseola

Roseola infantum is a rose-colored rash. Called just roseola, it is a viral infection usually seen in babies six months to three years of age. The disease often starts with a sudden high fever (103°-105°) and irritability. The fever continues for two to three days, then as it drops, a red rash which looks like measles appears on the face and trunk. The rash fades in 24 hours.

Two things are worth noting about this disease. First, there is a slight possibility of convulsions occurring since the fever is so high. Second, if penicillin is incorrectly prescribed at the onset of the fever, the child could be incorrectly diagnosed as having a penicillin allergy when the rash occurs.

Home Treatment

- Lots of liquids
- Lower the temperature as you would for any high fever to reduce the risk of convulsions, i.e., sponge baths or acetaminophen (Tylenol).
- If a convulsion occurs, see treatment on page 126.

When to Call a Health Professional

- See the same warning signs under convulsions, page 125.

The Fifth Rash

In addition to chicken pox, measles, roseola and rubella, there is one more common and highly contagious rash of childhood. Its name is erythema infectiosum, but it is known as the "fifth disease."

Symptoms:

- Pink rash on cheeks first, then back of arms and legs.
- No fever.
- No feeling of illness.
- Highly contagious. The rash appears 6-14 days after exposure.

Home Treatment:

- None. This rash causes no known problems. Watch for a fever which may mean that fifth disease is not the problem.
- It gets brighter in response to heat. It will usually be gone in four or five days, but can recur off and on for a few weeks.

Rubella (German, Three Day, or Soft Measles)

Rubella is a relatively minor disease in a child. It is contagious for one week before the rash appears. Symptoms occur 12-21 days after exposure and include a mild, low-grade fever, muscular aches and pains and occasionally a headache. The lymph glands in the neck may swell and the eyes may be slightly inflamed. A rash of tiny pimples will then appear, usually first on the face and neck. The rash will cover the whole body in 12-24 hours. Rubella usually lasts three days.

Rubella is a dangerous disease when a woman contracts it during the first three months of pregnancy, since it can cause severe fetal damage. An adult woman can be tested to determine if she has immunity to rubella. If a woman who has not had rubella wished to start a family, she should discuss vaccination with her health professional. Some health professionals are reluctant to immunize since a women shouldn't become pregnant for at least three months after vaccination.

Home Treatment

- To relieve itching, see page 109.
- Avoid exposing a woman who could possibly be pregnant.

When to Call a Health Professional

- If the patient appears to becoming sicker and sicker each day.
- When fever is greater than 102°.
- If patient has convulsions.
- If patient is extremely listless or lethargic.

Rubeola (Red Measles or Regular Measles)

Regular measles can be serious and is very contagious. Symptoms appear 8-12 days after exposure. Initial symptoms are fever, runny nose, hard dry cough, and red eyes. After a few days a spotty rash will appear and the fever will rise and continue until the rash has covered the body. The rash appears first on the face and neck, and covers the whole body within three days. These spots will later fade from the head down. The disease is contagious from just before the rash appears and will continue to be contagious while the rash remains.

Encephalitis, or inflammation of the brain, is a possible complication of regular measles; see page 84. Protect your child from measles and any complications by immunization.

Home Treatment

- Give plenty of liquids.
- Humidify the room to help the dry cough.
- Limit television viewing and reading books as the eyes are unusually sensitive.

When to Call a Health Professional

- If any sore throat occurs, especially with a rise in fever. This could be strep throat.
- If the temperature is nearly normal for two days, then rises above 101°. It is possible that a secondary infection has developed.
- If difficulty in breathing occurs. This could be a sign of pneumonia.
- If the child has a convulsion.
- If an earache develops.
- A blue, gray, or purple color to the lips or beneath the nails might indicate pneumonia.
- Thick, discolored mucus out of the nose could be a sign of a sinus or ear infection developing.

Recommended Reading for Infant and Child Health

For more on infant and child health see Resource #G1 on page 269.

Behind every successful woman is herself.

New American Proverb

Chapter 10

Women's Health

Women have always been health experts. Throughout history, women have been the chief providers of health and healing to others. Even now, when hospitals, clinics and a vast array of health professionals are available to treat illness and injury, a full eighty percent of all health problems are still treated in the home, usually by moms and grandmoms.

Women need to be health experts for themselves, too. From puberty to menopause, women must cope with health care problems that are unique to them. This chapter covers health issues of special concern to women and what women can do to better manage them. By becoming knowledgeable about the female body and how to take care of it, women can take greater control of their health, and with it, their lives.

For an excellent guide to women's health issues, see Resource #U1 page 270.

Breast Health

If you are female, over age 18 and interested in keeping healthy, one of the most important things you can do for yourself is a monthly breast self-exam. Breast cancer is the number one cancer killer among women. However, if caught early, breast cancer is highly curable. Most breast lumps are discovered by women themselves, often quite by accident. The breast self-exam is a simple technique to help you learn what is normal for you and to become aware of any changes.

Breast Self-Exam

Establish a regular time each month to examine your breasts. A good time is a few days after your

Breast Self-Exam - continued

menstrual period; your breasts will not be as swollen or tender. Menopausal women and women who have had hysterectomies can examine their breasts the first day of each month.

Most women's breast tissue has some lumpiness or thickening. This is normal. You can have any areas of concern or doubt checked by your health professional at your next scheduled visit. The important thing to do is to learn what is normal and customary **for you** and to report changes to your doctor.

The breast self-exam takes place in three stages.

Stage 1: In the bath or shower
Begin your breast exam in the shower or bath when your hands are wet and soapy and can glide easily over the skin. Using the flat surfaces of your fingers (not your fingertips), gently move over every part of each breast and armpit. Check for unusual lumps or thickening.

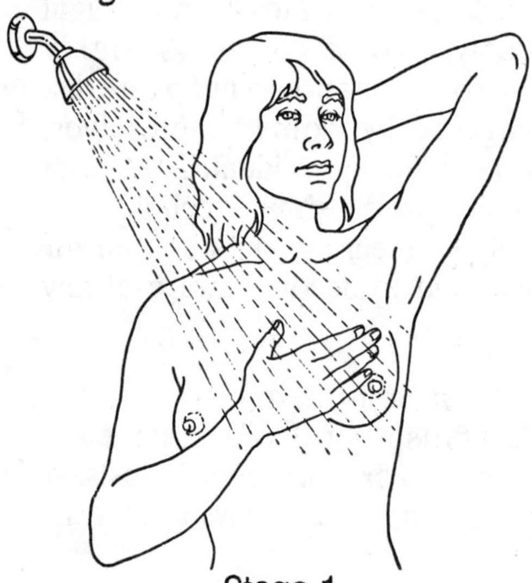

Stage 1

Stage 2: In front of the mirror
Examine your breasts visually before a mirror. Few women have breasts that match exactly. Learn what is normal for you. You are looking for any dimpling, puckering, retraction of the skin, or any changes in the contour and shape of the breast.

Place your palms on your hips and press down firmly to flex your chest muscles. Again, look for dimpling or any skin changes.

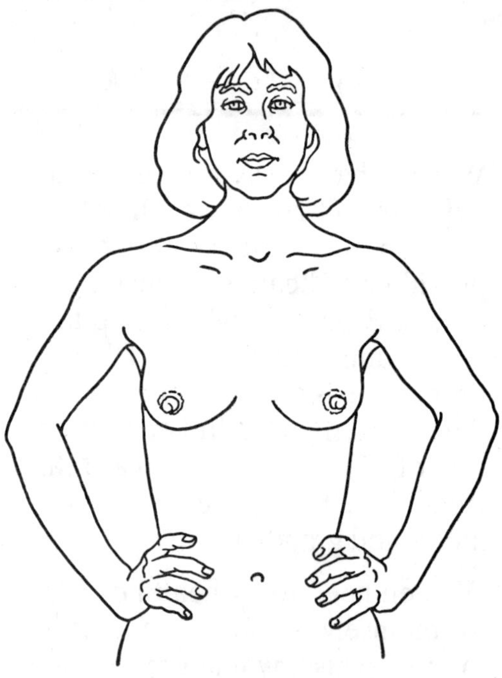

Stage 2

Next, squeeze the nipple of each breast gently between thumb and index finger. Look for a discharge.

Stage 3: Lying down
Place a pillow or folded towel under your left shoulder and place your left arm under your head. Use your right hand to examine your left breast. With fingers relaxed,

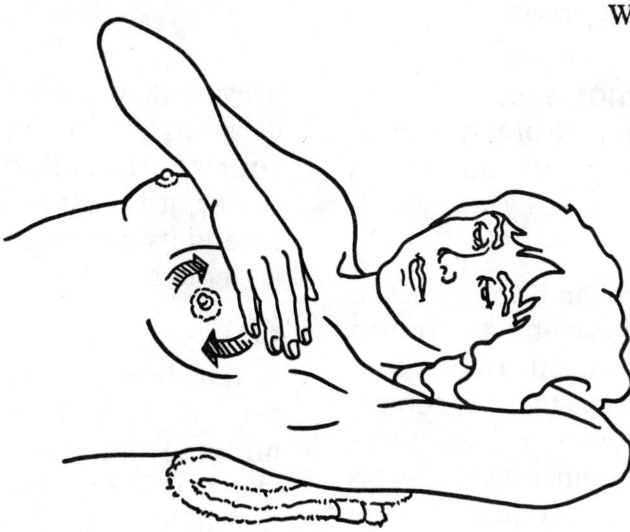

Stage 3

move the flat surface of your fingers in a gentle, circular motion to examine the breast. You are feeling for lumps, thickening, or changes of any kind.

To make sure you cover the whole breast, imagine that your breast is a clock. Start on the outside of the breast at 12:00, move slowly to 1:00 and then around the clock back to 12:00. Then move one inch in toward the nipple and go around the "clock" again. Be sure to include the nipple, the breastbone and the armpit in your exam.

Move the pillow or towel to the other shoulder and repeat this procedure for the other breast.

If you discover any unusual lumps, thickening or changes of any kind, you will need to report these to your doctor immediately. Remember, most lumps are not malignant, but you will need your doctor to make a diagnosis.

If you start a habit of examining your breasts monthly, you will learn what is normal for you and quickly recognize when something is amiss. The breast self-exam does take some practice. Ask your doctor for help in learning the technique.

Breast Health Tips

- Do your breast self-exam every month. Most breast lumps are discovered by women themselves. If detected early, breast cancer can be cured 90% of the time.
- Have a periodic mammogram. See the Breast Exam Schedule for frequency.
- Eat a low-fat diet. The American Cancer Society recommends cutting down on fried foods and high fat dairy products and eating food containing vitamins A and C (dark green and orange vegetables). Cruciferous vegetables (broccoli, cabbage, kale) are also recommended.
- Reduce caffeine. While no connection has been found between caffeine and breast cancer, women who eliminate all caffeine from their diets may decrease or get rid of their breast cysts.

About Mammograms

A mammogram is a breast x-ray. It helps to find breast tumors too small to be detected by breast self-exam.

Mammograms can be an effective cancer detection method in women over the age of 50. Because of radiation risks and the lower detection rates at younger ages, mammography for women aged 35-49 is recommended only if there is a family history of early breast cancer among close relatives.

When to Arrange for An Appointment

- Schedule your exam more than one week but less than two weeks after your period.
- Do not wear deodorant, perfume or powder.
- Wear two-piece clothing so you only have to remove your top.

Gynecological Health

Pelvic exams and Pap smears are vital components of women's health. These exams are important because they can give you early indications of any abnormalities in your reproductive organs. Of course, it is best to catch any disease in its early stages; it is much easier to treat then.

Self-Exam

A female's genitals include two sets of lips: the inner (labia minora) and the outer (labia majora). These lips form around the urinary opening, the vaginal opening, and the clitoris.

Periodically exam your entire genital area for any sores, warts, red swollen areas, or discharge. A healthy discharge will be white to yellowish-white and smell slightly like vinegar. It can be either thick or thin and present in large or small amounts; every woman is different. During ovulation (the mid-point between periods) there is often a large amount of clear and slippery mucus. If your discharge seems unusual in either amount, smell or texture, consult the entry on Vaginitis on page 151.

BREAST EXAM SCHEDULE

Age	Procedure	How Often
18 and over	Breast self-exam	Every month
Over 40	Breast exam by physician	Every year
Over 50*	Mammogram	Every 1-2 years

*Begin at age 35 if there is family history of breast cancer.

There should be no pain or straining on urination and the urine should come out in a fairly steady stream. The color should be pale yellow and there should be no strong ammonia smell. If you experience pain or burning on urination, read the entry on Urinary Tract Infections, page 149.

Self-exams will help you better understand your own body and what is normal for you. It is possible to conduct your own vaginal exam using a plastic speculum (the duck-billed tool a health professional will use for a pelvic exam), a mirror and a flashlight. See Resource #A3 on page 268.

The Pelvic Exam

A pelvic exam given by a health care professional will consist of an external genital exam, a Pap test and a manual exam, generally in that order.

The Pap test is the screening exam for cancer of the cervix. Pap smears detect 90-95% of cervical cancers, making it a reliable and important test. The clinician will insert a speculum into your vagina and gather some cells from your cervix and vagina. You may experience some discomfort. Be sure to tell the clinician if you feel any pain. She may be able to make some adaptations to the speculum to ease the discomfort.

The cells are put on a slide and sent to a lab for classification. There are five classes. If your cells are classed at III, IV or V, your doctor will ask you to return for further evaluation. In any case, your doctor should let you know the results of your Pap test.

With the manual exam, the clinician inserts two gloved and lubricated fingers into your vagina and presses on your lower abdomen with the other hand in order to feel the ovaries and uterus.

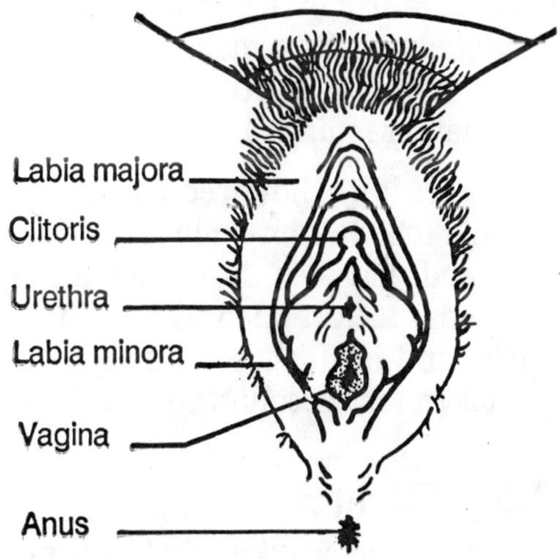

Female Genitals

Preparing for a Pelvic Exam

Schedule the exam when you are not bleeding. One to two weeks after your period is a good time. Do not douche, have intercourse or use feminine hygiene products before the exam as they can alter the test results.

How Often Should You Schedule an Exam?

There are conflicting view points on the subject of how often you should have Pap tests. As far as the first exam goes, there appears to be a connection between level of sexual activity, especially with multiple partners, and cancer of the cervix. Therefore, a 16 year old girl who is having sexual relations should have an exam at 16.

The American Cancer Society recommends Pap smears every 2-3 years until the age of 65 after two normal screenings.

The decision of how frequently you should schedule an exam rests with you and your health professional. Personal factors such as age, lifestyle, and health history can then be taken into account.

Birth Control

Choosing and using a reliable form of contraception is an important aspect of self-care. Birth control can protect you against unwanted pregnancies, the risk and trauma of abortion and sexually-transmitted diseases (if you use a barrier method). Best of all, it allows you a measure of control over your body, your health and your life.

There are pros and cons that go along with all birth control methods. In choosing the right method for you and your partner, many factors such as age, health history, lifestyle, and religious belief need to be considered. It is a good idea to get professional advice, either from your physician or a family planning center.

Pregnancy and Childbirth

Pregnancy and the actual birth of your child is a very emotional and personal experience. For this reason it is important to take the time and energy to choose a doctor or midwife whose views reflect your own. Are they in favor of natural childbirth? Are they comfortable having your spouse or other family member present? What tests do they consider necessary and why? To help you make this first decision, a guide for interviewing a health care professional can be found on page 5 of this handbook.

Once you have chosen your physician or midwife you will begin to schedule regular visits. During these visits they will check on the baby's growth and your overall nutritional, physical and mental wellness needs. Remember, the healthier you are, the healthier your baby will be. See Resource #U2 and U3 page 270.

Nutrition. Everyone will have an opinion on how much weight you should gain and what you should be eating and drinking. A good rule is to take in enough healthy food to replenish your energy needs and include some vital extras to help you grow a healthy baby. Your doctor will prescribe a prenatal vitamin supplement and you should eat three well balanced meals a day.

If you are a heavy smoker or drinker, STOP NOW! Not only will you feel and look better, but so will the baby. See page 220 for nutrition guidelines.

BIRTH CONTROL

Method	Effectiveness*	Risks
Sterilization: Tubal ligations (women) Vasectomies (men)	99.6%	Consider it permanent
Oral contraceptive: (the pill)	97	Increased risk of circulatory disorders and high blood pressure for smokers or women over 35
IUD: (intrauterine device)	94	May cause bleeding and cramping. May be expelled without being noticed. Increased risk of pelvic infection
Barrier Methods:		Increased risk of unwanted pregnancy when used improperly
Condom and foam	95	
Condom alone	88	
Cervical cap	82	
Diaphragm	82	
Vaginal sponge	80-90	
Spermicides: Foams, creams, jellies	79	Increased risk of unwanted pregnancy
Fertility awareness: Basal body temperature, mucous method, rhythm/ calendar method	80	Increased risk of unwanted pregnancy
Withdrawal	82	Increased risk of unwanted pregnancy
No method (chance)	11	High risk of unwanted pregnancy.

*Percent of women having no accidental pregnancies during 12 months of use.
Source: Robert Hatcher, et. al., Contraceptive Technology, 1988-1989, Irvington, New York, 1988.

Pregnancy - continued

Exercise. Always check with your physician first, but chances are you can continue with the same exercise routine you had before your pregnancy. While this is not the time for non-runners to start training for a marathon, it also is not the time to spend nine months perfecting your couch potato techniques. Regular exercise will help you tone and strengthen your muscles which will give you more stamina and muscle control during labor. A

BIRTH PLAN

Pre-Delivery

1. Place of delivery: hospital, home, birthing clinic
2. Environment: soft lighting, labor/birthing room, delivery room
3. Natural childbirth: Lamaze, Leboyer, etc.
4. Presence of partner

Labor

1. Enema: none, self-administered, hospital
2. Prep: partial, clip or shaving of all pubic hair
3. Onset of labor: spontaneous or induced
4. Mobility: ability to move around, walk, kneel or squat
5. Monitoring fetal heart: as labor changes, throughout labor
6. Pain relief: relaxation techniques, medications
7. Vaginal exams: as labor changes, regularly
8. Rupture of membranes: spontaneous or induced

Delivery

1. Position: squatting, semi-reclined (on back or side), prone
2. Perineum: intact (massage)
3. Need for forceps or vacuum extractor

Post Delivery

1. Bonding: place baby on mother's abdomen, amount of time with mother
2. Cutting the cord: by partner or doctor, before/after pulsating stops
3. Delivery of placenta: spontaneous, encouraged, manual extraction
4. Visitation by family members
5. Flexible rooming-in
6. Breast-feeding: on demand
7. Circumcision: none, parents present, anesthesia

Cesarean Birth

If planned, check on the various options regarding: partner's presence, anesthesia, participation, and contact with baby.

"Fitness Formula" and exercise guidelines can be found on page 208.

Relaxation. Pregnancy is an exciting and happy time, and it can also be stressful. Your body is changing and your hormones are raging. As each month progresses, the prospect that you are bringing a new life into this world becomes more real. Take time to learn some relaxation techniques to help you keep a positive and healthy frame of mind. Relaxation exercises will help you throughout the pregnancy and will be invaluable during labor. Not only can it help reduce pain, but it will allow you to conserve your energy. Specific relaxation techniques can be found on page 215 of this handbook.

The Birth Plan on page 142 is a check list which covers issues you will want to discuss with your health care professional prior to delivery. Supply your physician or midwife, hospital or birthing center, and your coach with a copy of your birth plan to insure there will be no confusion regarding your desires and expectations throughout the delivery and birth.

Bleeding Between Periods

Many women experience bleeding between their periods. It does not necessarily indicate that a serious condition is present. If the bleeding is not heavy and if it occurs only occasionally, apply home treatment. If you have an IUD (intrauterine device), you may increase your chances of spotting.

Home Treatment

- Use tampons or pads.
- Avoid using aspirin as this may prolong the bleeding.

When to Call a Health Professional

- If accompanied by unusual pain or cramping.
- If the bleeding is heavy.
- If the bleeding lasts more than three days in a row.
- If the bleeding occurs three months in a row.
- If you have already undergone menopause.

Menopause

Menopause occurs for most women between the ages of 45 and 55 when the production of "female hormones" (estrogen and progesterone) is greatly reduced. With these hormonal changes, you can expect to experience lighter and irregular menstrual periods before they stop altogether. You may also experience hot flashes, vaginal dryness and mood changes.

Irregular Periods may mean lighter or heavier than usual menstrual flows, either shorter or longer intervals between flows, or spotting. Some women experience irregular periods for years in association with menopause. Others

Menopause - continued

have regular periods until they suddenly stop. Every woman is unique and will experience menopause differently.

Hot Flashes are sudden periods of intense heat, sweating and flushing. They are experienced by 75-80% of women going through menopause. They may occur as frequently as once an hour and last as long as three to four minutes. A hot flash usually begins in the chest and spreads out to the neck, face and arms. Most hot flashes cease within one or two years.

Vaginal Dryness, the loss of lubrication and moisture in the vagina, may lead to soreness during and after intercourse.

Mood Changes are brought on by the hormonal and physical changes of menopause. Symptoms such as nervousness, lethargy, insomnia, moodiness or depression are not uncommon.

With menopause, many women fear emotional upheaval and the loss of sexuality. On the other hand, many women look forward to the freedom that menopause brings, particularly freedom from the discomfort associated with the menstrual cycle and freedom from contraception.

Understanding what is happening to you and using home care techniques to relieve any discomfort will help you in your efforts to make the most of menopause.

Home Treatment

Hot Flashes:

- Keep your home and work place cool.
- Wear loose clothing that can be easily removed.
- Drink lots of water and juices.
- Avoid caffeine and alcohol if they bring on hot flashes.
- Exercise regularly. This will help to stabilize hormones and lessen insomnia.

Irregular Periods:

- Keep a written record of your periods in case you need to confer with a health professional later.

Vaginal Dryness:

- Use a water-soluble vaginal lubricant such as K-Y Jelly or Surgilube. Vegetable oil will also work. Do not use a petroleum based product such as Vaseline.

Mood Changes:

- The best thing you can do for yourself is to realize you are not alone. Discuss your symptoms with other menopausal women. Give yourself, and ask from others,abundant amounts of love, caring and understanding.

When to Call a Health Professional

- If you experience prolonged irregular bleeding, particularly if you are overweight.
- If you are considering estrogen replacement therapy (ERT). Estrogen therapy has been

shown to reduce many of the symptoms of menopause. However, ERT may increase a woman's risk of uterine cancer. Other studies link ERT to an increase in risk of heart disease, high blood pressure and stroke.

The decision to use estrogen is a personal one. The increased cancer risks and only temporary relief of symptoms (they reappear when estrogen is stopped), suggest ERT may best be left for severe menopausal symptoms or cases of documented osteoporosis. Knowing the facts, a woman should make her own decision. See page 146.

Menstrual Cramps (Painful Periods)

Many women suffer from painful menstrual cramps or dysmenorrhea. Symptoms include mild to severe cramping in the lower abdomen or thighs, backache, headaches, diarrhea, constipation, nausea, dizziness and fainting.

Menstrual cramps are caused by prostaglandins, chemicals naturally produced in the human body. Women with severe cramps have higher than average concentrations of prostaglandins in their menstrual fluid.

Home Treatment

- Exercise. Regular workouts decrease the severity of cramps. See Chapter 15.
- Use heat (hot water bottles, heating pads or hot baths) to relax tense muscles and relieve cramping.
- Take a recommended dose of aspirin or ibuprofen, such as Advil or Nuprin. Take these with milk or food as both aspirin and ibuprofen can upset stomachs.

  Over-the-counter medications for menstrual pain, such as Midol or Pamprin, can contain aspirin or acetaminophen, caffeine, an antispasmodic and a diuretic.
- Herbal teas, such as chamomile, mint, raspberry and blackberry are good for soothing tense muscles and anxious moods.
- Try using a sanitary napkin instead of a tampon.

When to Call a Health Professional

- If painful cramping suddenly occurs after years of less painful periods.
- If you suspect that your IUD (intrauterine device) is causing the cramping.
- If bleeding is very severe and fails to respond to home treatment.
- If cramping does not cease when menstrual flow stops or if cramping begins five to seven days before your period begins.
- If your period is accompanied by sudden high fever, diarrhea, or skin rash.

Osteoporosis

Osteoporosis or "brittle bones" is a condition that affects 25% of women over 60 years old. Osteoporosis is much less common and severe in men. It is brought about by loss of bone mass and strength and it can lead to serious problems with broken bones.

High risk factors for osteoporosis include thin body frames, sedentary lifestyle, and a family history for this disease. Women who drink or smoke are at greater risk. Osteoporosis is a "silent" disease; there are no symptoms until a bone is broken and the condition recognized after x-rays. The first indication may be hip or low back pain or painful swelling of a wrist after a minor fall.

X-rays which measure bone density are available. These may be especially useful for women at high risk of osteoporosis in determining who will benefit from estrogen replacement therapy. Ask your doctor about your need for this test.

Home Treatment

- Get regular weight bearing exercise, such as walking. Bones get bigger and stronger with exercise. See Chapter 15.
- Take about 1,500 mg of calcium a day. The average American diet contains 500 mg. The extra 1,000 mg can be obtained either

ESTROGEN REPLACEMENT THERAPY

The Pros

Helps prevent osteoporosis and associated risks

Relieves menopausal symptoms such as hot flashes and vaginal dryness

Reduces depression and fatigue for some women

The Cons

Increased risk of uterine cancer and gallbladder problems

Increased risk of heart disease, high blood pressure and stroke

Provides only temporary relief; must be taken continuously

Possible side effects including: fluid retention, breast tenderness, weight gain, nausea and others

Who Should Consider ERT

Women at high risk for osteoporosis

Women with severe menopausal symptoms

Who Should Not Take ERT

Any woman with:
- Breast cancer
- History of blood clots, heart attack or stroke
- High blood pressure
- Diabetes
- Gallbladder problems
- Uterine cancer or fibroids

by a large increase in dairy products (one quart of skim milk would add 1,100 mg of calcium) or by calcium supplements. Five 500 mg calcium carbonate tablets, such as TUMS, will yield 1,000 mg of calcium. Space them out over the day and take them with meals or milk.

When to Call a Health Professional

- If you are considering estrogen replacement therapy. See the Estrogen Replacement Therapy chart on the preceding page.
- You experience sudden and severe back pain.

Premenstrual Syndrome (PMS)

Premenstrual syndrome or PMS occurs seven to ten days before the menstrual period begins. It is estimated that 90% of women have had some of the symptoms associated with PMS. Some women have severe problems with PMS.

Over 150 physical and psychological symptoms are associated with PMS. Physical symptoms include: headaches, backaches, weight gain, breast tenderness, water retention, food craving and increased appetite, diarrhea or constipation, dizziness and fainting, clumsiness.

Psychological symptoms include: irritability and anger, mood swings, anxiety, sudden bouts of crying, sadness, fatigue, poor concentration, diminished sex drive, aggression. Symptoms generally improve with the onset of bleeding.

To determine if you have PMS consider:

- Do the same symptoms occur each month?
- Do symptoms improve or disappear when bleeding begins?
- Do you have at least one symptom-free week per month?

Keep a menstrual diary charting your symptoms, their timing and severity. If symptoms appear fairly consistent over several months, chances are you have PMS.

Home Treatment

- Eat healthy foods. Try to avoid junk foods high in sugar, fat and salt. Salt causes water retention. Caffeine causes breast tenderness. See Chapter 16.
- Get some exercise. Regular exercise will help minimize PMS symptoms. See Chapter 15.
- Try relaxation techniques such as yoga and deep breathing. See Chapter 15.
- Be good to yourself. Reduce your stress level as much as possible.
- Talk with others. Your PMS affects not only you but those you live and work with. Join a PMS self-help group. You can ask for information and referrals from your local hospital.

PMS - continued

When to Call a Health Professional

- If psychological symptoms are very severe and you feel out of control.
- If symptoms do not stop with onset of menstrual bleeding.

Sexually Transmitted Diseases

Sexually transmitted diseases (STDs) or venereal diseases (VD) are infections passed from person to person through sexual intercourse or genital contact. Gonorrhea, genital herpes, chlamydia and genital warts are among the most common of STDs. The most virulent and deadly of all STDs, AIDS (Acquired Immune Deficiency Syndrome) is discussed on page 155.

Gonorrhea, also known as clap, drip or GC, is caused by bacteria spread through intimate contact. Untreated gonorrhea in women may lead to pelvic inflammatory disease which in turn can cause sterility. For women, it is not always easy to tell if you have been infected. You may have no symptoms, or symptoms such as vaginal discharge, painful urination and irregular menstrual bleeding, that can be confused with other problems. Gonorrhea-infected men may have a thick discharge from the penis and burning on urination or no symptoms at all.

Genital Herpes is caused by a virus and is easily spread through sexual contact and other direct skin contact. There are two types of herpes simplex virus: Type 1 and Type 2. Type 1 generally shows up in cold sores and fever blisters on the mouth, face and lips. Type 2 appears as sores and blisters around the genitals. Either type may infect the genital area.

Symptoms show up within two days to four weeks after contact with an infected person. The first sign of infection is generally an itching, burning or tingling sensation in the genitals, then sores and blisters will appear. You may also experience swollen lymph nodes, fever, headache and fatigue. It is also possible to be infected with herpes and have no symptoms at all. There is no known cure for herpes at this time. Once infected, you may suffer from recurrent outbreaks.

There is medication available to decrease the severity of outbreaks and to prevent frequent recurrences. Ask your doctor.

Chlamydia (kla-mid-ee-uh) infects millions of men and women every year. It is spread through sexual contact with an infected person. Symptoms may be so mild that the disease goes unnoticed and undiagnosed. In fact, 80% of all infected women are without symptoms until complications, such as pelvic inflammatory disease, set in. If symptoms show up at all, they may occur two to four weeks after exposure. Symptoms for women may include vaginal discharge, stomach pain, and pain on urination. In men, chlamydia can cause inflammation of the urethra, penile discharge and painful urination. Many infected men have no symptoms.

Genital Warts are caused by a virus similar to the one that causes common skin warts. They generally appear as small bumps (which can grow larger if they are not removed). In women, the warts can be located in the vagina, on the cervix or around the anus. Of most concern to women is the link between genital warts and cancer of the cervix. Luckily, wart infections of the cervix can be detected by a Pap smear early on. Genital warts in men are usually found on the penis or scrotum. All genital warts need to be removed by a health professional.

Prevention

With STDs in particular, prevention is far easier than treating an infection once it occurs.

If you are beginning an intimate relationship, take the time, before having sex, to talk with your lover about STDs. Find out if he or she has ever been infected or exposed. Remember that it is quite possible to be infected without knowing it.

The most foolproof method is avoiding sexual or intimate contact with anyone who has the symptoms of a STD or who has been exposed to a STD. Be aware of any unusual discharge, sores, redness, or growths.

Use a diaphragm or condom during sexual relations. They put up an effective barrier to STD organisms. However, they must be used from the very beginning of contact. Contraceptive creams and jellies appear to have some preventive effect on STDs, but these should not be your sole source of protection.

When to Call a Health Professional

All STDs need to be diagnosed and treated by a health professional. Venereal disease clinics and public health agencies can provide STD diagnosis and treatment for low cost. If you notice any unusual discharge or sores, or if you suspect that you have been exposed to a STD, make an appointment as soon as possible. Your sexual contacts must be treated, even if they do not have symptoms. They may reinfect you and develop serious complications themselves.

Urinary Tract Infections

Urinary tract infection (UTI), also called bladder infection or cystitis, is a common health problem for women.

Early symptoms are a burning sensation during urination, itching, or pain in the urethra, the tube

Urinary Infection - continued

through which urine is expelled from the bladder.

Urinary infections are generally caused by bacteria, E. coli, which are normally present in the digestive system. Because of the closeness of the anus and the urethra in women, they are much more susceptible than men to the infection.

Any mild irritation to the vaginal area may increase the likelihood of bladder infection. Lovemaking, diaphragms, infrequent urination, perfumed soaps and powders, even spicy food may contribute to the problem.

Most urinary tract infections can be eliminated by home treatment methods in about three days. Untreated, some infections may go on to infect the kidneys and cause permanent kidney problems. Because of this danger, pain upon urination should always be treated promptly.

Prevention

- Women should wipe from front to back after going to the toilet. This will reduce the bacteria spread from the rectum to the vagina.
- Avoid frequent douching, use of vaginal deodorants or perfumed products.
- Drink more fluids; water is best.
- Women susceptible to urinary infections should urinate before and after intercourse. Drinking extra water after intercourse may also help prevent infection.
- Urinate frequently.
- Wear cotton underwear, cotton lined pantyhose and loose clothing.
- Drinking cranberry juice without sugar seems to protect against infection-causing bacteria.

Home Treatment

- Examine vagina and check temperature twice daily. See home physical exam, page 18.
- Drink lots of fluids to wash out the infection.
- Avoid alcohol, coffee, and spicy foods.
- If abdominal pain or vaginal burning and redness occur in a young girl, consider the possibility of an allergy to bubble bath or soap.
- Get extra rest.
- Use a home self-test to detect E.coli bacteria in the urine. Nitrate dip strips and urine dip cultures are inexpensive and can be found at a pharmacy.

When to Call a Health Professional

- If there is no improvement after two to three days.
- When pain on urination is accompanied by any of the following symptoms:
  - Chills and/or fever over 101°
  - A frequent inability to urinate when you feel the urge
  - Pain or tenderness in the thighs
  - Backaches
  - Bloody urine

Vaginitis

Vaginitis is any vaginal infection or inflammation characterized by a change in vaginal discharge. Healthy women have a small amount of odorless, non-irritating discharge. The amount varies from woman to woman and may increase in certain times of the menstrual cycle. General symptoms of vaginitis are a marked change from the normal discharge, sometimes accompanied by itching, burning on urination, and pain during intercourse.

Vaginitis is caused by organisms that are normally found in the vagina along with other protective bacteria. The vagina usually has a slightly acid pH (the measure of acidity and alkalinity) which resists infection. If something happens to upset the balance of bacteria or the usual pH, vaginitis can result. This can happen by:

- Excessive douching which allows the other organisms to take over after washing away protective bacteria. Too much douching may also upset the vaginal pH.
- The use of antibiotics which kill protective bacteria.
- Infectious organisms which may be introduced through sexual intercourse.
- Tension, pregnancy and birth control pills which can change the hormonal balance and upset the normal vagina.

Vaginitis is common and is not necessarily a symptom of a sexually-transmitted disease. It is not very serious and some women seem more susceptible than others. An aggravating fact about vaginitis is that it can recur.

Prevention

- Wear cotton underpants. The organisms which cause vaginitis grow best in warm, moist places. Nylon underwear and pantyhose retain heat and perspiration. Avoid pants that are tight in the crotch and thighs.
- Avoid douching frequently. A healthy vagina will clean itself.
- Avoid using feminine deodorant sprays and other perfumed products as they may irritate tender skin.
- If you have to take antibiotics, it is sometimes possible to prevent bacterial vaginitis by including plenty of yogurt or buttermilk in your diet.
- Change tampons at least three times a day or alternate tampons with pads.

Home Treatment

- A bacterial or non-specific vaginitis may go away by itself in three to four days.
- A mild yeast infection may be cured by a boric acid suppository. Use 600 mg in a size 00 capsule daily for 14 days. This will help restore an acid pH in the vagina.
- Avoid scratching. Itching can be relieved by a cold water compress.

Vaginitis - continued

- Make sure that the cause of the vaginitis is not a forgotten tampon, or other foreign body.
- Abstain from sex until the infection is cleared. Although the infection does not usually cause symptoms in men, you may become reinfected later by your sex partner.

When to Call a Health Professional

- If you recognize a yeast infection and it is mild, then try the boric acid suppository. Otherwise, see a health professional for any symptoms of vaginitis. A lab test will identify the organism causing the infection.
- Antibiotics can be prescribed to clear up the infection. See page 261, which describes appropriate use of antibiotics.
- If the discharge is accompanied by abdominal discomfort.
- If the discharge and other symptoms are very uncomfortable.
- If the discharge lasts more than two weeks.
- If you suspect that you have been exposed to a sexually transmitted disease.

What to Expect at the Doctor's Office

- If you need to see a health professional, do not douche or have intercourse for 24 hours before the appointment since it may make diagnosis difficult.
- Expect a pelvic exam. Your doctor will take a sample of the vaginal discharge and a culture of the cervix. Depending upon the cause of the problem, your doctor may prescribe a suppository, cream, or antibiotic. See page 261 for information about the appropriate use of antibiotics. Your sexual partners may need to be treated as well.

TYPES OF VAGINITIS

Type	Symptoms
Yeast or monilia	White, curdy discharge like cottage cheese, burning on urination, itching. May cause skin rash on thighs and vulva.
Trichomonas	Severe itching, pain, and profuse yellow-green frothy discharge with a foul odor.
Non-specific or bacterial	Itching, discharge and sour odor.

Man who say it cannot be done should not interrupt man doing it.

Old Chinese Proverb

Chapter 11

Men's Health

If you are a man, you are at a great disadvantage when it comes to health. Your life expectancy is seven years shorter than that for women. Have you ever wondered why?

Risky Lifestyles

Just look at the five most common causes of death for a man 40 to 50 years old.

1. *Heart Attack*
    - Men are 10% less likely than women to limit salt in their diet.
    - Men are 14% less likely than women to limit fat.
    - Men are 15% less likely to limit cholesterol.
    - Men are 14% less likely to eat plenty of fiber.
    - Men are 25% more likely to smoke.
2. *Suicide*
    - Men are far less likely than women to seek mental health services.
3. *Homicide*
    - Men are over twice as likely to own guns.
4. *Injuries*
    - Men are 19% more likely to drink and drive.
    - Men are 17% more likely to exceed the speed limit.
    - Men are 8% less likely to use seat belts.
5. *Cirrhosis of Liver*
    - Men are 12% more likely to drink too much.

5+*AIDS (which will soon make the list)*
- Most closely related to male-to-male sexual practices and needle-sharing for drug

Risky Lifestyles - continued

purposes, another male dominated behavior.

If men have a health disadvantage, it is largely because of the way they live. Men can gain back much of the longevity gap simply by pursuing healthier lifestyles.

While this chapter is entitled Men's Health, its purpose is not to address the primary areas of nutrition, stress management and safety that men must learn to deal with if they are to close the longevity gap. Rather, this chapter focuses on specific health problems that are of particular interest to men.

Genital Health

Daily cleaning of the penis, particularly under the foreskin of an uncircumcised penis, can prevent bacterial infection and reduce the already low risk of penile cancer. Routine exams for genital health include an annual exam of the prostate and a monthly testicular and penile exam.

Monthly Testicular and Penile Self-Exam

A three-minute exam of the penis and testes once a month can allow early treatment and cure of testicular and penile infections and cancers. The best time is after a warm bath or shower when the scrotal skin is relaxed.

- Stand and place your right leg on an elevated surface. A tub side or toilet seat works fine.
- Explore the surface of the right testicle by gently rolling the testicle between the thumb and fingers of both hands. Feel for any hard lumps or nodules.
- Notice any enlargement of the testes or a change in its consistency.
- Notice any pain or dull ache in the groin or lower abdomen.
- Repeat, lifting the left leg and examining your left testicle.
- Feel for the spongy tube (epididymis) on the top and down the backside of the testicle. Pain in the tube could indicate an infection.
- Examine the foreskin of the penis and the glans (head of the penis) for any sores, warts (see page 149), redness or discharge.

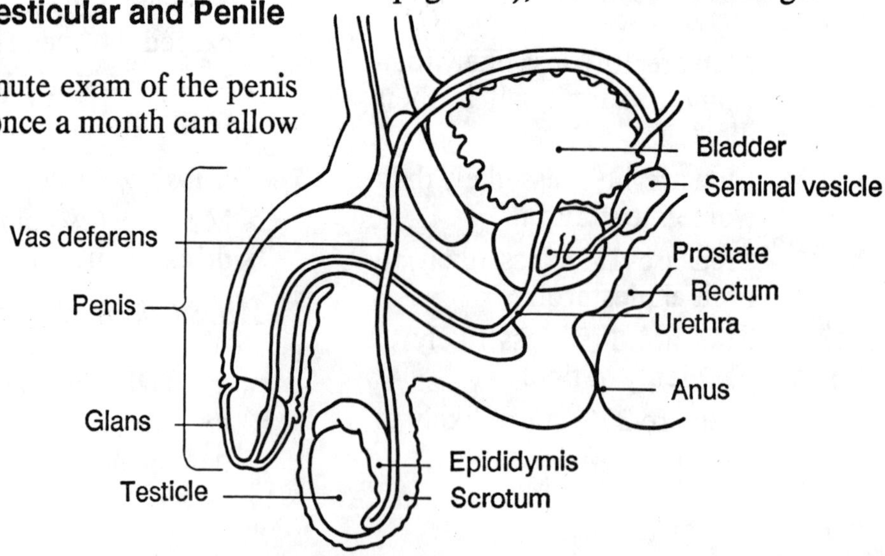

Male Genitals

- If any testicular lumps or nodules are found, call for an immediate appointment with your doctor to rule out testicular cancer. Because testicular cancer can spread within a few months, prompt action is important. Even very small nodules should be reported. Unexplained enlargement of a testes or groin pain should also be discussed with your physician.
- If you notice any penile discharge, see page 148 and discuss it with your physician.

Birth Control

Both morally and legally, men have as much responsibility for birth control as their partners do. See the discussion of birth control in the Women's Health Chapter, page 140.

There are three basic methods of birth control available to men.

1. *Condoms (rubbers)*

   Condoms used alone are about 90% effective. Of 100 couples using condoms regularly, only ten women are likely to get pregnant in a year. By using a condom and contraceptive foam, the effectiveness is improved to 95%.

2. *Withdrawal*

   Withdrawal or "pulling out before ejaculation" is a very risky form of birth control; 18 of every 100 couples practicing this method for a year will have a pregnancy. The effectiveness is low both because of failure to pull out before ejaculation and because some sperm can be transferred in the clear liquid that comes out of the penis before ejaculation.

3. *Vasectomy*

   Vasectomy is a male sterilization operation performed under local anesthesia. It involves cutting the vas deferens, a tube that allows the sperm to mix with the semen. Vasectomies are simple operations with a low rate of major complications and near perfect effectiveness rates in preventing pregnancy. However, they should only be considered by men who are sure that they do not want any, or more, children. Vasectomies can be reversed in over half of the cases. But, the reversal surgery is more expensive, less reliable, and prone to more complications.

Even if you rely primarily on your partner for birth control, you can help her insure success. Encourage her to use her method every time you have sex and give her time to use her method.

AIDS (Acquired Immune Deficiency Syndrome)

AIDS, caused by the HIV virus (human immunodeficiency virus), greatly reduces the body's natural defenses against disease. As the immune system fails in patients

AIDS - continued

with AIDS, infections which normally are rare and minor become common and often fatal.

AIDS spreads when blood cells infected with the HIV virus pass from one person to another. Blood cells can be transmitted anytime blood, semen, vaginal fluids, or breast milk is ingested or enters the blood stream through a cut or scratch.

Behaviors that spread AIDS include (in descending order of riskiness):

1. Sharing injection needles and syringes with someone who has the HIV virus.
2. Rectal entry intercourse with someone who has the HIV virus. Rectal entry sex often tears the rectal blood vessels allowing contamination to occur.
3. Unprotected sexual intercourse with someone who has the HIV virus.
4. Receiving blood transfusions, blood products, or organs donated by someone who has the HIV virus. The risk is dropping dramatically as blood testing and blood product treatment improves.

Babies born to or breast-fed by women who have the HIV virus are also at high risk of contracting AIDS.

AIDS Symptoms

People can carry and spread the HIV virus for years without having any symptoms. When AIDS does develop, the symptoms vary according to which illnesses the reduced immunity has allowed to develop. Common symptoms are as follows:

- Periods of extreme and unexplainable fatigue.
- Rapid weight loss of ten or more pounds.
- Bruising more easily than normal.
- Repeated diarrhea.
- Recurring fevers and night sweats.
- Swelling of glands in the throat, groin or armpit.
- Deep dry coughing, unrelated to other causes.
- Shortness of breath.
- A whitish coating on the tongue.
- Unexplained bleeding from growths on the skin.
- Severe numbness or pain in the hands and feet.
- A personality change or mental deterioration.

Each of these symptoms can be caused by many illnesses other than AIDS. However, if any symptom develops without a good explanation, you should see your doctor.

AIDS Testing

Simple blood tests available through all physicians, hospitals and health departments can tell if someone carries the HIV virus. While a confirmed, positive test does not mean that you will get AIDS, it does mean that you are capable of spreading AIDS and that you should take steps to protect others around you.

Prevention

- Avoid unprotected intercourse with anyone who may have had other sex partners or may have shared needles for drug use anytime since 1979.
- Insist on using condoms with any sex partner whose sexual history you do not know to be risk-free. Use spermicidal foam, jelly or cream with condoms for even greater protection.
- Never share needles or syringes. Even needles that have been boiled can remain contaminated. If reuse cannot be avoided:
    1. Flush syringe and needle four times with alcohol or a one to four part solution of chlorine bleach and tap water.
    2. Separate the plunger, syringe and needle.
    3. Let the separated parts stand in the bleach solution for 15 minutes.
    4. Flush with tap water four times before storage or reuse.
- Do not share toothbrushes, razors, tattoo needles or other personal devices that could be contaminated with blood.

If you follow these prevention steps, your risks of receiving the HIV virus will be cut to almost nothing. Being coughed and sneezed on, touched by, hugged by, or even lightly kissed by someone with AIDS will not transfer the HIV virus to you. You can work next to an AIDS carrier for years and so long as you practice the prevention behaviors above, you will have virtually no risk of contracting the HIV virus.

AIDS and Blood Donation

There is no AIDS or HIV virus risk in **donating blood.** Blood banks use disposable needles so there is no way for another person's blood to contaminate the donor. Although all blood donations have been tested for the HIV antibodies since 1985 and are now treated so that they are HIV-free, there remains a very low risk of HIV transfer from donors who were infected within a short time of donating blood. The risk is estimated at about 1 in 100,000. Even that very small risk can be avoided through self-donation programs available through most blood banks.

For more information about AIDS, call your local health department or look in the yellow pages for a local AIDS hotline. Also see Resource # C1 page 268.

Other Sexually Transmitted Diseases

The same protective behaviors used to prevent AIDS will also be effective in preventing gonorrhea, herpes and other sexually transmitted diseases. More information on the symptoms, self-care recommendations and other treatments for these problems can be found as follows:

- Gonorrhea: page 148
- Herpes: page 148
- Chlamydia: page 148
- Genital warts: page 149

Erection Problems

Erection problems are common and generally solvable by self-care remedies. By definition, an erection problem is a difficulty in raising or maintaining a penis capable of intercourse. While about half of all erection problems have a physical component to the cause, psychological factors almost always play some role as well.

Prevention

Most erection problems can be prevented by a more relaxed approach to lovemaking and a close watch for possible side effects from medications or illnesses. While the ease of gaining and sustaining erections does generally decrease with age, with the right foreplay and environment, there is no age limit to the ability of healthy men to have erections.

Home Treatment

- Rule out medications first. Scores of drugs can cause erection problem side effects. Many blood pressure medicines, diuretics, and mood-altering drugs are particularly troublesome. Ask your doctor or pharmacist to look up the possibility of sexual side effects in the PDR (Physician's Desk Reference), or look it up yourself. See Resource #A2 on page 268.
- Try for more foreplay. Let your partner know that you would enjoy some stroking. Slow down, then slow down some more.
- Listen to the wisdom of the penis. Sometimes, your penis pays attention to things that your consciousness has not registered. If you are grieving over a loss or change in a relationship, your inner self may not be ready for erections. Take some time to let the stress pass.
- Do the penile stamp test to determine if the problem is physically or psychologically based.

Nocturnal Penile Stamp Test

Most healthy men have spontaneous erections during the REM (rapid eye movement) phase of sleep. If you can confirm that those erections are occurring, the cause of an erection problem is more likely to be psychological than physical. The Nocturnal Penile Stamp Test can help you make a determination.

1. Avoid alcohol or sleep medication for two days before the test.
2. Wear brief-type underwear with a fly opening. Bring your penis through the fly to keep most of the pubic hair out of the way.
3. Wrap a strip of four to six stamps snugly around the shaft of the penis forming a partially overlapping ring. Wet the overlapping stamp and seal it to the stamp ring.
4. After the stamp has dried, replace the penis inside your underwear and go to sleep.

5. Upon awakening, check to see if the stamps are broken along the perforations.
6. Repeat for three nights.

If on any night, all of the perforations between any two stamps are broken, you are physically capable of having an erection and should concentrate on psychological solutions to the problem. If the stamps are not perforated, call your physician to pursue possible physical causes.

For more information on this test, see Resource #A3 on page 268.

When to Call a Health Professional

- If you think that a medication may be causing the problem. Substitutes are almost always available.
- If you have a negative penile stamp test or think that your problem may be a physical one.
- If you are still having problems after a few months of self-care, consider using the services of a psychological therapist. Therapy can be successful in about 80 percent of cases.
- After all other options have been tried for several months without success, you may wish to talk with your doctor about penile implants or erection-producing medications.

Hernia

An inguinal hernia occurs when part of the intestine protrudes down the inguinal canal into the scrotum. The condition is caused when exertion increases the pressure of the intestine against a congenitally weak spot in the abdominal wall. The exertion could be a result of heavy work, weight lifting or even straining during bowel movements.

A hernia is called reducible if the bulge can be pushed back into place inside the abdomen; irreducible if it cannot.

The symptoms of inguinal hernias vary. Sometimes the onset will be gradual, with the symptoms increasing slowly. Other times, the hernia will occur suddenly with the feeling that something has "given way." Even then there may be varying degrees of pain.

Symptoms can include:

- A feeling of weakness or pressure in the groin
- Occasional pain or aches
- A gurgling feeling
- Visible bulges just above or within the scrotum. These bulges are easier to see if the person is coughing.

Strangulated hernias occur when irreducible hernias get so pinched that the blood supply is cut off and

Hernia - continued

the tissue dies and swells. Rapidly worsening pain in the inguinal region is a signal that the hernia is strangulated. The dead tissue quickly becomes infected and can lead to a life or death situation in a matter of hours.

Prevention

- Avoid activities that strain your abdominal area.
- If you lift weights, use a wide weight lifting belt to support the abdominal wall and prevent hernias.
- Avoid straining during bowel movements.

Home Treatment

- Follow even more closely the advice in the prevention section.
- Pay close attention to increasing pain or other signs of strangulation.

When to Call a Health Professional

- If you suspect a hernia, you should see your physician for a full diagnosis and evaluation of the risk.
- If you experience progressive abdominal, scrotal or inguinal pain.
- If low level pain in the inguinal area continues for more than one week.

Prostate Problems

The prostate is a doughnut-shaped cluster of glands that lies at the bottom of the bladder about halfway between the rectum and the base of the penis. The prostate encircles the urethra, the tube that carries urine from the bladder out through the penis. The prostate produces most of the fluid in semen.

Prostate problems can develop in four ways: prostatitis (infection), prostatosis, benign overgrowth, and two forms of cancer (one mild and one dangerous). The chart on the following two pages presents the symptoms and home treatment guides for each.

See Resource #N1 page 269.

PROSTATE PROBLEMS

Description	Symptoms	Care Guidelines
Prostatitis (Infection) Prostatitis is a bacterial infection of the prostate. The condition is easily treated with antibiotics and does not lead to prostate cancer. Tests for chlamydia, mycoplasma and trichomonas as well as gonorrhea and E. coli may be appropriate.	A C D E F	• Hot baths. • Stress reduction (see page 215). • Avoid coffee, tea, alcohol, and spicy foods. • Drink at least eight glasses of water a day. • See health professional right away for bacterial tests and antibiotic prescription.
Prostatosis (Undiagnosed penis pain) This is a "we don't really know" diagnosis when penis and ejaculation pain does not respond to antibiotic medications. Prostatosis may be caused by a chronically stressed urinary sphincter, the muscle valve just above the prostate that controls the flow of urine from the bladder. Stress can cause this muscle valve to remain chronically tense. Prostatosis may also be aggravated by diet, particularly alcohol, coffee, tea, and spicy foods.	A B C	• Same home treatment as for prostatitis. • Call your health professional if other symptoms appear or if a month of your self-care treatment has not helped.

SYMPTOMS KEY

A. Pain in or near penis
B. Pain on ejaculation
C. Frequent urination
D. Fever
E. Pain on urination
F. White pussy discharge
G. Hard, lumpy, fixed nodules
H. Low back pain
I. Blood in urine

PROSTATE PROBLEMS - continued

Description	Symp-toms	Care Guidelines
Overgrowth (Benign Prostatic Hypertrophy) By age 65, virtually all men's prostates will be enlarged. Some men may have no symptoms. For others, as the prostate enlarges, it presses on the urethra. The stream of urine becomes smaller and slower. The bladder may fail to empty completely which, in turn, may lead to bladder and kidney infections. Urinary flow may also be obstructed. Medical or surgical care is required. TURP (Transurethral Resection of Prostate) surgery is a non-incision surgery which restores full flow of urine without limiting erections.	C	• Use patience to maximize urination. Visualization helps some men. • See a health professional if other symptoms appear, if urination difficulties become extreme, or if you have not had a recent professional rectal exam. See page 32 for schedule.
Prostate Cancer There are two types of prostate cancer. Slow-growing prostate cancer is common and generally poses no threat to health or life. A third of all men in their sixties have some slow-growing cancerous cells in their prostate. Fast-growing prostate cancer is much less common, but still accounts for 10% of cancer deaths in males. A relatively simple biopsy can tell whether a cancer is fast or slow-growing. Even if it is the fast-growing type, prompt treatment can be effective.	A C E G H I	• Call your doctor for an immediate evaluation if symptoms are present.

SYMPTOMS KEY

A. Pain in or near penis
B. Pain on ejaculation
C. Frequent urination
D. Fever
E. Pain on urination
F. White pussy discharge
G. Hard, lumpy, fixed nodules
H. Low back pain
I. Blood in urine

Jack and Jill went up the hill to fetch a pail of water. Jack fell down and broke his crown and Jill came tumbling after. Up Jack got and home did trot as fast as he could caper. He went to bed to mend his head with vinegar and brown paper. Jill came in and she did grin to see his paper plaster. Mother, vexed, did hold her next for causing Jack's disaster.

Mother Goose

Chapter 12

Injuries and Sports Medicine

Few of us make it through a year without some kind of minor injury, and it sometimes seems a child can't make it through a whole day without at least one "owwie." If you know how to treat these minor injuries, you can save money and unnecessary visits to your health professional.

An injured person may need calming down. Give reassurance and understanding along with first-aid. Dealing with injuries in a matter-of-fact way will help reduce anxiety.

You can treat many minor injuries with a minimum of tools. For example, the best treatment for bruises, strains, sprains, and burns is something almost everyone has: ice. Ice reduces swelling and pain. Keep a cold pack (see page 247), or a paper cup of ice in your freezer. When accidents happen, apply the ice as quickly as possible. Wrap the ice in a thin cloth or paper towel to avoid damaging the skin tissue.

Accidental Tooth Loss

If a permanent tooth is lost because of an injury, a dentist may be able to reimplant it in the mouth. Since a baby tooth probably cannot be reimplanted and has to come out anyway, it isn't worth the effort to save it. However, if a baby tooth is lost prematurely, the permanent teeth may grow in crooked in order to fill the opening. Call your dentist to determine if a spacer is needed to temporarily fill the gap.

Home Treatment

- Clean off the tooth and re-implant immediately, or wrap the

Tooth Loss - continued

tooth in a piece of milk-soaked gauze and place it in a small glass of milk.

- Immediately call your dentist for an emergency visit.

When to Call a Health Professional

- To reimplant the tooth. The sooner you reimplant the tooth, the better the chance the tooth will stay in. Your odds are best if reimplanting occurs within 15 minutes of the injury. After 24 hours there is little chance the tooth can be successfully reimplanted.
- If the tooth lost was a baby tooth. Schedule an appointment within two weeks to determine if a spacer is needed.

Animal Bites

When bitten by an animal, the main concern for most people is whether or not a rabies shot is needed. The main carriers of rabies are wild animals, especially skunks, foxes and raccoons. Pet cats and dogs rarely have rabies since most have been immunized at least once. If a pet has bitten you, the animal needs to be observed for ten days to see if it develops rabies symptoms. If the owners cannot be relied on to watch the animal, call the dog warden to catch and quarantine it.

Bacterial infections are common in animal bites that break the skin. Tetanus can occur if shots are not up-to-date.

Prevention

- Don't try to catch wild animals or provoke them to attack. Especially do not try to handle a sick or injured animal.
- Don't rush up to a dog without making sure it is friendly. It should be wagging its tail and not snarling or growling.
- Observe beware-of-dog signs.

Home Treatment

- Clean the wound thoroughly with soap and water. Treat it as you would a puncture wound (see page 175) if the skin has been penetrated. Watch for signs of infection.

When to Call a Health Professional

- If rabies shots may be needed. Below are some reasons rabies shots should be considered:
    - Any wild animal bite.
    - If the animal is a domestic cat or dog but is acting strangely, foaming at the mouth, or is very thirsty.
    - If the animal owner has no record of the pet having been vaccinated for rabies.
- If your tetanus shots aren't up-to-date. See page 264.
- If a human bite breaks the skin.

- If the bite is severe, particularly on the hand or face.

Blisters

Blisters are usually the result of persistent or repeated rubbing against the skin.

Closed Blisters

If a blister is closed and can be protected, it is best to leave it alone. While draining a closed blister can speed healing, it also increases the chance of infection.

If the blister is in a place that cannot be protected, puncture the blister at its edge with a sterile needle. Press the top of the blister to remove the fluid.

Open Blisters

If a blister is open and dirty, you will need to wash it and remove any dead skin. Use alcohol to wash your hands and a small pair of scissors. Clean the blister with alcohol, cut away the dead skin and cover the wound with a non-stick bandage. Take care to keep the area clean until the new skin is well established.

Blood Under a Nail

Fingernails and toenails often get crunched, bashed, or smashed. These injuries usually aren't too serious; although when swelling under the nail occurs, it can be very painful.

The throbbing and pain can be relieved only by draining the blood. To do that, you need to make a hole in the nail. This can be done at home rather than in a health professional's office. You may feel squeamish about trying this method, but it is the same thing a health professional would do.

Home Treatment

- As soon as possible after the injury, apply ice. This will minimize the swelling.
- If pressure and pain require a hole to be made in the nail, follow these steps:
  - Straighten a paper clip and heat the tip in a flame until it is red hot.
  - Place the tip of the paper clip on the nail and let it melt through. Do not push. This will not be painful as the nail has no nerves. A tough nail may take several tries.

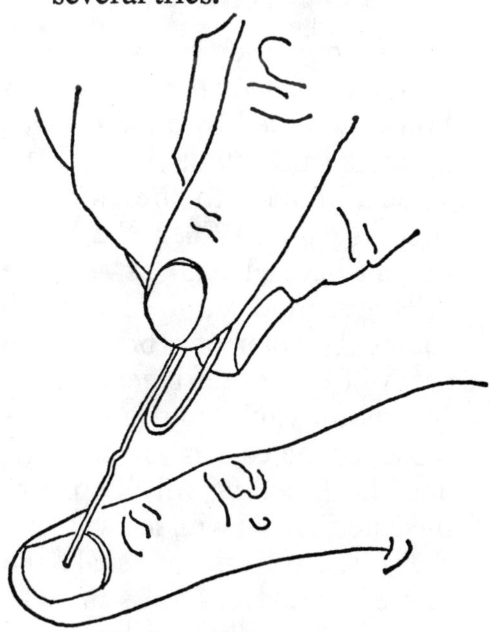

Relieve Pressure

Blood Under Nail - continued

- As soon as the hole is complete, blood will escape and the pain will be relieved.
- Soak the finger three times a day in a half and half mixture of hydrogen peroxide and warm water.
- If the pressure builds up again in a few days, repeat the procedure, using the same hole.

When to Call a Health Professional

- If the victim is uncooperative and won't let you try the procedure.
- If the nail appears infected. The nail is infected if it is red, hot, or has pus under it.

Bruises (Contusions)

When your body is battered or bumped, a bruise develops. A bruise is caused by a blow which ruptures small blood vessels. The vessels bleed into the soft surrounding area. When the blood doesn't have enough oxygen, the cells turn from red to blue which causes the color of a bruise. The area will either keep bleeding until the tissue can't hold any more blood, or the vessels will constrict and the bleeding will stop. Immediate first aid with ice will help the vessels constrict and make the bruise less severe.

A black eye is a type of bruise and needs the same treatment. Of concern here is the possibility that the eye itself is also injured. Inspect the eye and call a health professional if the white of the eye is very red or if vision is impaired.

Home Treatment

- Apply ice or cold packs for 20 minute intervals during the first 48 hours to help vessels constrict and to reduce the swelling. The quicker you apply ice after the injury the less bleeding will result.
- If possible, elevate the bruised limb. Blood will leave the area of the wound and there will be less swelling.
- Rest the limb so you won't injure it further.
- If the area is still painful after 48 hours, apply heat with warm towels, a hot water bottle, or a heating pad.

When to Call a Health Professional

- If signs of infection develop. The symptoms are:
  - increasingly severe pain
  - fever of 101° or more
  - marked swelling and surrounding redness
- If the bruise is a black eye and the white of the eye is very red or vision is impaired.

Burns

Burns are classified as first, second, or third degree depending on their depth, not on the amount of pain nor the extent of the burn. A first degree burn involves just the outer surface of the skin. The skin is dry, painful, and sensitive to touch. A mild sunburn is an example. A second degree burn involves the tissue beneath the skin in addition to the outer skin. The symptoms are swollen, puffy, weepy, or blistered skin. A third degree burn involves the outer skin, tissue beneath the skin, and any underlying tissue or organs. The skin is dry, pale white or charred black, swollen, and sometimes broken open. Nerves are destroyed or damaged, so there may be little pain except on the outer edges where there is a second degree burn.

Prevention

If you catch on fire, roll over and over on the ground to smother the flames. If another person catches on fire, roll the victim in a blanket, rug, or coat to stifle the flames. If the victim is allowed to run, air will fan the fire and make it worse. If a hose is handy, use it to put out the flames. Water will cool the burned areas and reduce the severity of the burns.

Home Treatment

For minor burns:

- For treatment of sunburn, see page 116.
- Ice or cold water is the best immediate treatment for minor burns. The cold lowers the skin temperature and lessens the severity of the burn. Immediately run cold tap water over the burn. While you do this, send someone to get some ice. Ice in a paper cup can be applied directly to a burn if you keep the ice moving around. The application of ice or a cold pack hurts for a while, but it is the best treatment.
- Do not put any salves, butter, grease, oils, or lubricants on a burn. They don't do any good and can irritate the skin more.
- Do not cover the burn unless it rubs against clothing. If it rubs, it is better to cover the wound than to break open the blisters. To cover a burn, remove any burned clothing. Wash the burned area and cover it with a single layer of gauze. Tape the edges of the gauze well away from the burned area. This dressing needs to be changed the following day and then every two days.
- Shock is often present with major burns especially if they involve the head, face, hands, feet, or genitals. See page 196 for prevention and treatment of shock.
- A third degree burn needs immediate medical treatment. Do not apply any salves or medication since these will have to be removed later for treatment and their removal may cause further harm.

Burns - continued

When to Call a Health Professional

- If a burn involves the face, hands, feet, or genitals.
- If the burn encircles an arm or leg or covers more than one-quarter of the body part involved.
- If the pain lasts over 48 hours.
- For all third degree burns.
- If an infection starts developing. Signs of infection are:
  - fever of 101° or more
  - increase in pain, redness and swelling
- If in doubt as to extent of burn or in doubt if it is a second or third degree burn.

Chemically Burned Eye

Chemical burns to the eye occur when something caustic, such as window-cleaning fluid, gasoline, or turpentine, is splashed into it. The eye appears reddened and watery. If the damage is more severe the eye appears whitish.

Home Treatment

- Immediately flush the eye with ordinary tap water to dilute the chemical. Fill a sink or dish pan with water, immerse the face of the victim in the water, and then open and close the eyelids to force the water to all parts of the eye. It may sometimes be necessary to move the eyelids with the fingers.
- Keep dunking under water until the eye stops hurting.

When to Call a Health Professional

- After flushing the eye, go immediately to an emergency center if there is major exposure to a strong acid, e.g., battery acid; or base substance, e.g., lye, or Draino.
- If after 20 minutes of home treatment, the eye still hurts.
- If the eye appears to be damaged. Symptoms include:
  - persistent redness
  - discharge
  - watering
  - any visual impairment such as double vision, blurring, or sensitivity to light

Cuts (Lacerations)

What concerns most of us when we see a cut is whether or not stitches or sutures are necessary. In general, stitches are used to hold the two edges of a wound together so that healing can occur with a minimum of scarring. The following table, Are Sutures Necessary?, gives specific guidelines as to whether or not you need to have a cut sutured.

If a cut doesn't need stitches, be sure to bandage it properly at home. Always put an adhesive strip across a cut rather than lengthwise. This will bring the edges into firm contact and promote healing.

To remove an adhesive bandage, pull it slowly in the direction of hair growth to prevent pain caused by pulling against the hairs.

Are Sutures Necessary?

Sutures Needed:

- The wound is deep and tends to gape widely.
- The cut is deep and is located on a part of the body that bends and puts stress on the cut. Examples of stress areas are elbows, knees, and fingers.
- A cut on the scalp tends to separate and usually needs stitches.
- Deep cuts on your thumb or palm of your hand may cut nerves affecting your sense of touch.
- A split lip needs suturing because it scars easily.
- Cuts to eyelids need stitches to prevent drooping.
- Whenever you are particularly worried about scarring, especially with facial cuts. A sutured cut usually heals with less scarring than an unsutured one.
- Cuts that go down to the muscle or bone.
- If bleeding, even from a minor wound, cannot be controlled with 20 minutes of direct pressure.

Sutures Not Needed:

- Cut edges of the skin tend to fall together.
- Cuts less than one inch long that aren't deep.

A butterfly bandage, very useful in holding together cut skin edges, can be made at home or purchased. The adhesive is on the outside edge, so the middle part over the cut isn't sticky. The following steps show how to make a butterfly bandage:

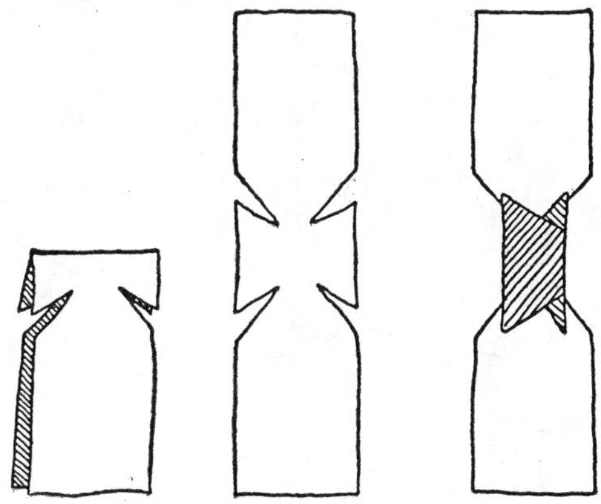

A Butterfly Bandage B

- Cut a strip from a roll of one inch adhesive tape and fold it sticky-side out. Cut wedges into the tape as shown in A.
- Unfold the tape, then fold the wedged pieces together sticky-side in as in B. The center of the tape will be non-sticky.
- Place one end of the tape on the skin, then pull the other end to tightly close the wound as in C.

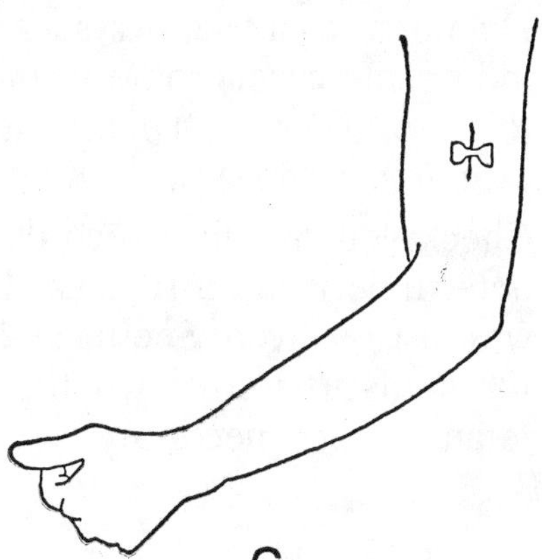

C

Cuts - continued

If the cut is long, you may need to use more than one bandage as in D.

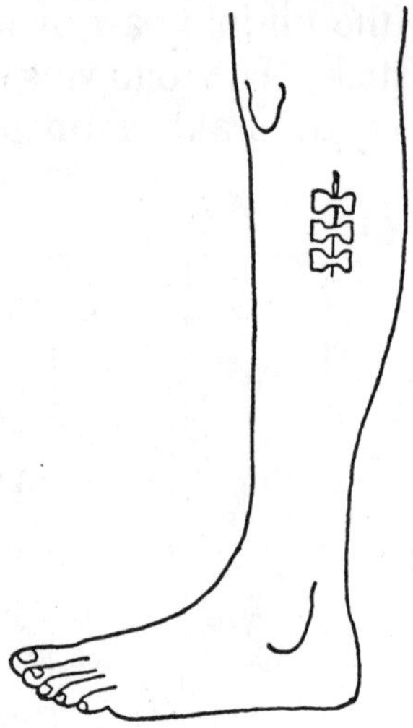

D

Home Treatment

- Wash the cut with soap and water.
- Stop the bleeding by applying direct pressure to the wound. If bleeding is severe, maintain pressure for a full ten minutes without peeking or dabbing at the wound. See page 187.
- Use a regular adhesive strip or butterfly bandage to continue the pressure.
- Do not use antiseptics such as iodine, mercurochrome, or merthiolate. These can harm delicate tissues and slow healing.
- Check your medical records to determine when a tetanus shot was last received. See page 264 for a discussion of whether a tetanus shot is necessary.

When to Call a Health Professional

- If the cut needs to be sutured.
- If the cut becomes infected. Symptoms of infection are:
  - increasing pain
  - tenderness
  - swelling
  - fever of 101° or more
  - red streaks leading away from the wound
  - redness around the cut

Fishhook Removal

Sometimes in the excitement of fishing, fingers are hooked instead of fish. It is convenient to know how to remove a fishhook by yourself, or for a fishing companion, especially if you are far from medical help.

Home Treatment

- Remove the hook as follows:
  - Use ice or cold water, or hard pressure to provide temporary numbing.
  - Tie a piece of fishline to the hook near the skin surface. See step A.
  - Grasp the eye of the hook with one hand and press down about $\frac{1}{8}$ inch to disengage the barb. See step B. While still pressing the hook down (barb disengaged), jerk the line parallel to the skin surface with the other hand so that the

hook shaft leads the barb out of the skin. See step C.

Step A

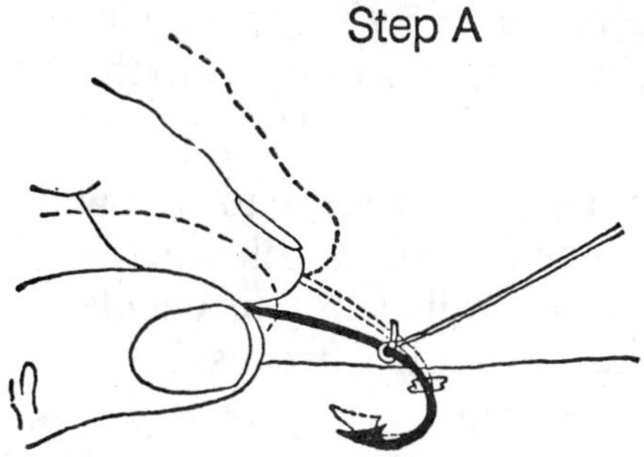

Step B

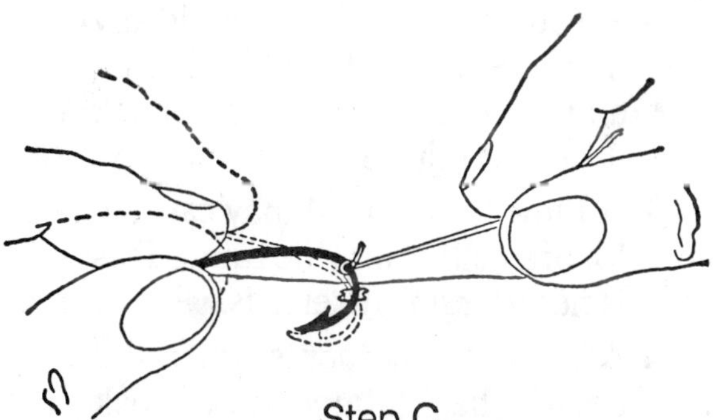

Step C

Removing A Fishhook

- Wash the wound thoroughly. Use soap if available.
- Do not remove the hook if it is in the eye.

When to Call a Health Professional

- Puncture wounds are susceptible to tetanus infection. See page 264 for a discussion of whether a tetanus shot it necessary.
- If the wound becomes infected. Symptoms are redness, pus, or heat around the wound.
- If hook is in the eye.

Fractures

Fractures and sprains are often confused. Both are painful and shouldn't have any weight put on them. Sprains can be treated at home, as described on page 177. Fractures need to be seen by a health professional. When you do have a fracture, call your health professional rather than rushing to the emergency room since they will have to call your doctor anyway. There is usually no immediate need to treat a fracture as long as it is immobilized and swelling can be kept at a minimum. See Splinting, page 177. A finger broken Sunday night can wait for treatment on Monday if initial treatment is started: reduce the swelling and don't use the finger. However, if you suspect nerve or artery damage below any possible fracture, see a physician immediately.

The following symptoms may be helpful in recognizing a fracture. X-rays will usually be needed to confirm the diagnosis.

When to Call a Health Professional

- If the limb is obviously bent out of shape or a bone is poking through the skin.

Fractures - continued

- If the limb is twisted unnaturally.
- If the victim can't move the injured limb.
- Run your finger along the bone line. If you feel an irregularity, it could be a fracture.
- *Gently* press the area of the injury. Pain is often centered at the site of a break. Pain from a sprain may be more spread out.
- If there is a *lot* of swelling and discoloration.
- If you are uncertain of the nature of the injury and the pain continues or increases.

Freeing Trapped Limbs

Fingers, arms or legs often get caught in objects such as bottles, jars, or pipes. Stay calm; panic will only make the situation worse.

Home Treatment

- Don't force the limb. This will only make it swell and become more difficult to remove.
- Try to get the victim to relax the limb. Relaxation alone will sometimes enable you to free the limb.
- If possible, elevate the limb.
- Apply ice around the exposed limb. This may reduce any swelling that has already occurred and allow the limb to be released.
- If ice doesn't work, dribble dishwashing soap or cooking oil down the limb. Turn the limb or the object so you "unscrew" it rather than pulling it out directly.

Head Injuries

Head injuries are frightening and can be very serious because of the potential for brain damage. However, not every head injury involves a concussion or injury to the brain.

There are certain steps to follow when someone suffers a blow to the head which will help you decide whether a health professional should be seen.

Home Treatment

- Treat the injury as you would any injury. Stop any bleeding, clean, and bandage the wound. Check for other injuries.
- A blow to the head may cause a lot of swelling and bleeding. This is not *necessarily* serious.
- After a few moments, when the person has calmed down, ask some questions to see if he or she is confused. Ask name, address, what day it is, etc.
- Observe the person frequently for the next 24 hours. *Immediately following the injury and every two hours for the next 24* (set your alarm during the night) *do the following checks:*
  - To check for alertness, ask questions, as above: name, address, age, what day it is. If the

person appears confused, call a physician.

- To check for pupil constriction: use a penlight in a darkened room and direct the light from the side into each pupil several times. If the pupils do not constrict, or one constricts considerably more than the other one, call a physician immediately. See page 24 for more information on the pupil constriction test.
- Check to see if the person can move arms and legs symmetrically.

When to Call a Health Professional

- If the person has lost consciousness at any time following the injury.
- If the person is very confused after the first few minutes following the injury.
- If there is nausea and vomiting *after* the first 2-3 hours following the injury. Limited nausea or vomiting at first is normal.
- If there is violent, persistent vomiting after the first 10-20 minutes.
- If the pupils do not constrict or do not constrict evenly. This indicates an *immediate* call.
- If the person has a loss of memory for more than a minute.
- If there is double vision.
- If there are seizures, similar to a convulsion.
- If there is weakness or numbness on one side.

Insect in the Ear

Getting an insect in your ear can be a frightening experience, especially for a child. It is sometimes difficult to know if an insect is in the ear rather than something else. Your child may say, "My ear is bumping around." Once you know for sure that it is an insect, there are a couple of tricks you can try to get it out.

Home Treatment

- Don't try to kill the insect by poking something in the ear. It will be much more difficult to get out and you may damage the ear.
- Insects are attracted to light, so they may be coaxed out with light. If you are outdoors, pull the earlobe gently to straighten the ear canal and aim the ear toward the sun. If indoors, shine a flashlight into the ear while pulling gently on the earlobe. The insect may crawl out toward the light.
- If the light method fails to work, dribbling a little mineral oil into the ear may cause the insect to float out. You must be *sure* that it is a bug in the ear before trying this method. If it is a bean, popcorn, or something similar, the object may swell and be difficult to remove.

When to Call a Health Professional

- If neither of the above methods work.
- If you decide that it is something other than an insect in the ear.

Nosebleeds

Nosebleeds can be inconvenient and messy, and they can be stopped with home treatment. Some common causes of nosebleeds are the common cold, allergies, blows to the nose, medication, high altitudes, blowing the nose, a foreign object in the nose, and low humidity.

Prevention

When a nosebleed occurs, try to figure out what caused it. You may save yourself from future occurrences by eliminating the cause. An example of this is a nosebleed caused by low humidity. Humidifying your house or at least the bedrooms and turning the heat down to 60-64° may prevent future nosebleeds.

Home Treatment

- Blow all clots out of the nose.
- Sit up straight and keep the head erect. Tilting the head backward may cause blood to run down the throat.
- Pinch the nostrils shut between your thumb and forefinger for ten full minutes. Watch the clock as you're doing this. Don't let go after a couple of minutes to see if it's still bleeding or you will have to start timing yourself again.
- After ten minutes, release the nose. If it is still bleeding, hold it for another ten minutes.
- After the bleeding has stopped, stay quiet for a few hours. This means no blowing of the nose, no loud talking, and no laughing.

When to Call a Health Professional

- If the bleeding hasn't stopped after three tries of ten minutes each.
- If the bleeding was caused by a fracture of the nose. Suspect a fracture if there is a deformity in the outline of the nose.
- If nosebleeds keep occurring and you can't find the cause.

Objects in the Eye

When something gets in an eye that tears can't remove, try not to rub it; you could scratch the cornea. You may have to restrain small children.

Home Treatment

- First wash your hands.
- If the speck is in the side of the eye or by the lower lid, moisten the tip of a twisted piece of tissue and touch the speck with the end. The debris should cling to the tissue.
- Gently wash the eye with cool water; an eyedropper helps.
- Never use tweezers, toothpicks or other hard items to remove any object; damage may result.
- If the object is under the upper lid, you may need to flip the lid.

- Ask the victim to look down at the floor.
- Grasp the eyelashes and pull the lid away from the eyeball.
- Place a cotton swab or wooden match stick across the outer surface of the lid near the lashes.
- Pull the lid forward and upward which will cause the lid to roll and fold back over the applicator. The lid will now remain rolled up and won't need to be held.

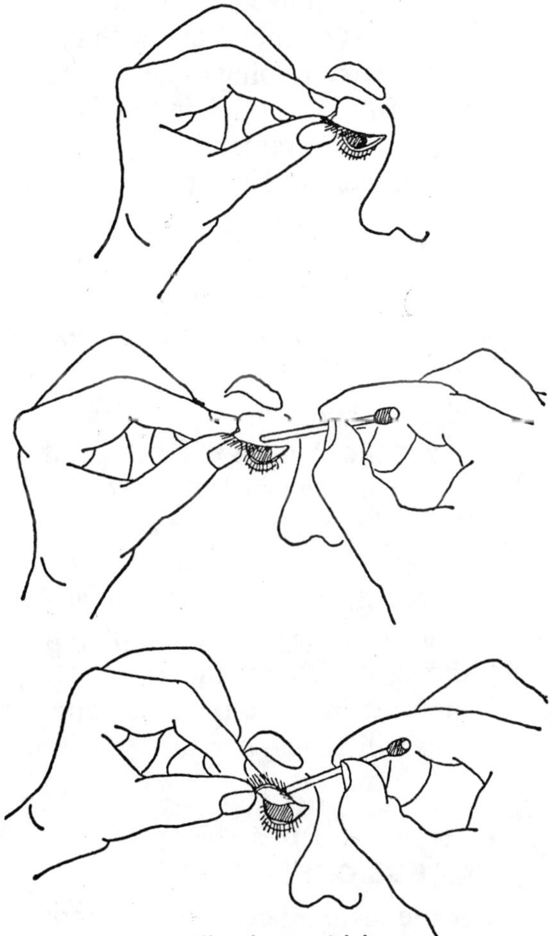

Flipping a Lid

- If the speck is on the eyelid, remove it with a moistened cloth or tissue.
- When you are through, the victim can look at the ceiling to allow the lid to drop in place.

When to Call a Health Professional

- If the object is on the eyeball rather than on the eyelid. You could damage the eye if the object severely scratches the eyeball. This is especially true if an object has penetrated the eyeball at all.
- If you cannot remove the object yourself.
- If the object has scratched the cornea. Although most corneal scratches are minor and self healing, pain that persists after the object has been removed should be checked out.

Puncture Wounds

A puncture wound is caused by sharp and pointed objects which penetrate the skin. Nails, pins, tacks, ice picks, and needles can all cause puncture wounds. There is greater danger of infection because the wound is more difficult to clean and provides a warm, moist place for bacteria to grow.

Home Treatment

- Check to make sure that nothing, such as the tip of a needle, has been left in the wound. Check the object to see if it is intact.

Puncture Wounds - continued

- Allow the wound to bleed freely to clean itself out unless there has been a large loss of blood or the blood is squirting out.
- Clean the wound thoroughly with soap and water.
- For the next four to five days, soak the wound several times a day in warm water. This will clean the wound from the inside out. If the wound is closed, an infection beneath the skin may not be detected for several days.

When to Call a Health Professional

- If the wound is in the head, chest, or abdomen, unless it is obviously minor.
- If the wound shows signs of infection, such as:
  - fever of 101° or more
  - pus or increased redness
  - swelling
- If the source of the puncture wound was dirty, such as barbed wire, a rusty nail, or a farm implement, you need a tetanus shot if yours isn't up-to-date. See page 264 for a discussion of whether or not a shot is necessary.

Scrapes (Abrasions)

Scrapes or abrasions happen so often that they seem unimportant. They need to be treated, however, to reduce the chance of scarring or infection.

Home Treatment

- The worst thing about scrapes is that they are usually very dirty. You need to remove all dirt and debris to prevent scarring and possible infection. Use a pair of tweezers to remove obvious pieces of debris, then scrub vigorously with soap and water and a washcloth to clean the wound. If you have a water sprayer in your kitchen sink, try using that on the scrape with additional scrubbing. The victim will probably complain loudly of the pain, but remember that you are preventing scarring.
- You may apply an antibiotic ointment, but it isn't a necessity. Neosporin and Bacitracin are a couple of over-the-counter examples.
- If the scrape is large, cover it with a non-stick bandage. This type of bandage won't stick to the scrape and is held in place by adhesive around the edges; Telfa is an example. If you apply a bandage and wish to use an ointment, put the ointment on the bandage, then the bandage on the scrape. This will be less painful.

When to Call a Health Professional

- If the scrape becomes infected. Signs of infection are:
  - swelling
  - increased pain

- red streaks leading away from the wound
- pussy discharge
- fever of 101° or more

Splinting

Splinting is used to immobilize a suspected fracture to prevent further injury. There are two general ways to immobilize a fracture: wrapping something around the injured limb, or tying the limb to some other part of the victim's body.

For the first method you can use rolled-up newspapers and magazines, an umbrella, a stick, a cane, or anything else that is stiff. Tie the stiff object to the injured limb with a rope, a belt, torn strips of cloth, or anything else convenient.

Position the splint so that the injured limb cannot bend. A general rule is to splint a joint above and a joint below the fracture. For example, if the forearm is broken, splint the arm from the elbow to the wrist.

The second method includes taping one broken toe to a healthy one or immobilizing an arm by tying it across the victim's chest.

Sprains and Strains

A *sprain* is an injury to the muscle, ligaments, tendons, and soft tissues in the region of a joint. Ligaments, tendons, and small blood vessels are stretched and sometimes torn when a joint is sprained. A *strain* is a muscle injury from over-exertion or stretching. Because treatment for both injuries is the same, they are presented here as one type of injury. For treatment of back strains specifically, see page 55.

Home Treatment

- If the sprain is to a finger or other part of the hand, immediately remove all rings. Rings may have to be cut off later if swelling occurs.
- Do not put weight on the injured joint. This can cause further damage. A sprain is just as painful as a fracture and needs just as much care. For a badly sprained ankle, use crutches. The inconvenience of crutches is justified by the faster healing of the ankle.
- Immediate application of ice or cold packs is needed to prevent or minimize swelling, especially for wrists and ankles. For difficult-to-reach injuries, a cold pack works best (see page 247. Apply ice, for periods of 20 minutes, for up to 48 hours after the injury.
- Elevate the injured limb while applying the ice treatment to decrease the swelling.
- Wrap the injury with an elastic bandage to immobilize the sprain. Be sure to loosen the bandage if the bandage gets too tight. A tightly wrapped sprain may fool you into thinking that you can continue using the joint.

Sprains and Strains - cont.

With or without a wrap, the joint needs total rest.

- After 48 hours of cold treatments switch to heat. A hot water bottle, warm towels, or a heating pad will speed up the healing process. Do not apply anything that is uncomfortably warm.
- If you did not remove the ring before the swelling started, try the following method to remove it:
  - Stick the end of a slick piece of string such as dental tape, under the ring toward the hand.
  - Starting at the knuckle side of the ring, wrap the string snugly around the finger toward the end of the finger, wrapping beyond the knuckle. Each wrap should be right next to the one before.
  - Grasp the end of the string that is stretched under the ring and start unwrapping it, pushing the ring along in place of the unwrapped string until the ring passes the knuckle.

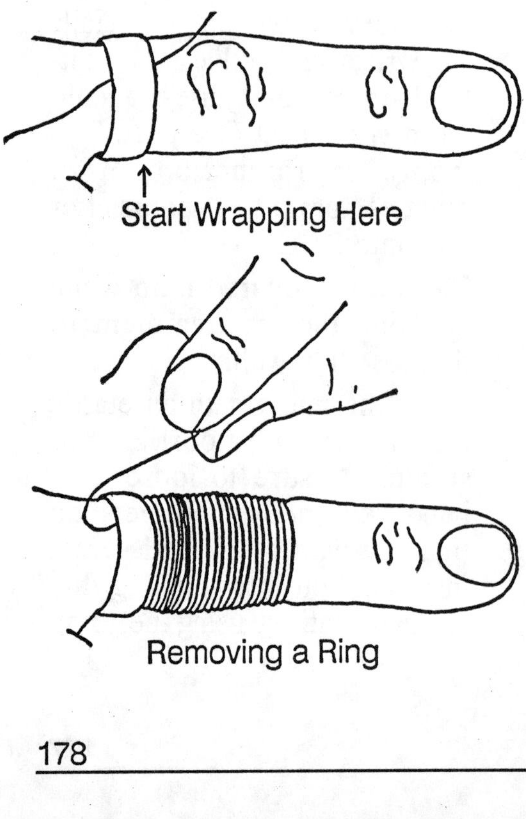

Removing a Ring

When to Call a Health Professional

- If the injury appears to be a fracture rather than a sprain. See Fractures on page 171 for symptoms of a possible broken bone.
- If the sprain is not improving after four days of home treatment.

Sports Injuries

Sports injuries are common among people who are trying to stay healthy. Most sports injuries are due to either traumatic abuse or significant overuse of the body.

Generally speaking, if the injury is to a muscle, ligament, tendon, or bone, the basic treatment is the same. It can be characterized in the six-step IRA/MSA process as follows:

I. Ice. As soon as possible after you notice an injury, cool down the injured area. The ice will reduce pain and swelling and lead to healing.

R. Rest. Injured muscle, ligament or tendon tissue needs time and rest to restore itself. Complete rest for 24 to 48 hours is usually enough to allow healing to begin in earnest.

Elevation of the injured area is also helpful during this phase.

A. Aspirin. Aspirin can be used after most injuries to reduce swelling and speed the healing process. Review aspirin guidelines on page 253.

After the injured area has begun to heal, the MSA part of the process should begin.

M. Movement. It's important to reestablish a full range of motion as quickly as possible after an injury. Maintaining flexibility during healing will insure that scar tissue formed by the injury will not limit functioning or performance later.

S. Strength. Once inflammation is controlled and a range of motion is reestablished, the injured part can benefit from gradual efforts to strengthen it.

A. Alternate Activities. After the first few days, but while the injured part is still healing, it is important to continue regular exercise using alternative activities or sports which do not place a strain on the injured part.

The IRA (ice, rest, aspirin) process is good to start immediately for most injuries. How soon you begin the MSA (movement, strength, alternate) process will depend on the location and severity of the injury. The chart on the following page describes what to do for most common sports injuries.

SPORTS INJURIES CHART			
Problem	**Reference**	**Prevention**	**Home Treatment**
Runner's knee	Bursitis, p. 95 Strains, p. 177	•Good shoes •Avoid slanted surfaces, jumping and hills	•IRA/MSA •Orthotics •Knee-strengthening exercises.
Heel spurs (plantar fasciitis)	Bruises, p. 165 Sprains, p. 177	•Good shoes •Achilles stretch, p. 211	•IRA •Heel pads •Orthotics •Massage
Tennis elbow	Bursitis, p. 95 Sprains, p. 177	•2-handed backhand	•IRA/MSA •Strengthen wrist
Muscle cramps	Back pain, p. 48	•Fruits, vegetables, salt, minerals •Stretching	
Pulled muscles (torn or strained)	Strains, p. 177	•Avoid overstress •Stretching, p. 211 •Balanced exercise p. 208	•Ice;24-48 hrs. then switch to heat •IRA/MSA
"Stitches" (sharp pain in side)	Curl-ups, p. 52 (for stomach muscles)	•Avoid exercise for one hour after eating	•Push fingers into cramp •Stretch abdominals
Stress fractures	Fractures, p. 171	•Good shoes •Gradual progress	•IRA/MSA
Sprained ligaments (ankles, knees, wrists, etc.)	Sprains, p. 177	•Gradual progress •Immobilize •Strengthen	•IRA/MSA
Low back pain	Back pain, p. 48	•Strengthen with exercise	•IRA/MSA
Blisters	Blisters, p. 165	•Good fitting shoes •Preventive taping	•Prevent infection

I: Ice **R:** Rest **A:** Aspirin / **M:** Movement **S:** Strengthen **A:** Alternate Activities

It is by presence of mind in untried emergencies that the native metal of a man (or woman) is tested.

James Russell Lowell

Chapter 13

Emergencies

An emergency is a sudden, unexpected occurrence demanding immediate action. Unfortunately, it can also be a time for panic and fear. We all dread coming upon an emergency and not knowing what to do. If you take the time to learn what to do now, you will be better able to cope during an emergency.

The most important thing to remember is to stay calm. By staying calm, you can better assess the situation and help the victim relax. Relaxing can help the victim by slowing bleeding, improving breathing and easing pain.

The next step in any emergency is to identify and prioritize the injuries. Carefully examine the victim. If the person is unconscious, check the pulse and respiration rates. Then look for bleeding, broken bones, and signs of shock. The most serious and life-threatening injuries will have to be treated first. While a cut on the head can produce a lot of blood and seem very serious, it is *relatively* unimportant if the patient is not breathing.

If you are needed in an emergency, give what assistance you can. Most states have a Good Samaritan law that protects people who, in good faith, help in an emergency. You cannot be sued for administering first aid or medical care unless it can be shown that you are guilty of gross negligence. Your local law enforcement office can tell you what protection your state's laws provide.

Good Reasons NOT to Call an Ambulance

- No emergency.
- The victim is conscious, breathing without difficulty, acting normal and has strong vital signs, and there is someone else to ride in the car to give comfort to the victim as you drive.
- Time. An ambulance is not a fast way to get a person to a medical facility; it usually has to travel both ways. You can usually get there at safe speeds faster by car.
- Anxiety. An ambulance ride can add to a victim's anxiety about the injury.
- Cost. Emergency medical services are extremely expensive. Most insurers pay for such services only if the problem can be shown to be a true emergency.
- Consideration. Emergency services should be saved for true emergencies. Inappropriate use can slow the response to people whose lives depend on speedy treatment.

Good Reasons TO Call an Ambulance

- You are alone with the victim who needs care. It is impossible for you to drive a car and care for another person.
- You or the victim is having symptoms of a possible heart attack. These symptoms are severe chest pain, sweating, or shortness of breath.
- You suspect a spinal or neck injury. See page 196 for symptoms of these injuries.
- The victim is having severe breathing difficulty.
- There is severe bleeding. Have someone else call for help while you continue to apply pressure to the wound.
- You cannot cope with the emergency.

Ambulance and Emergency Medical Services

Modern ambulance services have become extremely proficient in providing on-site treatment of medical emergencies and trauma. They are invaluable when fast medical action is needed to save life or limb.

On the other hand, the inappropriate use of ambulances can provide care that is neither high quality nor reasonable in cost. Good judgment in choosing when to use emergency medical services is important both in obtaining quality care and in avoiding unnecessary costs. The guidelines listed on this page can be helpful.

Using Emergency Rooms

Hospital emergency rooms are staffed and equipped to offer sophisticated lifesaving services to those in need. They are designed to handle serious medical emergencies. Unfortunately, many people use emergency departments for minor problems. This will cost them more than a visit to a physician's office and involve a longer wait for treatment.

Emergency departments are not set up to deal with minor illnesses. They do not follow a first-come, first-served procedure. They take patients according to the severity of their illnesses. A cold, flu, or earache may have to wait for hours while a string of more critical problems are treated.

Emergency department services are also expensive because of the high cost of facilities and personnel needed. A family physician can treat an earache much more quickly and at a much lower cost. A family physician also keeps medical histories of each patient so possible allergies or drug interactions will be noted.

Try to rationally assess any illness or injury to determine if you can wait until the next day to see your health professional. However, if you feel you really do have an emergency and cannot reach your health professional, then do go to the emergency department for experienced help.

Artificial Respiration and CPR

Warning: Improper CPR or CPR for a person whose heart is still beating can cause serious injury. Never perform CPR unless:

1. Breathing has stopped.
2. There is no heartbeat.
3. No one with more training in CPR is present.

Be prepared; take a CPR course from the American Red Cross or the American Heart Association.

With basic life support, think ABC: airway, breathing and circulation, in that order. You must establish an open airway to start breathing and you must reestablish breathing before you can begin the external compression needed if the victim's heart has stopped.

Step 1: Is the person conscious?

- Grasp the victim's shoulders and shout, "Are you okay?" If the victim may have suffered a spinal injury be careful not to flex or twist the neck. Move the victim only if necessary. Gently roll head, neck and shoulders together as a unit, as if the person was a log, until he is on his back.
- If the victim does not respond, call for help. When help comes, send that person to call 911 or an ambulance.

Step 2: Is the person breathing?

- Put your cheek next to the victim's mouth to feel air passing through the lips. At the same time, look at the chest and abdomen to see if either is moving. If these signs aren't present, the victim is not breathing and you should proceed to open the airway.

Step 3: Open the airway.

- Turn the head to one side and clear the mouth of any foreign material with your fingers.

Artificial Respiration - cont.

- Open the airway by pushing down and back on the forehead and lifting up on the chin. *See illustration A.*
- Sometimes, just opening the airway is enough to get the victim breathing again. Check again for air movement from the mouth and nose and in the chest and abdomen. If the victim does not promptly begin breathing, begin rescue breathing immediately.

Step 4: Begin rescue breathing.

- Pinch the victim's nostrils shut with your hand still on the forehead.
- Place your mouth over the victim's, making a tight seal. *See illustration B.* If the victim is an infant, cover his nose and mouth with your mouth.
- Slowly blow in air until the person's chest rises. Use 1-1½ seconds to deliver each breath. Remove your mouth and allow time for the victim to exhale normally before the second breath.
- When you are able to deliver 2 breaths and observe a good chest rise, check the pulse.

Step 5: Check for the pulse.

- Locate the carotid artery in the neck:
  - Find the voice box or Adam's apple.
  - Slide the tips of your index and middle fingers into the groove beside it.
- Hold your fingers in place for 5-10 seconds.

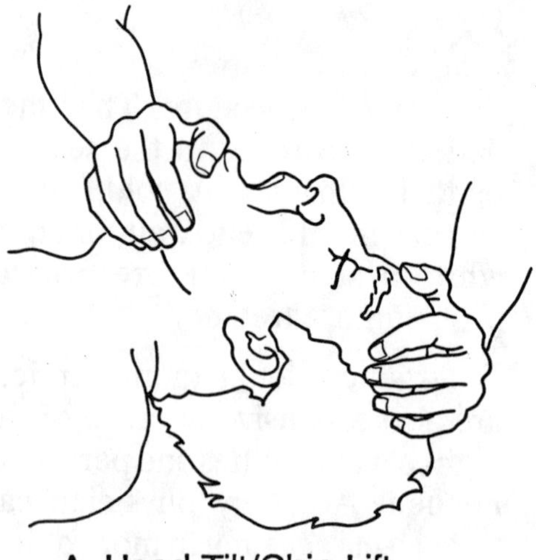

A. Head-Tilt/Chin-Lift

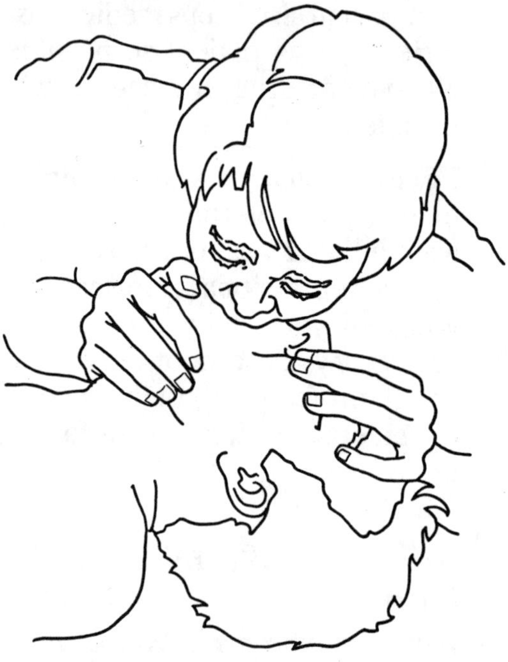

B. Slowly Blow in Air

Step 6: If pulse is present--rescue breathe only.

- Do NOT do chest compressions on someone who has a pulse.
- Blow air into the lungs:
  - 12 times per minute for an adult (once every 5 seconds).
  - 15 times per minute for a small child (once every 4 seconds).
  - 20 times per minute for an infant (once every 3 seconds).

- Check the pulse once per minute to make sure the heart is still beating. Continue breathing as long as necessary. A revived victim still needs to be seen by a health professional. This is important because a person can easily go into shock after breathing has stopped.

Step 7: If pulse is absent--perform chest compressions.

- Place the heel of one hand over the shaded area, about 1-1½ inches above the bottom tip of the sternum. *See illustration C and D.*

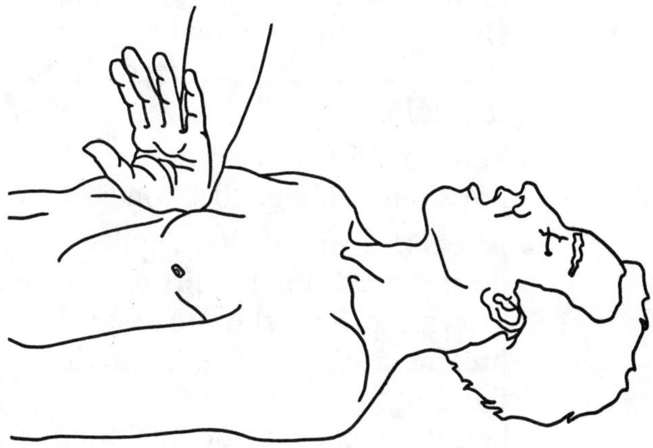

D. Placement of Hand

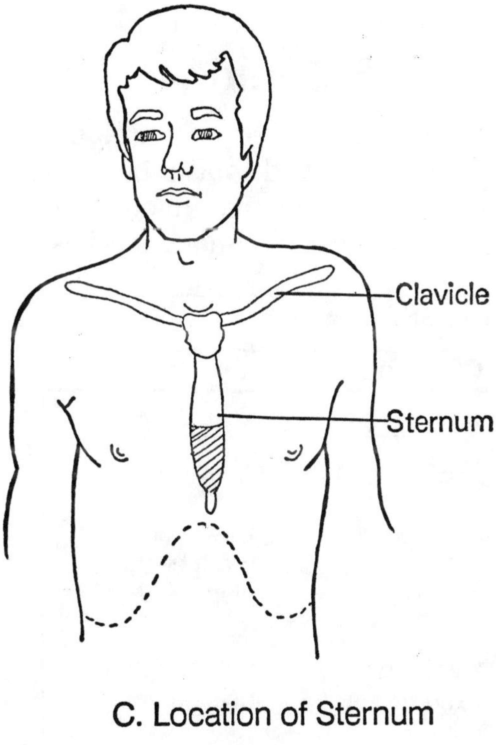

C. Location of Sternum

- Place your other hand on top of the one that is in position.
- Do not allow your fingers to touch the chest as that may cause undue damage to the ribs. *See illustration E.*

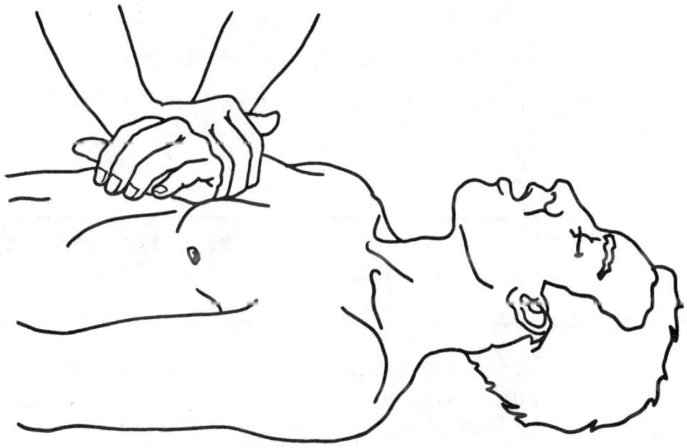

E. Hand Position to Avoid Rib Damage

- Lock your elbows into position, straighten your arms and put your shoulders directly over your hands so that the thrust for each compression goes straight down on the sternum.
- Push down with a steady, firm thrust. Push hard enough to press the lower end of the sternum 1½-2 inches for an adult.

CPR - continued

- Lift your weight from the victim, then repeat the compression. DO NOT lift your hands from the victim's chest during the relaxation.
- Perform 15 external chest compressions in about 10 seconds.
- After 15 compressions, quickly do the head-tilt/chin-lift on the victim, pinch the nose and breathe 2 full, slow breaths to fill the lungs (15:2 ratio). Remember, the chest must deflate after each breath.
- Continue with the 15:2 ratio at the rate of 80-100 compressions per minute. Check pulse again after 1 minute (4 cycles of 15:2). If there is still no pulse, continue with the compressions and breathing.
- If you are alone, do 4 cycles of 15:2, then call for emergency help on 911. Resume CPR as quickly as possible unless the victim has begun breathing on his own or his heartbeat returns.

CPR with Infants and Children

Extra care is needed when giving CPR to infants and children. An infant's neck is so flexible that when opening the airway you must be careful not to tilt too far backward, thus blocking the airway or damaging the spine.

Bleeding

Severe bleeding from major blood vessels is referred to as a hemorrhage. Since even small amounts of blood loss can cause shock, it is im-

CPR READY REFERENCE

	Adults	Children	Infants
Rescue Breathing, Victim has a pulse Give one breath every	5 seconds	4 seconds	3 seconds
No pulse-locate compression landmark	Trace ribs into notch, one finger on sternum	Same as adult	One finger-width below nipple line
Compressions are performed with	2 hands stacked; heel of one hand on sternum	Heel of one hand on sternum	2 or 3 fingers on sternum
Rate of compressions per minute	80-100	80-100	At least 100
Compression depth	$1\frac{1}{2}$-2"	1-$1\frac{1}{2}$"	$\frac{1}{2}$-1"
Ratio compressions to breaths:			
1 rescuer	15:2	5:1	5:1
2 rescuers	5:1	5:1	5:1

Guidelines from the American Heart Association

portant to stop bleeding as quickly as possible.

Home Treatment

- Most bleeding can be controlled by direct pressure for 10 minutes. It is best to use a folded, clean cloth or towel, but if nothing else is available, use your bare hand. Find the place that is bleeding the most and concentrate your pressure directly on that area. It is important to maintain steady pressure for a full 10 minutes without peeking under the cloth or dabbing at the wound. If blood soaks through the cloth, apply another cloth without lifting the first. After applying direct pressure for 10 minutes, bandage the wound with the cloth still on to continue the pressure. If the wound is large, a firm bandage will be needed.
- If there is any ice available, apply some to the area surrounding the wound, but not directly on the wound. This should slow the blood outflow and speed the clotting process.
- If the bleeding is from an arm, hand, leg, or foot, elevate the injured limb as you apply pressure. Gravity will then help by not allowing as much blood to rush to the wound.
- As you control bleeding, look for and treat shock. See page 195 for the symptoms of shock.
- Tourniquets should be used only for severe, life-threatening wounds. This method is dangerous and the victim's limb may be unnecessarily sacrificed. Virtually all bleeding can be stopped by direct pressure although sometimes it's necessary to press very hard or to apply a tightly wrapped bandage over the dressing. Make sure that direct pressure cannot stop the bleeding before resorting to a tourniquet.

When to Call a Health Professional

- If a cut requires stitches. See Are Sutures Necessary? page 169. Stitches are sometimes necessary to control bleeding that direct pressure cannot stop, even in small cuts.
- If a small cut continues to bleed through bandages after 20 minutes of direct pressure.
- If the victim has gone into shock, even if the bleeding has stopped. See Shock, page 195.

Blunt Abdominal Wounds

Blunt abdominal wounds caused by a blow to the stomach can cause severe bruising of the abdominal wall and internal bleeding from the abdominal organs. Such injuries are often caused by automobile, bicycle, tobogganing, and skiing accidents where the victim is thrown into something or to the ground.

The symptoms of abdominal injury are similar to those of external bleeding. Signs of shock will be

Blunt Abdominal - continued

present such as a rapid pulse, low blood pressure and cold, clammy skin. The abdomen may become rigid or tender. The victim may become confused and unable to recognize or describe the injury.

Home Treatment

- Home treatment for an abdominal injury is limited to making the victim comfortable and observing the symptoms. Watching the victim's pulse and blood pressure are the best indicators of serious internal injury.

When to Call a Health Professional

- If abdominal pain, tenderness, rigidity, or signs of shock develop up to 48 hours after a blow or injury to the abdomen. Internal bleeding from an abdominal injury can become a serious emergency. Should you have any questions about the symptoms you observe, call a health professional without delay.

Choking

Thousands of people choke to death each year.

The signs of choking are:

- Person cannot talk.
- Person cannot breathe.
- Person is turning blue.

The cause is usually food or an object stuck in the windpipe. You may have only four to eight minutes to save the person's life by popping out the food or object using the Heimlich Maneuver as described in the Choking Rescue Procedure.

Prevention

- Don't drink too much alcohol before eating. A person with dulled senses may not chew food properly and may try to swallow too large a portion of food.
- Don't eat and laugh at the same time. Food can be sucked into the windpipe.
- Take small bites. Cut meat into small pieces.
- Chew your food thoroughly.
- Don't give children under five years of age peanuts, popcorn, gum, or hard candy. Their molars have not developed and can't thoroughly chew these types of snacks. They can easily choke on these foods.

When to Call a Health Professional

- Call even if the food has been dislodged from a choked victim. There could be abdominal damage from the maneuver or the throat could be damaged by the object.

ADULT - CHOKING RESCUE PROCEDURE (Heimlich Maneuver)

WARNING: Do not begin choking rescue unless the person cannot breathe or is turning blue.

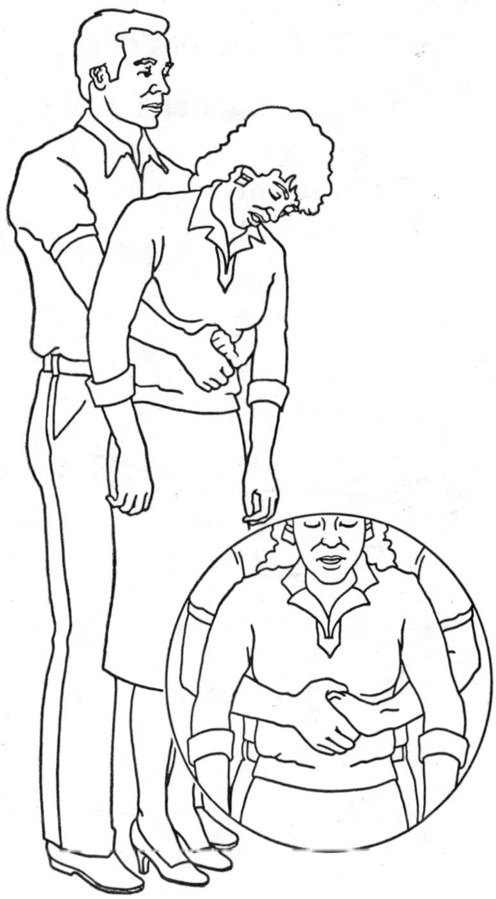

Illustrations A and B

ADULT: If victim is standing or sitting:

1. Stand behind the victim.
2. Wrap your arms around his waist as in illustration A.
3. Place your fist against the person's stomach just above the navel but below the rib cage. See illustration B.
4. Keep the thumb side of the fist against the stomach and grasp the fist with the other hand.
5. Thrust your fist upward causing object to pop out.
6. Repeat thrust up to 10 times until airway is cleared.

ADULT: If victim is on the floor:

1. Turn the victim face up.
2. Straddle the person on your knees next to his hips.
3. Place one of your hands on top of the other with the heel of your bottom hand on the victim's stomach above the navel but well below the rib cage. See illustration C.
4. Thrust in and upward suddenly to pop out object.
5. Repeat up to 10 times until airway is cleared.

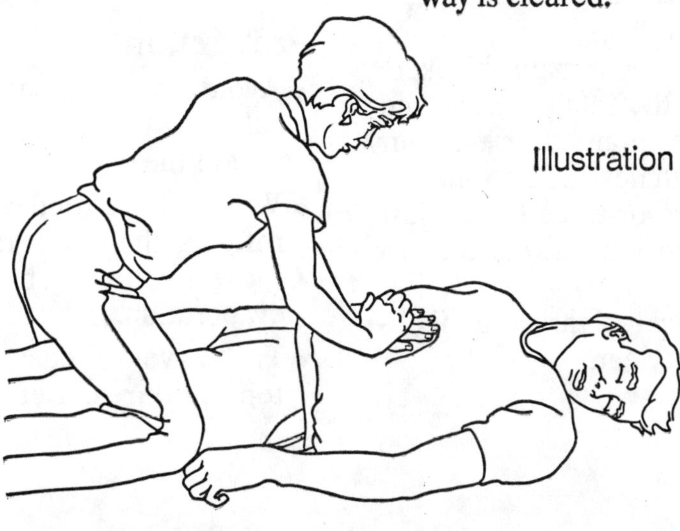

Illustration C

Heimlich Maneuver-cont.

CHILD: Infant under 1 year of age.

1. Hold infant as shown in illustration A.

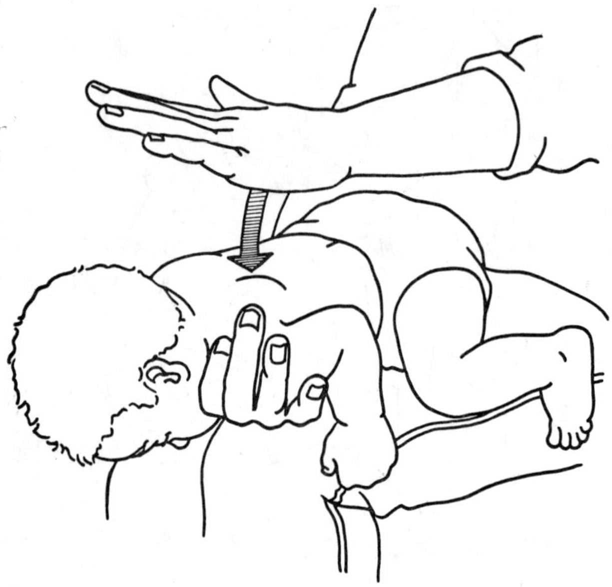

Illustration A

2. Use the heel of one hand to jar the child between the shoulder blades in an attempt to dislodge the object.
3. Repeat 4 times.
4. If the airway remains blocked, support the infant's head and turn the infant over on your thigh with head still down.
5. Place two or three fingers just below the line between the two nipples.
6. Repeat up to 4 thrusts until object pops clear.

CHILD: One year or older.
Follow the same steps as for an adult, but use less pressure. For a one year old, thrust very gently. Use more force for larger children.

Heat Exhaustion

Heat exhaustion is also called heat prostration or heat collapse. It is a serious condition, caused by the loss of vital body fluids.

Any time you work or play in hot weather, you perspire. The perspiration evaporates and cools your skin. If you didn't perspire, your body would get hotter and hotter until you died. Perspiration is made up of water and salt. If your body is low on these elements and thus cannot perspire, heat exhaustion can occur.

Heat exhaustion does have warning signals. You may become dizzy, nauseated, or weak. You will appear pale and your skin will be cool and clammy. As soon as you feel any of these symptoms, get out of the sun immediately and begin home treatment.

Prevention

- Avoid strenuous outdoor physical activity during the hottest part of the day.
- Wear light-colored clothing that reflects the sun's rays and is loose-fitting for better sweat evaporation.
- Try to avoid sudden changes of temperatures. Before getting

into a car that's closed up and parked in the sun, open the doors and wait a few minutes. This is especially true if you just dashed out of an air-conditioned building.

- Drink plenty of water. You need to replace the fluids you are losing in sweat.
- Do not take salt tablets to prevent heat exhaustion. Your body usually loses more water than salt when you perspire so you need water rather than the salt.

Home Treatment

- Get out of the sun to a cool spot.
- Drink lots of water.
- Eat salty foods such as crackers or salted nuts.
- If you are nauseous or dizzy, lie down awhile in a cool spot and then start taking water a little at a time.

When to Call a Health Professional

Heat exhaustion can sometimes lead to heat stroke. Although heat stroke is not common, it can be fatal if professional treatment isn't found. If you find any of the following symptoms, seek immediate help:

- The skin is dry, even under the armpits.
- The body temperature is high and keeps rising.
- The victim becomes unconscious.
- The skin is bright red.

While waiting for help to arrive, start cooling the victim off.

- Remove the victim's clothes and sprinkle water over the body or apply wet, cold towels. Encourage evaporation by placing the victim in front of an air conditioner or by fanning him.
- Try rubbing ice cubes over the victim's arms and legs.

Hyperventilation

Hyperventilation is breathing too fast. Too much oxygen is taken in and the level of carbon dioxide is lowered in the blood. Hyperventilation is usually caused by anxiety and can also be a reaction to severe abdominal pain.

The victim of hyperventilation breathes fast and cannot seem to get enough air. Other symptoms include tingling or numbness of the skin around the mouth, feet, or hands. In severe cases there can be chest pain, spasms of the heart muscles, or even unconsciousness.

Prevention

If you know someone has a history of hyperventilation and you notice fast breathing, bring it to the person's attention. In the final stages of hyperventilation, victims may not be aware that they are breathing fast. After the initial stages, victims are unable to control breathing voluntarily. So when you first notice it, try to get the person to only take a breath once every 5 seconds.

Hyperventilation - continued

Home Treatment

- The victim needs to increase the amount of carbon dioxide in the lungs. This can be done by breathing into a paper bag which covers the nose and mouth. Continue this treatment intermittently for 5-15 minutes.

When to Call a Health Professional

- If hyperventilation occurs in a person who doesn't appear tense or anxious. Sometimes, however, it can be difficult to determine if someone is tense or anxious. See Chapter 17, page 235 to help you determine if a person is anxious.

Hypothermia

Hypothermia is the lowering of the temperature of the body's inner core. It occurs whenever the body is losing more heat than it can produce. Air temperature, wind, and wetness all affect the rate at which heat leaves our bodies. Muscle activity such as exercise, or even shivering, burns up stored body fats to produce heat and warm the body. When several cooling conditions combine, as in a cold wet wind, the body's heat production methods are hard-pressed to keep up with the heat loss. If heat loss continues, the body temperature will drop and hypothermia will set in.

Hypothermia can occur at outside temperatures as high as 45° F. Cold weather with a damp wind can rob a poorly-dressed person of heat in just a few hours. Extreme cold, especially with a wind, can cause hypothermia much more quickly.

Early recognition is very important in the treatment of hypothermia. Often one hiker will lose heat to a very critical degree before others in the group notice anything wrong. If anyone begins to shiver violently, stumble, or will not coherently respond to questions, suspect hypothermia and warm the person quickly.

Prevention

Any time you plan to be out-of-doors for several hours in cool or unsettled weather the following precautions should be taken:

- Dress warmly and carry wind and water-proof clothing. Wear fabric that remains warm even when wet, e.g., wool.
- Wear a warm hat. An unprotected head may lose up to one-half of the body's total heat production at 40° F.
- Eat well before going out and carry extra food.
- Head for shelter if you get wet or cold.
- Don't drink alcohol while in the cold. It causes the body to lose heat faster.

Home Treatment

- The best treatment is to put the victim in a tub of water at 110° F.

Since this is not always available, try the methods below and maintain the warmth until help arrives.

- Get the victim out of the wind and rain as best as possible.
- Remove wet clothing and replace with dry or wool clothing if possible.
- Use body heat to warm the victim. Get inside a sleeping bag with the victim or wrap yourself in a blanket with the victim. If several people are with you, have everyone huddle around the victim.
- If the victim is conscious, administer warm fluids such as sweetened tea, broth, or juice. Have the victim eat candy and other quick-energy foods.
- Do not give food or drink if the victim is unconscious.
- Do not give alcoholic beverages in any circumstance.

When to Call a Health Professional

- Get the victim to medical care as soon as possible if:
  - The victim seems confused. This is one of the first signs of hypothermia.
  - The body temperature does not return to normal.
  - The victim is a child or is elderly. It's a good idea to call regardless of the severity of the symptoms.

Poisoning

FOR ANY POISONING: GIVE MILK and CALL 911 or your LOCAL POISON CONTROL NUMBER IMMEDIATELY.

Children will swallow just about anything, including poisonous substances. When in doubt, assume the worst. Always believe a child who indicates that some poison has been swallowed, no matter how unappetizing the substance. You will not harm anyone who has not swallowed poison by following the steps in Home Treatment.

If you suspect food poisoning, see page 41.

Prevention

- About 80% of childhood poisonings occur to children aged one to four. Infants grow so fast that sometimes they are crawling and walking before we have had time to prepare to protect them. Develop habits of poison prevention before your child is born and certainly before she is crawling.
- Many poisonings happen when someone using a poisonous product walks away for a "moment" to answer the phone, etc. Train yourself to take any open containers with you until you can put them away.
- All drugs need to be locked from curious children. This includes aspirin. The most common source of childhood poisoning is aspirin, especially the chewable,

Poisoning - continued

flavored baby aspirin. No matter how often you give a dose of a drug, lock up that drug between doses.

- Check under your kitchen sink for any poisons such as drain opener, dishwasher detergent, oven cleaner, or plant food. Remove poisons and put them completely out of reach of children. Dishwasher detergent is an especially dangerous substance.
- Always use original containers. Children recognize shapes and colors rather than labels. If you put plant food in a pop bottle, a child will think the bottle contains pop and may drink it.
- Use childproof latches for your cupboards. These plastic latches for your cupboard can be purchased at a hardware store and easily installed in each cupboard. These latches are especially useful for cupboards with magnetic or touch releases.
- Use "Mr Yuk" stickers and train your child to recognize them.

Home Treatment

- Give the poisoned victim a glass of milk. This will dilute poisons that shouldn't be vomited and will do no harm if the poison should be vomited.
- Call a Poison Control Center, hospital, or health professional to learn treatment for specific products and to determine if it is safe to induce vomiting.
- Do not have the victim vomit if she:
  - is having convulsions
  - is unconscious
  - has a burning sensation in the mouth or throat
  - is known to have swallowed a corrosive agent or a petroleum product, e.g., dishwasher detergent, lye, bleach, disinfectants, drain openers, floor wax, kerosene, or grease removers.
- If suggested by Poison Control, induce vomiting by:
  - Syrup of Ipecac, if available (see pg. 258)
  - placing a spoon or finger at the back of the throat
- When vomiting begins, place the victim's head lower than the chest to prevent the vomited material from entering the lungs.

When to Call a Health Professional

- Whenever a poisoning is suspected call your poison control center.

Seat Restraints

It is unsafe to ride in a motor vehicle without a safety restraint of some kind. An abrupt crash at 30 miles per hour creates the same force as falling head first from a three story building. Your arms are just not strong enough to brace against that kind of force; seat belts can.

The use of seat belts reduces the risk of serious injury by 50% and fatality by 65%.

Proper Use of Safety Belts

Safety belts should always be kept snug and as close to the body as possible. If a lap/shoulder belt is available, always use both parts even if the shoulder belt lies across the throat or face. (Sitting near the lower side of the seat belt helps.)

Air Bags

An air bag is a safety device that quickly inflates from the steering wheel and dash board of your car in the event of a sudden impact. Air bags are very reliable and extremely effective in protecting the front seat occupants and rarely inflate unless needed.

Even if your car is equipped with air bags, you still need to wear seat belts.

Seat Belts for Children

Regular use of infant car seats, booster seats and safety belts will protect your children from serious injury in the event of an automobile accident.

Infants under 20 pounds need infant car safety seats that are semi-reclined and face to the rear.

Over 20 pounds, the child will need a toddler seat that is forward facing and with either a shield or a harness. Some models can be easily converted from an infant seat to a toddler seat. Toddler seats can be used until the child grows too large for the seat (until his ears stick over the back of the seat).

When the child outgrows the toddler seat at age $2\frac{1}{2}$ to 3, switch to a booster seat which elevates the child so that he can see out of the car and use regular lap and shoulder belts.

Finally, for children who outgrow the booster seats, insist that they use the adult safety belts whenever they are in the car.

Shock

Shock occurs when vital tissues of the body do not get enough blood. It can happen after severe injuries because of blood loss. The leak in the circulatory system causes the blood pressure to drop below that needed to push blood to the brain and other organs.

Shock can also occur when the injury appears minor and insignificant. In such cases the body is so stunned by the injury that it loses control of the circulatory system. The blood vessels relax and expand instead of pushing the blood on through. Again, the blood pressure drops and vital organs are deprived of their needed blood supply. This condition can also occur when there has been no injury at all such as when a person is emotionally shocked by bad news. Fainting is very similar to shock, but a person quickly recovers from fainting.

Shock - continued

The symptoms of shock are the same regardless of the cause. They include cold and clammy skin; a fast, weak pulse that increases in rate; lowering blood pressure; paleness in the face; dizziness; nausea; and dilated pupils. Restlessness and anxiety often precede or accompany other symptoms. As shock progresses, the victim may slur his or her speech.

Shock must be considered a serious threat to life. The longer the condition is allowed to worsen, the greater the danger. Prompt action may well save the victim's life.

Prevention

Since shock can occur any time there is an injury or serious emotional shock, preventive measures should be started even before symptoms appear. The steps under Home Treatment should be followed.

Home Treatment

- Have the victim lie down.
- Elevate the legs 2 inches or more off the ground. If injury is to the head or chest, keep the legs flat.
- Treat all injuries and splint fractures. See Splinting, page 177.
- Keep the victim warm, but not hot. Place a blanket under the victim and cover with a sheet or blanket depending on the weather.
- Allow the victim to drink small amounts of water unless there is possible abdominal injury, vomiting, or unconsciousness.
- Take and record the victim's pulse every 5 minutes.
- Comfort and reassure the victim to relieve anxiety.

When to Call a Health Professional

- Anyone with significant symptoms of shock should be evaluated by a health professional as soon as possible. These symptoms are:
  - cold and clammy skin
  - fast, weak pulse or a pulse which increases in rate
  - low blood pressure
  - paleness in the face
  - dizziness
  - nausea
  - dilated pupils
  - slurring of speech
  - related to serious traumatic injury

Spinal Injury

Any accident involving the neck or back must be considered a possible spinal injury. Permanent paralysis may be avoided if the victim is immobilized and moved correctly.

Symptoms of a spinal injury are pain; bruises on the head, neck, shoulders, or back area; increased pain with the slightest movement; loss of sensation or movement in hands, feet, arms, or legs; a "tingly" feeling in the limbs; weakness or numbness on one side of the body; or tenderness at one point along the neck.

Home Treatment

- If you suspect a spinal injury, do not move the person unless there is an immediate threat to life, such as fire. Don't drag victims from automobile wrecks. If the injury was a diving accident, float the person face up in the water until skilled medical help arrives. The water will act as a splint and keep the spinal column immobile. Don't pull the victim from the water as you may cause permanent damage.
- Seek medical help to transport the person.

When to Call a Health Professional

- Whenever a spinal injury is suspected.

Unconsciousness

An unconscious person is completely unaware of what is going on and is unable to make purposeful movements. Fainting is a form of brief unconsciousness while a coma is a deep, prolonged state of unconsciousness.

Causes of unconsciousness include stroke, epilepsy, fainting, heat exhaustion, diabetic coma, insulin shock, head injury, suffocation, drunkenness, shock, bleeding and heart attack.

Home Treatment

- It is important that the unconscious person can breathe sufficiently. Check for breathing and if necessary, open the airway and begin artificial respiration. See page 183.
- Check the pulse. If there is none, start cardiopulmonary resuscitation (CPR). See CPR, page 185.
- Treat any injuries.
- Keep the victim lying down.
- Do not give the victim anything by mouth.
- Look for medical identification. The victim may have a bracelet, necklace, or card that identifies the medical problem such as epilepsy, diabetes, or allergy to certain drugs.
- If you find that the victim is a diabetic, he or she may have insulin shock (insufficient sugar in the blood) or be in a diabetic coma (too much sugar in the blood). The symptoms of a diabetic coma are red, dry skin; weak, rapid pulse; and gasping for air. Symptoms of insulin shock are pale, moist skin; normal pulse; and shallow breathing. If the person is a known diabetic and starts to lose consciousness, give something sweet to eat or drink. This will help if they are experiencing insulin shock and won't hurt if they are going into a coma. Remember, though, do not give anything to an unconscious person.

Unconsciousness - continued

When to Call a Health Professional

- A victim of a head injury needs to be carefully observed. See Head Injuries, page 172. See a health professional if the person loses consciousness after the injury.
- Unconscious victims always need to be seen by a health professional.

Be true to your teeth or your teeth will be false to you.

Dental Proverb

Chapter 14

Dental Care

The goal of good dental care is to keep your natural teeth all your life. It's a goal that almost anyone can achieve.

Dental disease is a preventable health problem. With good home care and regular professional visits, you just don't have to lose your teeth.

Dental Problems

Plaque and Tooth Decay

Bacteria are always present in the mouth. When well-fed and undisturbed, bacteria adhere to the teeth and multiply into larger and larger bacterial colonies called plaque. It appears as a sticky but colorless film on your teeth.

This sticky plaque does two unfortunate things. First, food particles, especially refined sugars, stick to it. The plaque uses that food to grow more bacteria and to produce acid. You wouldn't think that a little acid, even from a million germs, could eat through tooth enamel, especially with all that saliva in the mouth to dilute it. It couldn't --- if it were diluted. That's where plaque comes in again. It holds the acids against the tooth surface and prevents the saliva from mixing with it. Even swishing with water cannot get to the acid under its sticky blanket of plaque.

Fortunately, it takes about 24 hours for enough bacteria and acid to build up to do damage to your teeth, enough time for you to get the plaque off your teeth and to wash away the acid. But if you eat a lot of sugar, especially between-meal sugary snacks such as candy, cake, or chewing gum, plaque can build up very quickly. Then cleaning the plaque and acid off your teeth may be required more frequently.

Plaque and Gum Disease

Bacterial plaque is also the cause of gum disease. The toxins and acids damage the healthy layers of skin that touch the teeth right at the gum line. Irritated gums become swollen, tender and likely to bleed. Gums which bleed frequently are a definite sign of gum disease.

As gum disease progresses, the skin and fibers that fasten the gums to the teeth are destroyed. The gums then pull away from the teeth leaving deepening pockets between the gums and teeth. These pockets are perfect breeding grounds for more bacteria to form and damage the newly exposed portions of the teeth and gums. The bone of the jaw which holds the teeth is slowly dissolved by the toxins. The teeth then get looser and looser.

Calculus or dental tartar is also caused by plaque. Actually, tartar is formed from mineral deposits which get trapped by the plaque and are eventually deposited on the tooth. Once this happens, professional help is usually needed to remove it. Although the tartar itself is not the cause of gum disease, it harbors the bacteria and irritants and indirectly contributes to the problem. Of course, if the plaque is regularly removed in the first place, there will be much less opportunity for the tartar to form.

Preventing Dental Problems

Dental diseases can be prevented through proper self-care and regular visits to the dentist. The following are ways to keep your teeth and gums healthy.

Fluoride

Fluoride is a mineral that strengthens the tooth enamel and helps to prevent tooth decay. It also reduces the harmful effects of bacterial plaque.

The regular use of fluoride toothpastes, mouthrinses and topical applications at the dentist's office are recommended. Fluoride drops or tablets are also available through prescriptions by your dentist or physician.

Although fluoride is a natural part of almost all foods and water supplies, fluoride levels may be too low to fully protect the teeth. Infants and children in low fluoride areas will greatly benefit by fluoride supplements.

Fluoride supplements are valuable from birth onward. Fluoride helps to harden teeth even while they are developing in the jaw.

Talk to your dentist and your pharmacist about fluoride. It's a good way to prevent cavities in your children's teeth.

Brushing

Brushing should remove dental plaque from the outer, inner, and chewing surfaces of the teeth. A soft-bristle toothbrush is most effective in removing the plaque. Ideally, each bristle should be rounded at the tip.

Having a good brush is very important, but it's what you do with it that really makes the difference. The following method of brushing is one that is recommended for effective tooth care:

1. Use a toothpaste with fluoride. Only a small dab (pea size) is needed. Tartar-control toothpastes will slow the formation of tartar.

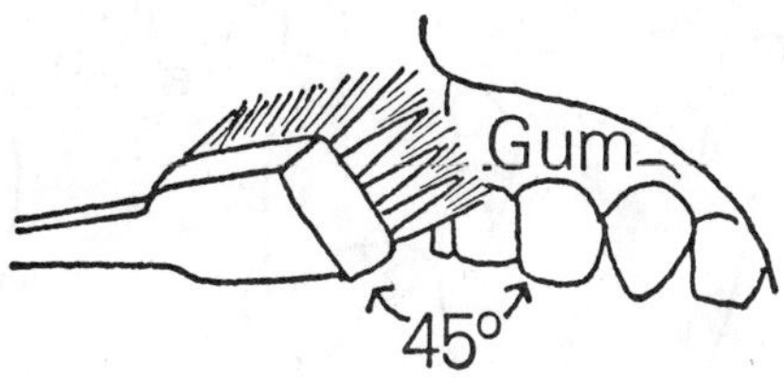

Brush at 45° Angle

2. Place the brush at a 45° angle where the teeth meet the gums. Press firmly, and gently wiggle or rock the brush back and forth using small circular movements. Do not scrub if you have a stiff-bristle brush. Vigorous brushing can cause the gums to recede and the teeth to show abrasion.
3. Brush all surfaces of the teeth; tongue-side and cheek-side. Give special attention to the front teeth and behind the back teeth since they are the most often overlooked.
4. Brush the chewing surfaces vigorously with short back and forth strokes.
5. Brush the tongue. Plaque on the tongue can cause bad breath and is a nursery for bacterial growth.
6. Use disclosing tablets periodically to see if any plaque is left on the teeth.

Disclosing Tablets

How well do you clean your teeth? You should be removing all the dental plaque from every tooth at least once a day. Unfortunately, it's hard to tell how well you are doing by just looking in the mirror. Remember, plaque is a colorless film.

Disclosing tablets are small, chewable tablets that help you see plaque. Chew the tablet, then swish with water. The tablets will color any plaque that remains on your teeth. By using a flashlight and a dental mirror you can see for yourself where you or your children have been missing the plaque.

Disclosing tablets are not expensive and can be found at most drugstores. Once you properly clean your teeth, they leave no stain or trace of color. These tablets provide the immediate feedback you and your children need to develop good home care habits. Adults should use tablets as they think necessary. Children should use them at least once per month to reinforce good brushing habits.

Flossing

Brushing properly can remove most but not all of the dental plaque. To thoroughly remove all plaque, aids must be used to clean between the teeth. These aids include dental floss, toothpicks, rubber

Flossing - continued

tips, and special interdental brushes.

Daily flossing is the best way to prevent gum disease between the teeth. Unfortunately, most people either have never learned how to floss or have never figured out how to make it part of their daily routine.

Many people believe the only purpose of flossing is to remove particles of food that get caught between the teeth. Not so. The real purpose of flossing is to scrape off the dental plaque which forms between the teeth and just under the gum line.

Flossing does require some dexterity and a little practice. It should be done once a day at a regular time. After learning to floss in front of a mirror, try flossing without one. That will make it a lot easier to fit flossing into a regular daily routine. Try flossing while watching television or while soaking in the tub.

There are many different kinds of dental floss on the market today: waxed floss, unwaxed floss, extra fine floss, flossing tape, and flossing ribbons. Each has its own advantages. Select the type that works best on your teeth.

How to Floss

There are a number of effective ways to hold the dental floss. Following is a description of two methods:

1. The finger-wrap method: Cut off a piece of floss 18-20 inches long. Pinch the end of the floss between the left thumb and the middle of the left middle finger. Wrap the floss around the finger several times and repeat this procedure on the right hand, until the two hands are a thumb-length apart.

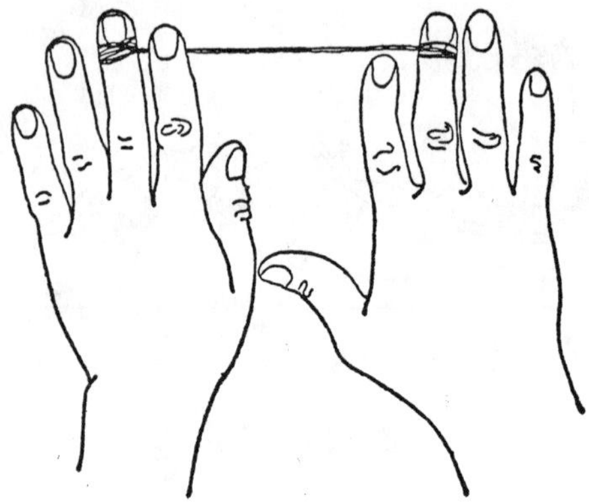

Wrapping Dental Floss

2. The circle method: Cut off a piece of floss 12 inches long. Tie the ends together to form a loop about the size of an orange. If the loop is too large, wrap the floss around the middle fingers to make it smaller.

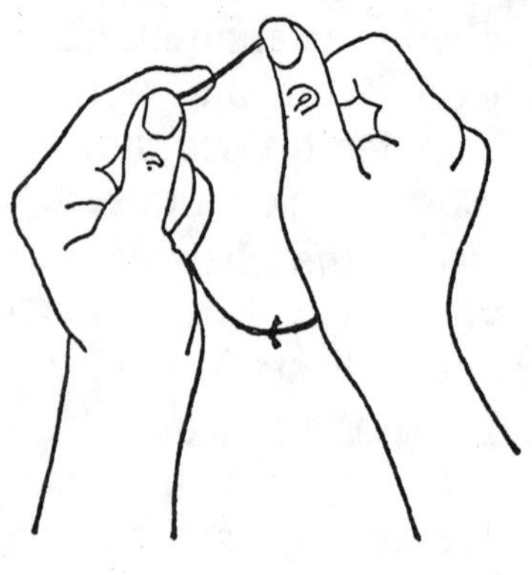

Flossing the Upper Teeth

For the upper teeth use a thumb of one hand and forefinger of the other as shown in the figure.

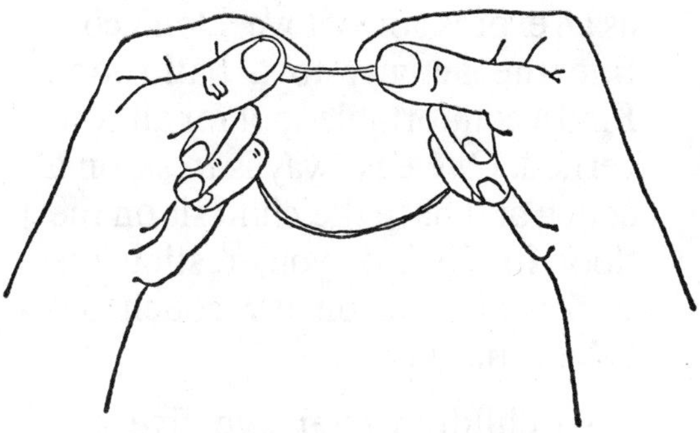

Flossing Lower Teeth

For the lower teeth use both forefingers to guide the floss. The fingers should be close together (about $\frac{1}{2}$ inch apart).

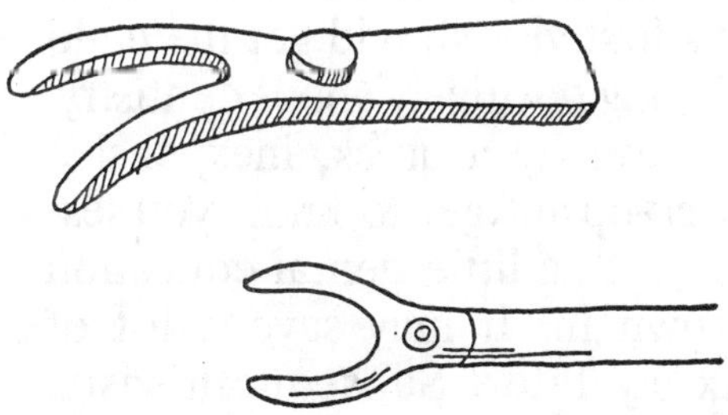

Flossing Tools

A variety of flossing tools are available for those who prefer them. They are particularly handy when an adult flosses a child's teeth since it's hard to get adult-sized fingers in a child-sized mouth. Many adults find them equally helpful for their own teeth. Flossing tools can do a good job of cleaning if care is taken to curve the floss around the tooth and partly under the gum line. Again, it is the scraping action that yields the benefits.

The most important thing about flossing is to curve the floss around the tooth being cleaned and to gently slide the floss under the gum line. With both fingers holding the floss firmly against the tooth, move floss up and down several times to scrap the plaque off. Often the teeth will sound "squeaky clean." Popping the floss in and out without using the scraping action will not remove much plaque.

At first, flossing may be awkward and slow, but continued practice will increase skill and effectiveness. Any bleeding should subside as the gums become healthy.

Sealants

Sealants are a plastic coating applied to the biting or chewing surfaces of the back teeth. They protect the grooves and crevices from developing decay. Sealants are especially good for permanent molar teeth when they first grow into the mouth. Permanent molar teeth are the large teeth which come in behind the baby teeth around age six and again at age eleven. Combining sealants with the decay preventing action of fluoride can prevent nearly all tooth decay.

Dental Care for Children

Efforts to save your children's teeth should start long before their permanent teeth arrive. In fact,

Dental Care/Children - cont.

dental care really starts in pregnancy. A baby's first teeth begin to form before birth. Good nutrition for the mother is very important.

From birth on, the child begins to develop lifelong habits of dental care. Do not give infants and small children bottles of fruit juice, jello water, or even milk to go to sleep with or to constantly suck on. Constant contact between the young teeth and the sugar in the liquids can cause rapid dental decay.

Eliminating all bottles by age one is a good goal. The use of a "tippy cup" can be very helpful.

Toothbrushing should begin when the teeth come in. Then, for the next four to five years, the parents must take the responsibility of brushing the child's teeth. Only after children develop enough dexterity to tie their own shoelaces, should they take over the entire brushing routine. Even then, use disclosing tablets often to determine if a child is able to remove all the plaque. A good training method is to have the child brush in the morning and the parent at night until the art of brushing is mastered. Then, a once-a-day routine can be started. Always use a fluoride toothpaste.

Flossing, too, should be started as soon as the child has teeth that touch each other. Flossing tools may be particularly helpful in doing a good job in a small mouth. A child cannot usually take over the flossing job until around eight. The actual timing depends a lot on the child's dexterity and motor skills.

Brushing and flossing provide a special opportunity for parents and children to feel close to each other. Try to look on it not as drudgery but as an expression of love. Don't confine the activity to a bathroom. Find a comfortable spot for all concerned. One easy way is to sit on a couch and have the child sit on the floor in front of you, resting the neck and head on the couch between your knees.

Also children over age five can benefit from the use of a fluoride mouthrinse either at home or in a school program. This is especially beneficial if the home drinking water is low in fluoride.

Professional Dental Care

Every child should visit the dentist early in life, at age two or three. This first visit should get the child thinking positively about dentistry. It is usually a quick, inexpensive check-up and get-to-know-you session with a little dental education thrown in. It may save a lot of anxiety later. Subsequent visits might include a more thorough examination with or without dental x-rays.

After that, even if all is well, your dentist will probably recommend six month check-ups for both you and your children. Since many of us do not take proper care of our teeth, a check-up every six months is not too frequent. On the other hand, if you and your child do take good care of your teeth and have had a few perfect check-ups in a row, ask your dentist if less frequent appointments might be adequate.

During the check-up, your dentist will evaluate the need for a cleaning, topical fluoride application, and other preventive or restorative treatments.

Preventive Orthodontics

Orthodontics is a specialty in dentistry which deals with the straightening of teeth. Most people equate orthodontics with wearing braces so that teeth will look pretty, but there is more to it than that. Healthy teeth require contact with other teeth if they are to stay healthy. Therefore, poorly arranged teeth not only affect appearance but also influence the life and usefulness of the teeth.

Sometimes potential orthodontic trouble can be spotted early, while the baby teeth are still in the child's mouth. Preventive treatment then can often reduce or eliminate the need for braces later.

Dental x-rays are often effective in finding orthodontic trouble early. It's another of the many good reasons why professional dental check-ups should start early in a child's life.

How to Choose a Dentist

Use your phone in your search for a prevention-oriented dentist. Call the dentist's office to find out what is involved in the initial visit. A thorough exam will include a medical history, a full mouth series of x-rays, a check of the gums as well as the teeth, an oral cancer exam, and an evaluation of the straightness and placement of the teeth in the mouth. Ask about fee arrangements. Know the cost of treatment before it is begun. Most importantly, ask if the dentist has a regular prevention program to teach and reinforce your family in good dental care.

Bleeding Gums

If your gums bleed, you probably have gum disease. Other signs of gum disease include red, swollen gums, pus, loose teeth, and bad breath. Gum disease is often painless until it has progressed and done some damage.

Prevention

- Proper daily brushing and flossing to remove plaque. See page 201.
- Avoid sugary snacks.
- Eat green and yellow fruits and vegetables. The A and C vitamins in them promote gum health.

Home Treatment

- If your gums bleed once in a while when you brush or floss, it is not a good sign, but it won't take too long to get back to normal.
- Brush and floss your teeth every day. Start now!

Bleeding Gums - continued

When to Call a Health Professional

- If your gums bleed when you push on them or bleed often when you brush your teeth.
- If teeth are loose.
- If pus is present.
- If gums are very red and swollen.

Toothaches

Toothaches are caused when the inside of the tooth, the dentin, is exposed. The pain may go away temporarily but the problem will not. Schedule an appointment with a dentist.

Home Treatment

- Take aspirin or acetaminophen (Tylenol) for pain relief.
- A cold pack applied on the jaw may also help.

When to Call a Health Professional

- If pain is severe or accompanied by fever or swelling.
- If area surrounding the tooth is red.

If exercise could be packed into a pill, it would be the single most widely prescribed, and beneficial, medicine in the nation.

Robert Butler, M.D.

Chapter 15

Feeling Fit and Relaxed

For most of us, our health becomes apparent only when we lose it, when a bad cold makes us feel miserable or a backache puts us in bed for a few days. The preceding chapters of this handbook have presented guidelines for recognizing and responding to these minor health problems that interrupt our day-to-day routines. By following these guidelines, you can confidently deal with common health problems in an effective and rewarding way.

But being "healthwise" is much more than just responding to problems as they arise. To be healthwise is to recognize that in the long run, our health is more affected by the way we choose to live. These next chapters will help you review your lifestyle and examine its positive and negative effects on your health. Then it's up to you, your friends, family and coworkers to support each other in making healthy lifestyle choices.

Once you decide that you want to, there are many ways to improve your health and well-being. By not smoking, by eating wisely, and by following basic safety rules, you can strengthen your chances for a long and healthy life.

The discussion in this chapter is focused on exercise and stress, two risk factors with significant impact on everybody's health. These factors are highlighted because they are so closely linked to how good we feel and how much we enjoy our lives. For many people, the way they cope with stress and the time they devote to exercise may become the most important keys for a healthier life. In this chapter, you will be invited to write a personal fitness plan that reflects your health goals, values and constraints.

Fitness and Exercise

Americans are getting off their duffs by the millions. Regular exercise is fast becoming a major priority in many people's lives.

This positive trend can be attributed to two major factors. First, as a nation we are becoming aware of the importance of exercise and fitness to our physical and mental health. Vigorous exercise increases alertness, reduces stress and enhances overall self-image. Second, Americans are discovering that exercise can be fun and greatly add to their enjoyment of life. In fact, "There is gain without pain."

Consider the facts on fitness, listed below, and find one, two or twelve reasons to begin or maintain your own fitness program.

The Facts on Fitness

- Relieves tension and stress
- Stimulates the mind
- Reduces body fat
- Controls appetite
- Boosts self-image
- Improves muscle tone and strength
- Improves performance
- Lowers blood pressure
- Helps you sleep better
- Improves flexibility
- Lowers cholesterol
- Increases resistance to illness

The Fitness Formula

No one exercise provides total fitness. You'll need to follow a simple, four-step "Fitness Formula:"

Warm-up/Stretching + Aerobics + Cool-down/Stretching + Strengthening = Fitness

Step 1: Warm-up/Stretching Phase (3-5 minutes)

The warm-up is designed to gradually warm and stretch the muscles, slowly increase the heart rate, and prepare all your joints for more vigorous activity. This phase is the most important for preventing injuries.

Try slow walking with gentle arm swings, slow bicycling, or slow swimming using different strokes. The key is to do something light.

Gradually increase your pace. Once you have warmed your muscles, you can do easy, comfortable stretches.

Step 2: The Aerobic Phase (20-40 minutes)

Aerobic conditioning, the major focus of your fitness routine, is the key to strengthening your heart and lungs. You will need two things to make this phase work for you: a rhythmic exercise that you can keep up for 20-40 minutes and your target heart rate.

Good aerobic exercises include brisk walking, jogging, swimming, bicycling, cross-county skiing, rope-skipping and aerobic dance. Choose an activity that you enjoy and one which you can do at least three times per week. Exercising on alternate days is best. Cross-training, doing a variety of aerobic activities, will help you avoid injuries stemming from overuse.

Target Heart Rate
Each of us has a specific range of heart rate in which we achieve the best effects from exercise: enough to promote health and fitness, yet not enough to overdo it. Exercising at a heart rate below the target range will provide only limited benefit to the cardiovascular system. Exercising at heart rates above the target range may stress the heart and lungs and have a damaging effect.

Follow the example and directions on page 210 to calculate your target heart rate. You will need to first measure your resting pulse (see page 20). If you are a new exerciser, it's a good idea to check your pulse before you exercise, then again about every three to five minutes during exercise until you get the same count three times, and then when you are about to cool down. The key is to bring your pulse rate into the target range and keep it there for 20 minutes or more. Checking your pulse means you will have to stop for ten seconds each time you take your pulse but then just pick up at the same pace again.

One simple way of making sure you don't overdo it is to use the "Talk Test." If you can talk while exercising without gasping and choking, then you are working aerobically. If you cannot, slow down.

Count again after three minutes of cool-down and finally after you have rested for ten minutes. At the ten-minute point, after moderate activity, you should be back to near your resting level.

Step 3. Cool-down/Stretching Phase (5-10 minutes)

The cool-down is just as important as the warm-up. It is designed to gradually cool the body, lower the heart rate, improve flexibility and reduce the chance of sore or stiff muscles and injuries. Do your cool-down in the reverse order you do your warm-up.

- Slow your aerobic activity to a gradual pace.
- Stretching is particularly important and productive during the cool-down phase when your muscles are warm and well lubricated.
- Try some stretching activities, such as those illustrated on page 211.

Remember:

- Do slow, gradual stretches. Hold for a count of ten.
- Don't bounce! Bouncing can cause injury.
- Exhale as you stretch, inhale as you relax. Don't hold your breath.
- Do some stretching every day. Try a stretch break instead of a coffee break.
- If it hurts, you have gone too far or you are doing it incorrectly.

For more on stretching, see Resource #K1 on page 269.

TARGET HEART RATE

Lower End of Target			Upper End of Target		
	220			220	
–	______	Age	–	______	Age
=	______		=	______	
–	______	Resting Heart Rate	–	______	Resting Heart Rate
=	______		=	______	
x	.6		x	.8	
=	______		=	______	
+	______	Resting Heart Rate	+	______	Resting Heart Rate
=	______	60-Sec. Heart Rate	=	______	60-Sec. Heart Rate
÷	6		÷	6	
=	______	10-Sec. Heart Rate	=	______	10-Sec. Heart Rate

(Example: Target Heart Rate for 50-year old with a resting pulse of 80 beats per minute.)

Lower End of Target			Upper End of Target		
	220			220	
–	50	Age	–	50	Age
=	170		=	170	
–	80	Resting Heart Rate	–	80	Resting Heart Rate
=	90		=	90	
x	.6		x	.8	
=	54		=	72	
+	80	Resting Heart Rate	+	80	Resting Heart Rate
=	134	60-Sec. Heart Rate	=	152	60-Sec. Heart Rate
÷	6		÷	6	
=	22	10-Sec. Heart Rate	=	25	10-Sec. Heart Rate

This person should keep his heart rate between 22 and 25 beats in 10 seconds to receive an optimum aerobic conditioning effect.

Attention: If you are on certain heart or blood pressure medications which lower your heart rate, check with your health care professional about appropriate target heart rates for you.

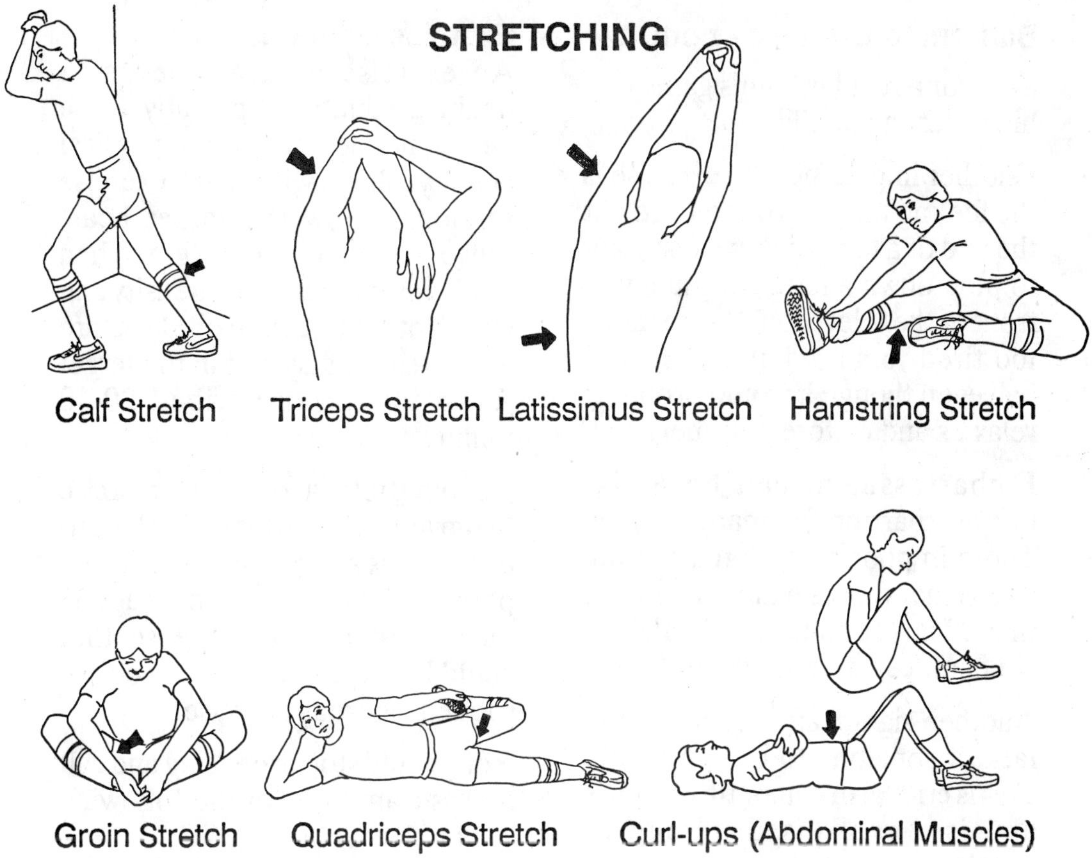

Step 4: Muscle Strength and Endurance Phase. (10-30 minutes)

The final phase of a good fitness routine is one to improve muscle strength and endurance. Muscle strength and endurance are important, not only for improving work or athletic performance, but also for avoiding fatigue and exhaustion from daily activities. Muscle tone exercises will also help you look better and feel more energetic.

One of the most popular and effective forms of muscular strength activities involves resistance training --- either with traditional weight sets or various types of strength and resistance training equipment. It is recommended you begin weight training with instruction by an exercise specialist from a YMCA or fitness center. Other forms of muscle strengthening are simple, safe and effective. Bent-knee curl-ups, as described on page 52, are excellent for firming stomach muscles and avoiding back injuries. Push-ups, side leg-lifts, chin-ups, and other calisthenics improve strength of the arms, legs, neck and shoulders. You can also use a two-foot piece of rubber tubing to strengthen arms and shoulders.

Barriers to Exercise

There are always barriers that work to limit the amount of exercise you get. Time is one of the biggest obstacles to regular exercise. We ride in cars and elevators rather than walk to save time. We can't get

Barriers to Exercise - cont.

away for a regular tennis game or a hike with the family.

Another impediment to exercise is the feeling that we're too tired. At the end of a tense day, we just want to plop down and relax, usually in front of the television. We're much too tired to go swimming or play ball even though it would probably relax us and restore our energy.

Embarrassment can be a significant barrier for many people. Those in poor condition are often afraid that others will make fun of them. They're embarrassed at their appearance, their ability, or both.

Another significant barrier is the lack of someone to exercise with. This is critical in competitive sports and is a real disadvantage in developing a regular exercise pattern around team activities.

Weather is also a barrier, particularly for the person who is limited to a specific sport or outdoor activity. Skiing or ice skating in the winter must be combined with summer sports to assure a year-round program.

Many exercise activities are costly. Sports equipment, club memberships, or getting into a skating rink may be too expensive to handle on a regular basis. If less costly activities are not substituted for expensive ones, the regular conditioning program will suffer. Identify your barriers and brainstorm some solutions.

Exercise Caution

An exercise program needs to begin gradually, especially for a person not accustomed to physical activity. Start with easy exercise sessions below the target heart range and of less duration. Then gradually increase the intensity and length of each session until you are able to safely stay within the target range for the prescribed 20-40 minutes.

Jumping into a rigorous exercise program without gradual conditioning is asking for trouble. Ten percent (10%) of males over age 35 have hidden heart disease that could be triggered by the shock of sudden vigorous exercise.

You should stop exercising and call a physician if any of the following symptoms occur:

- a sudden burst of rapid heartbeats,
- a very slow pulse when a moment before it had been in the target range,
- pain or pressure in the chest or the arm or throat related to exercise,
- abnormal breathing,
- nausea or dizziness.

Now go ahead and complete your own personal fitness plan. Take the leap to a better quality of life by completing page 213.

Stress and Distress

Stress is an emotional and physical condition that occurs whenever we require our bodies to adapt to

PERSONAL FITNESS PLAN

1. My fitness goal(s): ______________________________

2. My future image: ______________________________

3. Three fitness activities I will do regularly for 5 weeks.

	Activity	Where	Days/week	Time of day	With whom
a.					
b.					
c.					

4. Minutes I will spend on each element every time.

	Activity	Warm-Up/Stretch	Aerobics*	Cool-Down	Strength
a.					
b.					
c.					

*10-second target pulse rate ______.

5. Other activities I plan to do (example: fitness book, use of stairs, etc.): ______________________________

6. My greatest potential barriers and how I will overcome them: ______________________________

7. New resources I plan to use (equipment, shoes, class enrollment): ______________________________

8. How others can support me: ______________________________

9. One reward I will give myself when I succeed: ______________________________

I agree to follow the above fitness plan for five weeks.

______________________ ______________________
Signature Date

Stress and Distress - cont.

change. The body's normal stress response is to stimulate the heart rate, increase respiration, tense the muscles, and increase physical strength.

When physical danger induces stress, the body's stress reaction may be needed to divert the crisis. Then, when the danger has passed, the body relaxes and returns to its normal routine. Nearly everyone has felt that primitive fright when confronted by a vicious dog or shaken by an automobile collision.

In fact, the stress response is a well-developed, positive physiological reaction when we need to fight or to flee. In today's society, however, most dangers are more complex. Financial insecurity, changing relationships and emotional uncertainties are also threatening.

Although the threats are no longer physical, the body still reacts in a physical way. Muscles tense and blood pressure rises as the body prepares for the danger, but there is rarely an opportunity to fight or flee. This continual physical reaction with its subsequent build-up of stress hormones is what results in distress. The body is all charged up with no place to go.

Eventually, the wear and tear on internal organs and muscles results in health problems. The list of health problems associated with distress reads like a "Who's Who in Disease:" high blood pressure, ulcers, heart disease, asthma, headaches, backaches, and minor illnesses such as colds and flu. The degree of its impact on our health depends on how successful we are at recognizing and coping with stress.

Recognizing Stress

It's sometimes difficult to recognize or admit that stress is affecting your health. If you can learn to watch for the effects and to take corrective action quickly, you will be very much ahead in coping with your stress.

The signs of stress are classic. You can get headaches, a stiff neck, or nagging backaches, rapid breathing and sweaty palms. You can become irritable and intolerant of even minor disturbances. You can lose your temper more and find yourself yelling at your family without real cause. Your pulse rate can increase and you might feel jumpy or exhausted all the time. You may find it hard to concentrate.

When these symptoms appear, recognize them as signs of stress and think of a way to combat it. Just knowing why you're crabby may be the first step in coping with the problem. It is your attitude toward stress, not the stress itself, that most affects your health.

Managing Stress

Stress and tension affect our emotions and feelings. By expressing those feelings to others, we are able to better understand and cope with them ourselves. Crying can also serve to release tensions. It's part of our emotional healing process. Those people who develop a source of understanding in their spouse or good friend have an invaluable assistant in coping with stress in their lives. Expression through writing, crafts, or art may also be a good release.

Exercise is a natural response to stress; it is the normal reaction to the fight or flight urge. By brisk walking, for example, one can take advantage of the rapid pulse and tensed muscles caused by stress. The pent-up energy is expended in the exercise. After a long walk, the stress emotions are much more easily relieved and returned to normal.

Look over the following "Lifeplan for Managing Stress" and pick one general strategy that you can begin today.

Lifeplan for Managing Stress

- Recognize that you do indeed have stress and identify your own unique symptoms. (This is the key to the use of relaxation skills.) Write down stress-causing situations and your symptoms.
- Look for ways that you can modify your work and social environment to either eliminate or minimize the source of stress.
- Is the stress self-induced? Look for ways that you can modify your perceptions and attitudes to minimize stress.
- Learn and use relaxation skills.
- Nurture your body and mind through regular exercise, good nutrition, and time for play.
- Express yourself often.

The rest of this chapter is devoted to the skills and techniques that will help you increase your resistance to stress and better cope with those stressors you choose to accept.

Relaxation Skills

Regardless of whatever else you do to manage stress, you can benefit from the regular use of relaxation skills. Their effect is exactly opposite to the flight or fight response. When first learning these skills, it's critical that you remove yourself from all outside distractions. Once you've trained your body and mind to relax (two to three weeks), you'll be able to produce the same relaxation feelings on the spur of the moment.

Of the many methods of relaxation and meditation, the following three are among the simplest and most effective. They should be done for about 20 minutes twice a day. Pick a time and place where you won't be disturbed or distracted.

Roll Breathing

The object of roll breathing is to develop full use of your lungs. It can be practiced in any position, but is best learned lying down, with your knees bent.

1. Place your left hand on your abdomen and your right hand on your chest. Notice how your hands move as you breathe in and out.
2. Practice filling your lower lungs by breathing so that your left hand goes up when you inhale;

Roll Breathing - continued

your right hand remains still. Always inhale through your nose and exhale through your mouth.

3. When you have filled and emptied your lower lungs eight to ten times with ease, add the second step to your breathing: inhale first into your lower lungs as before, but then continue inhaling into your upper chest. As you do so, your right hand will rise and your left hand will fall a little as your stomach is drawn in.
4. As you exhale slowly through your mouth, make a quiet, whooshing sound as first your left hand and then your right hand falls. As you exhale, feel the tension leaving your body as you become more and more relaxed.
5. Practice breathing in and out in this manner for three to five minutes. Notice that the movement of your abdomen and chest is like the rolling motion of waves rising and falling in a rhythmic motion. Roll breathing should be practiced daily for several weeks until the roll breathing can be done almost anywhere, providing you with an instant relaxation tool any time you need one.

CAUTION: Some people get dizzy the first few times they try roll breathing. Get up slowly and with support.

Progressive Muscle Relaxation

The body responds to tense thoughts or situations with muscle tension. This muscle tension can cause pain or discomfort. Deep muscle relaxation reduces the tension in the muscles as well as general mental anxiety. You can use a pre-recorded tape to help you go through all the muscle groups or you can do it by just tensing and relaxing each muscle group. Deep muscle relaxation is effective in combatting stress-related health problems and often helps people get to sleep.

Muscle Groups and Procedures

Pick a place where you can stretch out comfortably, such as a carpeted floor.

Tense each muscle group for 4 to 10 seconds (hard but not to the point of cramping), then give yourself 10 to 20 seconds to release and relax. At various points, go back over the various muscle groups and relax each a little more. Arouse yourself thoroughly by counting backwards from five to one. Tense:

1. Hands by clenching them.
2. Wrists and forearms by extending them and bending the hands back at the wrist.
3. Biceps and upper arms by clenching your hands into fists, bending your arms at the elbows, and flexing your biceps.

4. Shoulders by shrugging them. (Review the arms and shoulders area.)
5. Forehead by wrinkling it into deep frown.
6. Around the eyes and bridge of the nose by closing the eyes as tightly as possible. (Contact lenses should be removed before beginning the exercise.)
7. Cheeks and jaws by grinning from ear to ear.
8. Around the mouth by pressing the lips together tightly. (Review the face area.)
9. Back of the neck by pressing the head back hard.
10. Front of the neck by touching the chin to the chest. (Review the neck and head area.)
11. Chest by taking a deep breath and holding it, then exhaling.
12. Back by arching the back up and away from the support surfaces.
13. Stomach by sucking it into a tight knot. (Review chest and stomach.)
14. Hips and buttocks by pressing the buttocks together tightly.
15. Thighs by clenching them hard.
16. Lower legs by pointing the toes back toward the face, as if trying to bring the toes up to touch the head.
17. Lower legs by pointing the toes away and curling the toes downward at the same time. (Review the area from the waist down.)

Relaxation Response

To get a relaxation response, you repeat a chant, phrase, or sound which helps to block tension-producing thoughts. Transcendental Meditation (TM) is a widely known and used relaxation technique of this type. Although TM and other methods differ in exactly what is done, they all are related to the general procedures discussed in the six steps below.

1. Sit quietly in a comfortable position.
2. Close your eyes.
3. Deeply relax your muscles as described previously using Progressive Relaxation.
4. Breathe from the abdomen and through the nose, remaining aware of your breathing. Breathe easily and naturally.
5. As you breathe out, say the word "one" or "om" (rhymes with home) silently and repeat this for 10 to 20 minutes. As you passively repeat the word or sound, other thoughts will come into your mind. Try to neither dwell on nor shut out these thoughts. Just let them come in and out and return to the repetition of the sound.
6. When you finish, sit quietly for a few moments with your eyes closed and later with your eyes open.

Practice the technique once or twice a day, but wait several hours after any large meal since digestion sometimes interferes with the relaxation response.

Relaxation Response - cont.

The regular practice of these techniques will begin to train your body in the art of relaxation. Developing this art can add a new and rewarding dimension to your life.

As you begin to feel tension in a stressful situation, you will be able to call upon your art to maintain or restore a relaxed state of both body and mind. Learning to relax is one of the best ways to enjoy life more; it is an important part of becoming healthwise.

For a more complete description of the relaxation response, see Resource #S1 page 270.

Never eat more than you can lift.

Miss Piggy

Chapter 16

Eating Wisely

Gardeners know you cannot raise a healthy plant without the proper nutrients. The right amount of water and fertilizer at the right time makes all the difference in the life and health of a plant.

Your body also needs the right nutrients in order to be healthy. The right fuel keeps your body operating at its best. Good nutrition also wards off illness and aids recovery from crises such as surgery or severe physical or mental stress.

Increasingly, research is showing that diet affects how likely you are to develop certain diseases. Along with smoking and high blood pressure, high levels of cholesterol in the blood has been accepted as a major risk factor for heart disease.

The American lifestyle, eating too much rich, fat food too quickly, increases the incidence of cardiovascular disease, cancer and all the diseases associated with obesity (including diabetes, gout, osteoarthritis, gallbladder disease and high blood pressure).

Diet and Disease

The average healthy person who has few, if any, risk factors does not need to make drastic dietary changes if the present diet is nutritious. Rather, small, easy-to-make improvements in what you eat can help you feel better and be healthier for the rest of your life.

This chapter gives some guidelines to good eating and some hints on how to help your children establish healthy eating habits. The best way children learn is by example, so you can help them most by practicing good nutrition along with them.

Nutrition Guidelines

There isn't a day that goes by without some media blitz on the perfect diet.

There is no ideal diet that could possibly meet the varying food needs of a population that has so many different ages, body sizes, physical activities, and health problems.

The message is clear. Beware of nutritional claims that promote the "perfect" or "ideal" food or diet.

Fortunately, there are some practical guidelines, based on scientific research that can help us make healthy eating choices. The following guidelines from the United States Departments of Agriculture and Health and Human Services are accepted as sound advice for good nutrition.

- Eat a variety of foods.
- Eat food high in starch and fiber.
- Avoid too much fat, saturated fat and cholesterol.
- Reduce sugar intake.
- Reduce salt intake.
- Maintain ideal weight.
- If you drink alcohol, do so in moderation.

Eat Real, Wholesome and Unprocessed Foods

Eating a variety of foods from those listed on the following page will assure you an adequate and healthy diet, if you are already a healthy person. These are the foods that are generally high in nutrients and low in sugar, salt, fat, and cholesterol.

Fruits and vegetables are excellent sources of vitamins, especially vitamins C and A. Whole grain and enriched breads, cereals, and grain products provide B vitamins, iron, and energy. Meats, poultry and fish supply protein, fat, iron and other minerals, as well as several vitamins, including thiamine and vitamin B-12. Dairy products are major sources of calcium, protein, riboflavin and other nutrients. Dry peas and beans, such as soybeans, kidney beans, lima beans, and black-eyed peas are good vegetable sources of protein and iron, and are high in fiber.

The 80-20 Rule

If you eat good foods 80% of the time, you don't need to worry about the occasional slice of white bread, doughnut or Twinkie. "Junk foods" won't hurt you if most of what you eat is wholesome, unprocessed food.

On the other hand, if most of what you eat is high fat, high sugar foods, a few "health foods" mixed in will probably not improve your health.

Eat More Carbohydrates

How many times have you heard that starchy foods are fattening? If you have been avoiding starch as a way to lose weight --- STOP and read this carefully.

- Starches are usually packed with nutrients and fiber.
- Starches have less than half the calories per ounce as fats.

• Starches are usually inexpensive.

Starchy foods like potatoes, rice, bread, and vegetables are mostly made of complex carbohydrates. Carbohydrates are the ideal fuel for most body functions. They are low in calories, high in nutrients and fiber, easily digested and comparatively low in cost.

It's not the starches that are fattening but rather what we put on them. Use less toppings and spreads on

NUTRITIOUS FOODS

Food group and serving size is noted

Breads (B: 1 slice)
Whole wheat/whole grain breads, muffins and rolls

Cereals (B: $\frac{1}{2}$ c. cooked, $\frac{3}{4}$ c. dry)
Whole grains and unsweetened

Cooked Dry Beans (P: 1 c.)
Garbanzo, Lentils
Navy, Soy
Peas, Pinto
Red

Dairy Products-Low-fat only (D: 1 c. or 1 oz.)
Milk
Cottage Cheese
Yogurt
Cheese:
- Mozzarella
- Farmer's
- Jarlsberg Swiss
- Ricotta
- Romano

Fish (P: $\frac{1}{2}$ c.)
Baked, broiled or steamed

Fruits (F & V: 1 piece or $\frac{1}{2}$ c.)
Fresh or canned in light syrup

Fruit Juices (F & V: $\frac{1}{2}$ c.)
Fresh, frozen or canned, unsweetened

Grains (B: $\frac{1}{2}$ c. cooked)
Whole grain products
Brown rice
Barley
Bran
Bulgur

Meats (P: 2-3 oz.)
Lean cuts-not fried

Nuts & Seeds (P: 2 Tb.)
Unsalted and no oil
Peanut Butter

Pasta (B: $\frac{1}{2}$ c. cooked)
Whole wheat or spinach noodles

Poultry (P: 2-3 oz.)
Chicken
Turkey
Wild birds
Baked or broiled --- not fried

Tofu (P: 1 c.)

Vegetables (F & V: 1 c. raw or $\frac{1}{2}$ c. cooked)
Raw, steamed, stir-fried, home-cooked, or frozen with little or no oil, butter, salt or sugar

Key to Food Groups
B = Bread/Grains
D = Dairy
F & V = Fruits/Vegetables
P = Protein

Carbohydrates - continued

your breads and potatoes or choose low fat alternatives.

Be aware that many popular bread products like croissants, muffins, cornbread and pastries have a great deal of fat baked in. These fats often double the calories. Proceed with caution.

Eat More Fiber

Fiber itself has no vitamins or nutrients, yet it is an important part of what we eat.

- Fiber aids in digesting and excreting food.
- Fiber and fluids together prevent constipation.
- A lack of fiber may lead to cancer of the bowels, constipation and diverticulosis.

If your bowel movements are large, soft and easy to pass, you probably are getting plenty of fiber. If they are small, hard and difficult to pass, you may be getting too little fiber or water.

One slice of whole grain bread per meal adds much needed fiber. Other high fiber foods include:

- unprocessed cereals (like bran, shredded wheat, oatmeal).
- brown rice, cooked dry beans or dry peas, nuts and seeds.
- popcorn (but beware of added fat).
- fresh fruits and vegetables (raw or lightly steamed).

Eat Less Fat

The American diet is high in saturated fat which causes high blood cholesterol levels and a higher risk of heart disease.

Here are some tips to avoid too much fat, saturated fat and cholesterol:

Tips for Eating Less Fat

- Broil, bake or boil rather than fry.
- Vary lean meat, fish, poultry and legumes as your entree.
- Limit your intake of eggs, organ meats, butter, margarine, hydrogenated oils, creams, etc.
- Brown lean meats in nonstick pans with little or no oil.
- Trim fat from meat and remove skin from poultry.
- Chill soups, stews, sauces and broths and remove congealed fat.
- In sauces and dressings, use low calorie bases (vinegar, mustard, tomato juice, fat-free bouillon) instead of high calorie ones (creams, mayonnaise, oils).
- Slice your butter or margarine thinner.
- Choose unsaturated fat products (liquid at room temperature) like corn, safflower, and sunflower oils over saturated fat products (solid at room temperature) like meat fats, shortening, butter, and "hydrogenated" fats. Coconut, palm oils and cocoa butter are also saturated fats.

Check Your Cholesterol

Cholesterol is fat produced by the body and found in animal products. High levels of cholesterol in the blood increase your risk of heart disease.

By checking your blood cholesterol, you can learn whether it is a problem for you. The National Institutes of Health recommends the cholesterol guidelines shown below.

Cholesterol tests are easy, quick and inexpensive. Ask your physician, health department, hospital or employer if a cholesterol screening can be arranged.

If you are solidly in the "Good" category, you need not be too concerned about avoiding high-fat foods. Others, in the moderate or high-risk group, may wish to read carefully the tips for reducing fat as listed on page 222. People in the high risk category should have the test repeated within the next six months and begin to modify their diets.

Your physician can help you diagnose your cholesterol problem and recommend a dietitian to help you set a self-care plan to reduce it. Medications can be tried if your self-care efforts are not successful. How often should you have a cholesterol test? Every 5-10 years if your last test was good. Twice a year if you are trying to lower it.

Oat Bran and Cholesterol

Oat bran, cooked dry beans, dry peas and lentils contain a high amount of **soluble** fiber that cholesterol sticks to in the intestine. Eating these foods on a regular basis can reduce your overall blood cholesterol levels.

On the other hand, **insoluble** fiber found in wheat bran, other grains (except oats) and most fruits and vegetables helps prevent constipation and diverticular disease. Once again, the research is showing the importance of a balanccd approach to nutrition.

More on Cholesterol

There are two important kinds of cholesterol in your blood: LDL and HDL (Low Density Lipoprotein and High Density Lipoprotein).

CHOLESTEROL GUIDELINES

Age	Good Level	Moderate Risk	High Risk
20-29	<180	200-220	220>
30-39	<200	220-240	240>
40+	<200	240-260	260>

Cholesterol - continued

LDL cholesterol acts like a fat delivery truck distributing fat to arteries all over the body. HDL cholesterol acts like a garbage truck, picking up fat in the arteries and hauling it away. While LDL cholesterol in your blood increases the risk of heart disease, HDL cholesterol reduces the risk. Tests that break down your blood cholesterol level into the two groups can be more accurate in predicting your heart disease risks.

Many experts believe that it is the ratio between total cholesterol and HDL cholesterol that best predicts the risk. The chart on this page describes the risk.

Your HDL level can be increased by exercise, weight control and stopping smoking. Monounsaturated fats (olive and peanut oils) help to lower total cholesterol levels without reducing HDL. Regular use of oat bran may increase HDL levels by 10%.

Fish Oil and Cholesterol

Most fish contain oils that provide some protection against heart disease. These Omega-3 fatty acids can help to reduce blood clotting and lower blood cholesterol and triglycerides. As a general rule, fish with darker flesh have more of the Omega-3 oils. Mackerel, lake trout, herring, fresh albacore tuna, sturgeon, whitefish, salmon and halibut are particularly good.

Two to four servings of fish per week is sufficient to reduce your risks. Most experts recommend eating fish rather than fish oil supplements. The research showing that fish oil supplements are effective is still incomplete.

Eat Less Sugar

The problem of too much sugar in our diets is a sticky one. The average American consumes well over 100 pounds of sugar each year. That's almost 500 calories per person per day from sugar alone. Can we stand that? The high incidence of obesity and dental disease and the fact that high sugar foods often replace other nutritious foods suggests that we eat far too much sugar.

Be wary of new cookbooks and products claiming "no sugar" or "all natural" ingredients. Many times these recipes or ingredients simply replace sugar with honey. There are essentially no known nutritional qualities distinguishing honey from white or brown sugar.

RISK RATIO of TOTAL CHOLESTEROL to HDL CHOLESTEROL*

	Men	Women
Low	4.0	3.8
Average	5.0	4.5
Moderate	9.5	7.0
High	23.0 +	11.0 +

* From the Framingham Study

Remember that an occasional sweet is not harmful. It's the 80/20 Rule, once again, that counts.

Tips for Eating Less Sugar

- Use cinnamon and vanilla instead of sugar as a sweetener.
- Cut sugar in recipes by 1/4 to 1/3. (It will still taste sweet.)
- Use fresh fruits or fruits canned without sugar or in light syrup or in their own juice.
- Try fresh fruits and vegetables as snacks instead of candy, soft drinks, ice cream, cakes, pies and cookies.
- Read food labels for clues on sugar content. If the words sucrose, glucose, maltose, dextrose, lactose, fructose (any word ending with "ose"), or syrup appear first, then there is a large amount of sugar. Also watch for many different forms of sugar which are often combined to avoid listing a sugar as the first ingredient.
- Eat less honey, brown sugar, white sugar, raw sugar, molasses, and syrups.

Eat Less Salt

The average American consumes twelve grams of salt a day. For people prone to have high blood pressure, that's way too much.

Salt, or sodium chloride, contains 40% sodium. Studies show that when sodium intake is reduced, blood pressure levels tend to drop. Half of the salt we eat is hidden, often as a preservative or flavoring agent that is added to processed foods.

Tips for Eating Less Salt

- Use herbs and spices instead of salt.
- Rediscover the taste of unsalted food.
- Eliminate salt from the table and reduce it in all recipes except those containing yeast.
- Moderate your intake of salty foods such as chips, pretzels, salted nuts, soy sauce, garlic salt, pickled foods, cured meats, ham, bacon, sausage and luncheon meats.
- Use fresh or frozen fish instead of canned varieties.
- Read food labels to determine sodium content. Watch for the words "sodium, brine and MSG."
- Cook without or only small amounts of added salt.
- "Light Salt" has only half the sodium of regular salt.

Eat More Iron-Rich Foods

Inadequate iron intake in infants, preschoolers, teens and menstruating women can lead to iron-deficiency anemia. Following is a list of foods which are good sources of iron. Regularly including these foods in the diet will help prevent iron deficiency. If anemia is suspected, a health professional can diagnose it by taking a blood test. Iron supplements may be prescribed along with a diet high in iron to correct the problem.

Foods Rich in Iron

- Oysters, sardines, shrimp
- Red meats
- Liver*

Iron-Rich Foods - continued

- Dried Peas and Beans
- Dark Green Leafy Vegetables
- Whole Grains
- Iron-enriched Cereals
- Dried Apricots
- Prunes
- Raisins

*Liver is a good source of iron, but also very high in cholesterol.

Weight Control

Most people are concerned about how much they weigh. For some, it is an obsession. For many more, weight control is a never ending battle of ups and downs that places stress on both their bodies and their self-esteem. For these people, weight control can become much easier if the following simple truths are used as guidelines:

- Focus on fat, not weight.
- Exercise.
- Never go hungry.
- Fat foods make you fat.
- Feed your mind first.

Focus on Fat

For health and looks, fat control is far more important than weight control. How much soft, mushy tissue you can pinch on your arms, legs and stomach tell a truer story than your bathroom scale. Of primary concern is how much of your total weight comes from fat. Too much body fat increases your risk of diabetes, heart disease and stroke.

Ideally, body fat is around 15% of total weight for men and around 22% for women. Body fat can be measured simply and inexpensively through testing by a trained fitness or nutritional counselor. (Check with your local YMCA or your health professional.)

Exercise

Aerobic exercise raises your metabolism, the rate at which your body burns calories. Your body continues to burn more calories for hours after you stop exercising. For regular exercisers, metabolism rate stays up indefinitely. Exercise makes it much easier to lose both weight and more importantly, fat. See page 208 for information on exercise.

Never Go Hungry

You may think skipping meals is an easy way to lose weight. Think again. Going hungry, even for a few hours, will cause your metabolism to drop. You will gain more weight with a single 1,800 calorie meal each day than with three 600 calorie meals. In fact, you can eat up to 20% more calories and maintain your weight if those calories are spread throughout the day.

Fat Foods Make You Fat

Cutting down on the fat in your diet is guaranteed to have a positive effect on your overall body fat. The emphasis here is on the amount of calories that come from fat, not the total amount of calories. Over time, if you shift from a 2,000 calorie diet, which is 50% fat, to a 2,000 calorie diet, with only 30% fat, your body fat will go down. See page 222 for nine simple ways to cut down on fat.

Feed Your Mind First

For many, food is more our comfort than our staff of life. Food is often linked to emotional rewards or sanctuaries from stressful situations. Successful weight control often begins with changes in the mind rather than the menu. By building self-esteem and developing a greater sense of personal power, many people find more success in liking both who they are and what they look like. For more information, see Chapter 17.

Nutrition for Children

Introducing a child to the world is fun, and teaching good eating habits can be part of that fun if you approach it correctly.

Once children leave home for part of the day, even if just for preschool or kindergarten, they start making food choices without their parents' guidance. If you start them from infancy with the right ideas about foods, they should make better choices when on their own.

Habits are learned. While some desire for sweet foods is inborn, generally, the "sweet tooth" is a learned habit. Parents who limit the amount of sugar in their infants' and toddlers' diets are pleased to see their children choose fruits over candy --- at least sometimes. It is easy to slip up and become lax about your child's eating patterns, but remember that you're helping your child establish the food habits which will affect your child's health, well-being, and possibly even length of life.

Try to avoid giving food as a reward or withholding it as punishment. A child given an ice cream cone as a reward for good behavior, or threatened with no dinner to curb bad behavior, starts to look at food as something really special that must be earned. Then, when the child feels the need of a reward or an ego booster, food seems the answer.

Offer your child a variety of foods, but don't force the child to eat an unwanted food. A small taste and the observation of others eating is the best strategy in getting a child to try new foods. Imitation is a much better teacher than force. If you enjoy a food and are willing to try new ones, your child is more apt to do the same. Also, if you avoid having sugary, "junk" foods in the home, a child simply cannot eat them, at least at home.

Don't become overly concerned about your child's food intake. If you serve your family a wide variety of nutritious food regularly in a pleasant environment, you can relax and feel that you're providing the best nutrition atmosphere possible. Then, an occasional food "jag" of peanut butter sandwiches for breakfast, lunch and dinner need not worry you. Continue to offer and serve other foods without making it an issue, and that food "jag" probably won't last too long.

Nutrition for Children - cont.

Remember, too, that each person is unique. Food likes and dislikes will vary in a family without harm, as long as good nutritional intake is kept up and as long as no one expects to be constantly catered to.

Child-Sized Environment

Imagine yourself eating at a giant's table. That's how a child can feel eating at an adult-sized table in an adult-sized chair. Booster seats or cushions can help equalize things. Child-sized utensils can be used too, if your child has trouble holding larger ones. Don't insist that your child hold utensils the way an adult does. Dexterity comes with age and the skill will improve with the desire to look like everyone else. In fact, don't fuss about utensils --- fingers are fine until a child can hold utensils easily.

Just as a child's legs are shorter than an adult's, so is a child's stomach smaller. A small plate with small servings is a good idea. Let the child ask for seconds. It will make the child and the cook feel better.

Because of their smaller storage capacities, coupled with high calorie requirements, children need snacks to supplement meals. These snacks should provide part of the child's daily nutrient needs, and should not be served so close to a meal that they interfere with the child's mealtime appetite.

Emotional Environment

Ideally, mealtimes should be pleasant family experiences, time for good conversation and relaxation. However, for today's busy families, dinner is often the only time the family is together and frequently that meal is made unpleasant by arguments or too much noise.

Try to make meals as enjoyable as possible by keeping conversation pleasant, instead of a daily report of everyone's problems. Having the television on makes conversation difficult and causes people to ignore what and how much they're eating.

Hardest of all, try to keep comments about your child's eating to a minimum. The child's meal and yours will be much more pleasant.

Anxiety about whether the child is getting enough to eat or making sure a child cleans the plate may inadvertently cause obesity. Children should be allowed to eat what they feel they need.

Healthy Snacks

Consider between-meal snacks as part of the day's total food intake, and be sure the snacks contribute more than "empty calories." This is especially important in a preschooler's diet because of the high nutrient need in relation to calorie need.

Fruits and fruit juices are good snacks as are chunks of cheese, meat, or a cup of soup. Carrot and celery sticks, raw zucchini, or green pepper all taste good and are nutritious. When you want to give cookies or other sweets, be sure they contain more than just sugar.

Oatmeal raisin cookies or carrot raisin cake are good substitutes for gooey-pastries.

Diabetes

Obesity is often linked with diabetes, an illness that interferes with the body's ability to fully use carbohydrates. The pancreas either does not make enough insulin or the insulin is prevented from entering the cells. Without sufficient insulin, sugar builds up in the blood and can seriously damage the eyes, kidneys, heart and other body systems.

There are two types of diabetes. Type I, or insulin-dependent diabetes, usually begins in young people. Typc II, or noninsulin-dependent, more often develops later in life.

People with either type of diabetes can benefit from diagnosis, monitoring, and both professional and self-care treatment of the condition. Symptoms of diabetes include frequent urination, excessive thirst and hunger, sudden weight loss, fatigue and drowsiness, nausea, blurry vision, numbness in legs, feet or fingers, slow healing of cuts and skin infections. For more information on diabetes see Resource #I1 on page 269.

Home Treatment

- Home treatment includes active monitoring of blood sugar levels and the adoption of good nutrition, fitness and stress management habits. While there is no known cure for diabetes, its symptoms and risks are highly manageable.
- For information, contact the American Diabetes Association, (800) 232-3472.
- Emergency Care: Type I diabetics who take too much insulin or too little food can sometimes go into insulin shock and lose consciousness. See Unconsciousness, page 197.

Osteoporosis

Osteoporosis is a condition in which the bones lose calcium and gradually become weaker. Getting enough calcium through your diet is one way to combat osteoporosis. Because this condition affects primarily women, it is discussed in more detail in the Women's Health chapter on page 146.

He who laughs, lasts.

Mary Pettibone Poole

Chapter 17

Mental Self-Care

Being healthy has more to do with how well you feel than with how well your body is working.

And, how well your body is working has more to do with your brain than with anything else.

Most of us think of our brains as our source of ideas, emotions and memories. We tend to overlook the brain's main function --- that of controlling our health.

This chapter, which is organized in two sections, will help you provide better self-care for your brain and help your brain provide better self-care for you.

Part 1: Self-Care For Emotional Problems

Mental health problems are a lot like health problems in general: everybody has them; most are quite minor and, with a little care and attention they will go away on their own. They will also benefit from informed self-care, whether or not professional care is needed.

Self-care for mental health problems begins with observing the symptoms. The symptom inventory on page 232 is a good place to start. Score each symptom on the inventory and record anything special that you have observed which relates to the symptom. Generally, the more symptoms which interfere with daily life, the more serious the problem. Descriptions of each symptom are presented below.

Alcohol or Drug Use

Increased use of alcohol or drugs may be a symptom of mental stress. If alcohol or drugs cause any difficulties at home, work or anywhere else, then you have a use problem. The chart on page 233

SYMPTOM INVENTORY for EMOTIONAL HEALTH PROBLEMS

Possible Symptoms	Interference Rating Never/Rarely	 Sometimes	 Often
Alcohol/Drug Use Does alcohol or drug use ever interfere with your school, work, friends or family?	1	2	3
Anger/Hostility/Irritability Does anger, hostility or irritability interfere with your school, work, friends or family?	1	2	3
Anxiety Do symptoms of anxiety interfere with school, work, friends or family?	1	2	3
Depression Do feelings of sadness, hopelessness or apathy interfere with school, work, friends or family?	1	2	3
Hyperactivity Does feeling "hyper" or continually excited interfere with school, work, friends or family?	1	2	3
Addictive behaviors Do overeating, gambling, smoking or other addictive behaviors interfere with school, work, friends or family?	1	2	3
Sleep problems Do you have difficulty sleeping or staying awake?	1	2	3
Suicidal signals Have you thought about suicide or wondered if life is not worth living?	1	2	3
Withdrawal Does withdrawal or excessive daydreaming interfere with school, work, friends or family?	1	2	3
TOTAL SCORE	______	______	______

Alcohol or Drug Use - cont.

may help you identify a problem that may be developing.

Even if alcohol or drugs are not causing any problems, increased use of either can be a sign of mental stress. Try to identify the underlying cause and deal with it directly.

Home Treatment

- Recognize your increased use as a possible problem.

ARE YOU A PROBLEM USER?

Answer the questions honestly for yourself. Check the appropriate box if the statement is true for you for alcohol or drugs (including prescribed, recreational, or illegal substances that can be described as mood-altering).

Question	Alcohol	Drugs
1. Have you ever decided to stop using alcohol/drugs for a week or so but only lasted for a couple days?	______	______
2. Do you resent the advice of others who try to get you to stop or cut down your use?	______	______
3. Have you tried to control your use of alcohol/drugs by changing from one type of drink/drug to another?	______	______
4. Do you envy people who can use alcohol/drugs without getting into trouble?	______	______
5. Has your use of alcohol/drugs impaired your family relationships, your work, your driving safety, or any other aspect of your life?	______	______
6. During the past year, have you missed days of work because of your use of alcohol/drugs?	______	______
7. Do you tell yourself you can stop using alcohol/drugs any time you want?	______	______
8. Do you sometimes go on binges with alcohol/drugs?	______	______
9. Do you ever have blackouts related to use of alcohol/drugs?	______	______
10. Have you ever felt that your life would be better if you did not use alcohol/drugs?	______	______
Total	______	______

If your totals in either column or both columns combined are four or greater, chances are you may now have or will have a serious use problem with alcohol or drugs.

Reprinted from: Kemper, et. al., Pathways: A Success Guide for a Healthy Life, Healthwise, 1985.

Alcohol or Drug Use - cont.

- Look for other symptoms of mental stress and take action to eliminate the cause.
- Develop other stress management patterns such as exercise or the relaxation response (page 217).

When to Call a Health Professional

- Score of four of more on "Are You A Problem User?"
- Also see Seeking Professional Help on page 241.

Anger/ Hostility/Irritability

Anger is a physiological signal to prepare for a fight. Hostility is remaining ready for a fight all the time.

Expressing anger can feel good because it releases built-up tension and anxiety. Generally, the relief is only temporary. Uncontrolled anger increases blood pressure and poses safety risks for yourself and others. Worst of all, it can cut you off from the people that can best help.

Home Treatment

The following six steps provide a good guide for dealing with anger.

1. Admit the anger to yourself. Ignoring your anger does not reduce its impact on your health.
2. Think about what made you angry and why. Ask yourself if the cause is worth getting angry over. If the real cause is something else, focus on that as the problem.
3. Apply tincture of time. Count to ten. Compose yourself. Ask for some time to calm down. This is a good time to practice the roll breathing relaxation technique described on page 215.
4. Express your grievance without attacking the other person. Make your statements with "I" instead of "you." "I feel angry when your plans do not consider my needs."
5. Forgive and forget. You may benefit greatly if you are able to forgive. Your blood pressure and heart rate will drop. You will feel more relaxed.
6. Look at the whole person. What symptoms other than anger are also present? Try using the communication techniques on page 240 to identify and resolve the problem.

When to Call a Health Professional

- If the anger has or could result in violence or harm to someone.
- If the anger or hostility continues to interfere with your work, school, home or friends.
- Also see Seeking Professional Help on page 241.

Anxiety

Anxiety is the presence of an undefined fear with the absence of an obvious or immediate source of danger. It involves overestimating the danger of a situation and underestimating your ability to manage it.

Anxiety symptoms can include:

- Feeling of weight on your chest
- General nervousness
- Headaches
- Irritable bowels
- Lightheadedness
- Loss of concentration
- Muscle tension
- Nausea
- Pounding heart
- Restlessness
- Shortness of breath
- Sleeplessness
- Stomach cramps
- Sweaty palms

Anxiety can be resolved by understanding and dealing with undefined fears and by practicing relaxation techniques for immediate relief of symptoms. Vigorous exercise can also provide quick relief from anxiety in most people.

Home Treatment

- Accept your anxiety. Say to yourself, "OK, I see the danger. Now I'll start to deal with it."
- Notice and track your anxiety symptoms. Anxiety decreases when you objectively analyze the situation and consider your options.
- Act as if you are not anxious. Accept your fears --- but force yourself to go ahead anyway.
- Practice the relaxation response. See page 217.
- Focus on what you want to happen.
- Look at the whole person (see page 239) for other symptoms and evidence that the symptoms are interfering with day to day life.

See Resource #D1 and D2 on page 268.

First Aid for Panic Attacks

A panic attack due to anxiety or a special fear or phobia will often result in the following physical symptoms: pounding heartbeat, sweaty palms, weak-kneed feeling, and labored breathing. Here are four ways to stop a panic attack if it happens to you.

- Look for a laugh. Laughter can break the tension and provide relief from the symptoms of panic.
- Tell someone about it. Expressing your fears will reduce the symptoms.
- Focus on your choices. If you know that there is a way out (even an undesirable one), you will be less likely to need to use it.
- Remember when you felt panicked in the past and how you managed to get through it.

Anxiety - continued

When to Call a Health Professional

- You are unable to break out of an anxiety state.
- Also see Seeking Professional Help on page 241.

Depression

Few people are happy all the time, but when feelings of unhappiness start to prevail and interfere with daily life, they indicate a state of depression. Depression involves a loss of self-esteem and interest in the world around you. It keeps you from enjoying life.

Not all sadness is unhealthy. Grieving for the death of a loved one or the loss of a job is a normal part of the emotional healing process. With time, grieving leads to a better understanding and acceptance of a loss.

Depression on the other hand freezes those emotions. There is no progress toward feeling better. The depressed person feels trapped in self-pity and hopelessness.

Symptoms of depression include:

- Apathy
- Boredom
- Fatigue
- Feelings of helplessness
- Guilt
- Hopelessness or despair
- Lack of interest in food, sex, or entertainment
- Loss of concentration
- Overindulgence in food or drink
- Restlessness
- Sleep problems (too much or too little)
- Suicidal thoughts
- Withdrawal

Self-care can help alleviate depression. Depression ranges from feeling "blue" to having symptoms completely take over your life. Any depression can benefit from tender loving care either from yourself or someone else.

Prolonged depression that does not respond to self-care may involve biological factors or deep emotional feelings which can best be managed with professional help.

Home Treatment

- When you first recognize that you feel down, arrange for a little tender loving care.
- Keep on going. It is easier to **do** yourself into **feeling** better than to **feel** yourself into **doing** better.
- Get some exercise. Regular, vigorous exercise helps to clear the mind.
- Ask for special support from your friends and family.
- Check your medicines. Sleeping pills, tranquilizers, blood pressure medication and many other drugs can cause depression. Ask your doctor or look them up yourself. (See Resource #A2 on page 268.)

- Look for a belly laugh. Laughter, like exercise, can restore chemical balance to your system.
- Develop positive self-talk that affirms your value and worth. See Resource #H1 on page 269.
- Tell yourself that this mood will pass. Then look for signs that it is ending.
- Work to improve communication. See page 240.

When to Call a Health Professional

- If signals of suicide are present. See below.
- See Seeking Professional Help on page 241.

Sleep Problems

While it is normal for sleep patterns to change as you age, (you wake up more often as you get older), sudden changes in your sleep habits can be either a sign or a cause of mental stress.

Home Treatment

If sleeplessness is part of your problem, and is not reduced by either regular exercise during the day or warm milk before bedtime, give the following six step formula a two-week trial.

1. Save your bed for sleeping. Don't eat, watch TV or even read in it.
2. Save your sleep for bedtime. Don't take naps.
3. Forget "bedtime." Go to bed when you feel sleepy and only when you feel sleepy.
4. Get up at the same time each day no matter how little sleep you get.
5. Get out of bed and leave the room any time you lie awake for more than 15 minutes.
6. Repeat the two steps above until it is time to rise.

(Adapted from Anne Simons, M.D., "Tossing and Turning," *Medical SelfCare Magazine,* March/April 1988.)

This sleep formula will cure about two-thirds of sleep problems without the side effects and addiction problems of sedatives and sleeping pills. It may cost you some sleep the first few nights, but for most, that will be repaid in full within the first few weeks.

If sleep problems do continue, consider possible side effects of caffeine or medications.

When to Call a Health Professional

- If you suspect side effects from medications.
- If sleeplessness continues after a month of continuous self-care efforts.
- Also see Seeking Professional Help on page 241.

Suicidal Signals

Many people have considered killing themselves at some time in their lives. While suicidal thoughts

Suicidal Signals - continued

most often pass quickly, the longer they linger and the more frequently they occur, the more they indicate a serious problem that requires resolution. Any suicidal signal should be treated seriously.

Home Treatment

- Use your common sense and a direct communication approach to determine if the risk of suicide is great.
  - Does the person feel that he is in a crisis with no way out?
  - Has he developed an actual suicide plan?
  - How does he plan to do it?
  - When does he plan to do it?
  - Who else has he told?
- Speak as matter-of-factly as possible and show concern but not undue anxiety.
- Show understanding and acceptance of the person. Try to help the person analyze the crisis and what caused it. A better understanding of the crisis may suggest other alternatives for resolving it.
- Arrange for yourself or some other trusted person to stay with the person for that day or night to show concern and offer support.

When to Call a Health Professional

- If a person indicates that adequate preparations have been made for the suicide, then the potential danger is great and you need to seek professional help immediately.
- If you have any questions or doubts of the suicidal risk of a person, refer them to a mental health professional for an in-depth evaluation. If the person resists seeing someone, then use the resource yourself. You could share your own anxiety and responsibility and have a professional clarify the risk of danger and offer alternative solutions. If you are unsure whom to contact, call a community mental health center, suicide prevention center, hotline, hospital emergency room or clinic.
- Also see Seeking Professional Help on page 241.

Withdrawal

Withdrawal is the continual desire to avoid other people. Withdrawal can be a passive person's attempt to make others feel responsible for him. Withdrawn people tend to stay in their rooms, talk less than they used to, and generally avoid group activities.

There are three basic reasons for withdrawal: depression, low self-esteem and shyness.

Withdrawal can also take the form of excessive daydreaming. Daydreams are generally a wonderful and healthy part of life. However, excessive daydreaming that cuts out time for other important activities can also become a form of withdrawal.

Home Treatment

- A withdrawn person is suffering from a breakdown in communication. Review and practice the communication techniques on page 240. Also see Resource #R1 on page 270.
- Provide continued support and caring even if it is not recognized.
- Consider the whole person. (See below).

When to Call a Health Professional

- See Seeking Professional Help on page 241.

Other Symptoms of Emotional Problems

Addictive Behaviors

An increase in overeating, gambling, risk-taking, smoking or other addictive behaviors can reflect mental stress or emotional problems. Addictive behaviors feel good because they tend to compensate for the sense of satisfaction that may be missing in life. Unfortunately, that satisfaction is usually short-lived and brings with it problems that undermine happiness.

Be aware of any changes in these addictive behaviors and use them as a sign that all is not well. Look at the whole person and work on communication skills as ways to assess and work through the cause of the distress.

Hyperactivity

Being "hyper" can be a symptom of emotional distress. Hyperactivity refers to a continuous increase in the level of your excitement beyond what is normal. You may be unable to sit still or speak without jumbling several ideas and points into the same sentence.

Causes of hyperactivity can be psychological, drug-induced, even tied to physical disorders. Frequently, it is directly related to anxiety or frustration. Mental stress should be suspected, particularly when the symptoms occur at school or work but not at home, or at home but not at school.

Consider the Whole Person

After reviewing the symptom inventory on page 232 and learning more about the problem, step back and look at the whole person. One good way is to apply the "Four Squares Assessment" shown on the following page.

The Whole Person - continued

WORK and SCHOOL	FRIENDS
Square 1: How is the person doing at work or school? Is work or school the source of constant complaints, anxiety and negative self-talk?	Square 3: How is the person doing with friends? Does she have friends she can trust? Are friends the source of constant concern?
HOME and FAMILY	**SELF**
Square 2: How is the person doing in the family? Does she feel accepted and liked? Is the family the source of constant complaints, anxiety and negative self-talk?	Square 4: How well does the person like herself? Does she often make cutting remarks about herself? Does she tend to reject compliments?

Combining the Four Squares Assessment with your inventory of symptoms can help you focus on the cause of the problem and how important it might be. Once you have targeted the problem, good communication can begin to identify ways to reduce it.

Home Treatment

Goals: Understanding and Acceptance

The following home treatment goals apply whether you are concerned about yourself or someone else.

Goal 1.
Understand the mental stress that is causing the problem. Once the stress is brought into the light, healthy solutions become much more obvious.

Goal 2.
Develop and express acceptance for the person's worth as a human being.

Goal 3.
Find ways to physically relieve stress (see page 215).

Communication Techniques

Understanding and acceptance require good communication with others. The following techniques are offered as practical tips for talking about emotional concerns.

- **Learn to listen.** Bite your tongue and listen. Look into the person's eyes and ask how she feels. Show that you want to understand her feelings rather than just the facts.
- **Restate the problem.** Repeat what you think you are hearing. It demonstrates that you are listening and it allows for quick correction of misconceptions.
- **Lecture less.** Lecturing creates defensiveness. If rules were broken, try to understand why and what can be done in the future.
- **Trade shoes.** Put yourself in the other person's place. Try to remove yourself from your own feelings and then ask yourself why you are acting the way you are.

- **Avoid the "blow-up syndrome."** Anger becomes a trap in family discussions. When anger is expressed to you, try first to understand it. Restrain your impulse to strike back.
- **Consider your role in the problem.** Are you part of the problem? Or is the problem really yours?
- **Use a go-between.** Perhaps a third person can help. Pick someone who is neutral and whom you both trust.
- **Write about it.** If face-to-face communication doesn't seem to work, try writing to each other. Some people can organize their thoughts and express themselves much better in writing.
- **Remember the home treatment goals.** The purpose of communication is to gain understanding and express acceptance. Review those goals often.

Seeking Professional Help

- When a symptom becomes severe or disruptive.
- When a disruptive symptom becomes a continuous or permanent pattern of behavior and does not respond to self-care efforts.
- When symptoms become numerous and pervasive in all areas of the person's life (work, home, friends, self) and do not respond to self-care and communication efforts.
- If you are too close to the problem and can not involve a neutral third person to help out.

Where to Find Help

- Your physician can be a good first step, particularly if existing medications or physical problems may be involved.

Cost Management Tips

Avoid just picking a name from the yellow pages. The old saying "talk is cheap" does not apply to most professional therapists and counselors. The following tips can help keep the costs down:

- Use mental health professionals to help you identify the real problem and develop a self-care plan to resolve it.
- Emphasize the importance of self-care as you would with any other health problem.
- The benefits of continuing professional therapy after your plan is in place should be evaluated after the first few weeks. Long-term assistance is often not needed.
- Cultivate special friends, join support groups or look for peer counseling opportunities to provide continuing understanding and acceptance as you work to resolve the problem. 12-step programs, such as Alcoholics Anonymous, Al-Anon, Overeaters Anonymous and scores of others, are free and available almost everywhere.

Where to Find Help - cont.

- Employee Assistance Programs (EAP) are now offered by many employers. EAPs generally provide high quality counseling either by phone or in-person at no cost to the employee.
- Psychiatrists, psychologists, psychiatric social workers, other licensed therapists, and clergy are all good sources for professional help. Ask your EAP program or local mental health association for help in selecting a professional right for your needs.

Part 2: Mental Self-Care for Physical Problems

The brain is a self-care tool. The human immune system is the most powerful healing force in the world --- and the brain controls it. We understand only a little about how the brain works, but we can use what we do know to good advantage. The next time you have a health problem, use these ideas along with the other specific self-care guidelines in the book to speed your recovery.

The Mind-Body Connection

The nervous system is not the only way that the brain controls the rest of the body. It also sends commands by releasing messenger molecules called neurotransmitters into the blood stream. These molecules act like keys that fit into and unlock other molecules throughout the body.

Each messenger molecule has its own special shape or key that fits the receptor lock that it is designed to open. The messengers float through the blood until they reach their receptor lock in some distant organ or gland. When it interlocks with the receptor, it causes the organ or gland to change the way it is operating.

This is how medication works, too. Its molecules have a shape that fits the same receptor locks as do the natural messenger molecules of the brain.

Someday, we will learn how to control the production of messenger molecules using mental self-care. This chapter can help you get a head start.

Provable or Pie-in-the-Sky?

The information on the next few pages may seem ridiculous to some and apparently inconsistent with the sound scientific foundation on which the remainder of this book is based. Certainly, visualizing little armies of antibodies and talking to your chicken soup have not been included in most first aid classes to date, but don't be too quick to judge. The ideas presented here are based on findings in the new scientific field of psychoneuroimmunology.

Much is still unknown about how thoughts and feelings bolster immunity. As studies continue at research centers, such as Ohio State University, University of Pennsylvania and University of Rochester, scientific understanding will improve and the guidelines presented here will be refined. For the present, however, you may find that these new concepts provide an added self-care tool that is far more effective than any you have used in the past. Be willing to experiment. See Resource #M1 and M2 page 269

Five Ways to Stimulate Your Immune System

Research studies consistently show that the body's immune system responds to thoughts, emotions and actions. The following five steps will help assure that the next time you need it, your immune system will be working at its best.

1. Create positive expectations for healing.
2. Create an environment for healing with good nutrition, movement and relaxation.
3. Order up large servings of love and laughter.
4. Use visual imagery to speed healing.
5. Appeal to the Spirit.

1. Create positive expectations for healing.

Mental and emotional expectations impact medical outcomes. They don't insure success, but they can help. The placebo effect in medicine accounts for at least 25% of medical cures. Positive expectations are behind much of the success in wart removal, faith healing and many folk remedies; negative expectations account for the horrifying effects of voodoo curses. By shifting your expectations from negative to positive, you give your immune system a boost in fighting its foes.

Four simple ways to boost your expectations include:

- Stop all negative self-talk. Censor any statements that do not promote your recovery.
- Develop and repeat positive affirmations. For example: "I am a healthy person." and "My back is strong and flexible."
- Become a cheerleader for your immune system. Talk to it. Encourage it to keep up the fight. Tell it that you are already feeling better because of its good work.
- Write your illness a letter. Tell it that you don't need it any more and that your immune system is now ready to finish it off.

2. Create a healthy environment for healing.

Movement, nutrition and stress reducers, which are always important to good health, take on an additional role when you are ill. In addition to their normal value in building strength and reserves, they can also provide a special boost to your immune system.

- Even if you have to curtail your regular exercise, keep up as much stretching and movement as your health problem will allow. Remind yourself that past exercise has strengthened your body so that you will recover sooner.
- Pay special attention to your diet. Ask your doctor or a nutritionist if certain foods would be good or bad for your condition. Whatever you eat, do it with ceremony. Dedicate each

Immune System - continued

spoonful of chicken soup to your improved health and visualize its nutrients going through your body.

- Minimize your mental stress during recovery. Put issues that upset you aside. Practice the relaxation response and other stress reducers on page 215. Use the "down time" to develop better skills of relaxation.

3. Order up large servings of love and laughter.

Positive emotions boost the immune system. Laughter not only helps us feel better, but it helps us heal better, too. Even viewing a positive film or hearing a heart-warming story can help.

- Watch movies that make you laugh. Keep an "emergency laughter kit" of funny videotapes, jokes, cartoon and photographs with your first-aid supplies.
- Ask your family or friends to help you reminisce about your favorite memories.
- Collect around you evidence that those you love also care for you, e.g., poems, flowers and pictures.

4. Visualize your return to health.

Visual imagery can sometimes be effective as a part of treatment for cancer and other diseases. It seems to work by boosting the effectiveness of the immune system. Try it for speed-healing your next cold.

- Set aside at least 20 minutes and arrange not to be interrupted.
- Use the relaxation response activity on page 217 to fully relax and clear your mind.
- Imagine that you are an observer inside your body, watching the battle going on between the cold virus and your immune system's antibodies which are trying to fight it off.
  - Be a spy on the side of your antibodies. Point out virus cells that may be hiding from them.
  - Yell up to your brain to send more white blood cells to one place or another.
  - Perhaps you can call for a flood of a warm soothing fluid to wash out the virus in a particular stronghold.
  - Use your imagination to boost your immune system in any way you want. If you like music, imagine that music is playing in your body encouraging your antibodies while causing the virus cells to fall peacefully asleep.
- Once your imaginary observer has returned, imagine that you are healed and that your body is once again at peace and in harmony. Return to the relaxation response activity for a few minutes before ending the session. By practicing visualization several times a day in addition to your other treatment, you improve the chances for a speedy recovery.

5. Appeal to the Spirit.

If you believe in a higher power, ask for support for your healing efforts. Prayer and spiritual beliefs often play a role in recovery. The entire immune system can be viewed as a miracle. Prayer to invoke its use in your behalf can be an important part of your recovery plan.

Hardiness

Some people have more basic protection from disease than others. Their immune system appears to be naturally more efficient. Researchers studying these people have identified three factors in their personalities that stand out.

1. Hardy people show a strong commitment to self, work, family and other values.
2. Hardy people have a sense of control over their lives.
3. Hardy people generally see change in their lives as a challenge rather than as a threat.

Developing a "Hardy Personality"

Can a person develop more commitment, control, and acceptance of challenges? Apparently so, particularly if you start at an early age. You can help your children become hardy by encouraging them in the following ways:

- Develop a sense of commitment by providing strong parental encouragement and acceptance. The more acceptance that a child feels, the more he will be able to commit himself to others.
- Develop a sense of control by continually providing a variety of tasks which are neither too difficult nor too simple. Experience with both success and failure followed by success helps to build the sense of control.
- Encourage children to see changes as opportunities for enrichment rather than losses. Accentuate the positive even while recognizing that some losses are a part of life.

Developing hardiness in adults is also possible. Training to develop more commitment, control and challenge has been shown to be effective.

Remaining Guiltless

There is no value in feeling guilty over health problems. While it is true that we can do much to reduce health risks and to improve the chances of recovery, it is also true that some illnesses develop and continue no matter what we do. Try to remain guiltless particularly in applying the mental self-care suggestions in this chapter. If what you do helps, well, terrific. However, if your illness continues in spite of your best efforts, don't blame yourself. Some things just are. Just do your best.

If I had known I was going to live this long, I would have taken better care of myself.

Eubie Blake

Chapter 18

Your Home Health Center

More health care happens in your home than anywhere else. Having the right tools, medicines, supplies and information on hand will improve its quality.

This chapter summarizes what self-care resources every home should have. Additional recommendations are included for tools, supplies, medicines and books that will help with special health problems or situations.

In developing your own home health center, it's a good idea to store all your self-care resources in one central location. A large drawer in a bathroom cabinet would do nicely. You may use the charts on tools, supplies and books in this chapter as checklists for keeping your home health center well stocked.

Note: If small children are around, be sure that your supplies are either out of reach or protected by childproof safety latches.

Self-Care Tools

Cold Pack

A cold pack is an envelope-sized package of gel that remains flexible at very cold temperatures. Buy a cold pack at your pharmacy and keep it in your freezer. Get it out for bumps, bruises, back sprains, turned ankles or any other health problem that calls for ice. Cold packs are much more convenient to use than ice and may become the self-care tool you use most.

Humidifier and Vaporizer

Humidifiers and vaporizers are devices which add moisture to the air. A humidifier increases the moisture with a cool mist while a vaporizer puts out hot steam. The two terms, however, are sometimes used interchangeably. A humidifier has several advantages: it can't burn you, it makes tinier particles of water which can go further into the respiratory system, it can't hurt

Self-Care Tools - continued

Self-Care Tools

For every household:
- Blood pressure cuff*
- Cold pack*
- Dental mirror
- Eyedropper
- Heating pad
- Humidifier*
- Medicine spoon*
- Nail clippers
- Penlight*
- Scissors
- Stethoscope*
- Thermometer*
- Tweezers

For homes with children, add:
- Bulb aspirator/syringe
- Rectal thermometer or temperature strips*
- Otoscope*

*Description in text

the furniture, and the cool air is more comfortable and doesn't "wilt" you. However, a humidifier is noisier than a vaporizer, and you need to clean it with a disinfectant cleaner after each use and rinse it thoroughly. A vaporizer's biggest disadvantage is that the hot water can give a severe burn to anyone who overturns it or gets too close.

Whichever you choose, your family can benefit from a humidifier or vaporizer. They increase the humidity in the air and moistened air has less tendency to dry sensitive membranes. Humidity in the air can soothe a scratchy throat, help the dry hacking cough, and make it easier for a person with a stuffy nose to breathe. In general, moisturizing the air of a home will help anyone feel more comfortable, especially in the winter when the home is closed and artificially heated.

Medicine Spoon

A medicine spoon makes giving the right dose of liquid medicine much easier. Medicine spoons are transparent tubes with marks for typical dosage amounts. While the spoons are convenient for anyone, they are a particular blessing for young children. The tube shape and large lip allow most of the medication to get inside the child without spilling. Buy one at your local pharmacy.

Otoscope

An otoscope is a flashlight with a special attachment for looking into the ear. With a little practice, your use of an otoscope can help you decide if an ear infection is present. Inexpensive, consumer model otoscopes are available. They can also be used as high intensity penlights. One good product is the Ear Scope which can be ordered for around $25 from Notoco, P.O. Box 300, Ferndale, CA 95536, (707) 786-4400.

Penlight

A penlight has a small intense light which can be easily directed. It is useful while giving a physical exam and is easier to handle than a flashlight.

Stethoscope

A stethoscope will make it easier for you to hear heart and chest sounds for a home physical exam. It is not an essential item for every home health center, however. If there is someone with hypertension in the family, it's a good idea to have a stethoscope and a blood pressure cuff to frequently monitor blood pressure. If you decide to buy a stethoscope, purchase the flat diaphragm model rather than the bell-shaped one. The flat diaphragm model makes it easier for you to hear.

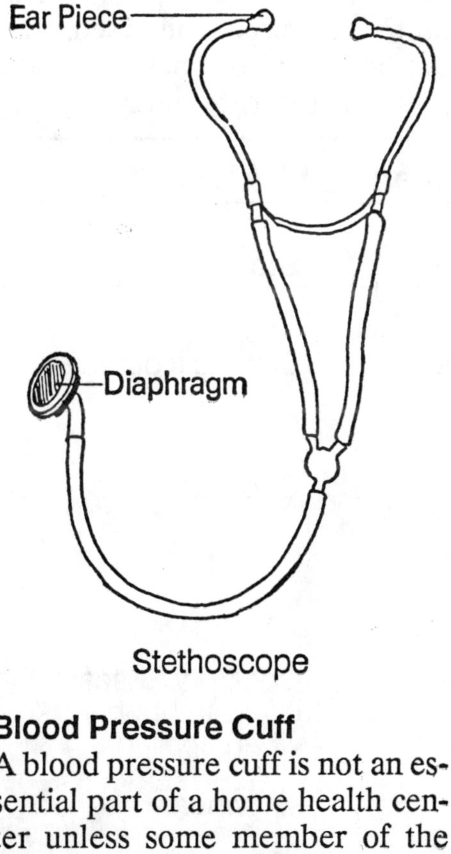

Stethoscope

Blood Pressure Cuff

A blood pressure cuff is not an essential part of a home health center unless some member of the family is a diagnosed hypertensive. It is then needed to take frequent readings of blood pressure. A cuff can, of course, also be used to determine normal blood pressure and tell when the pressure is rising or abnormal. For a description of how to use a blood pressure cuff, see page 21.

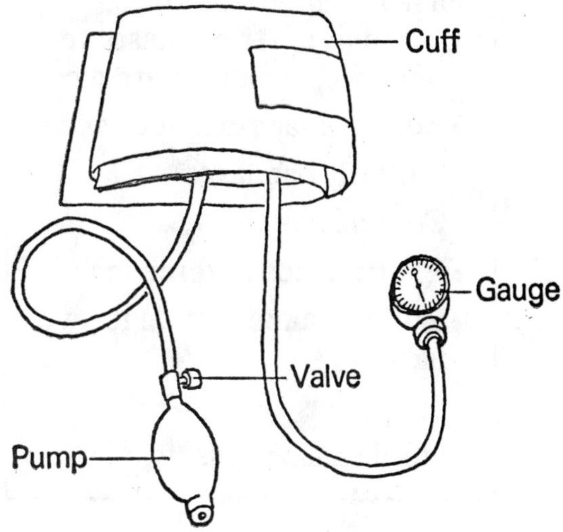

Blood Pressure Cuff

Thermometer

If you are shopping for a thermometer, buy one with easy-to-read markings.

Rectal thermometers with enlarged bulbs are available for use with small children. (See page 19 for cautions about using rectal thermometers.) Temperature strips, also available for children, are very convenient and safe but not as accurate as glass thermometers.

Self-Care Supplies

The chart on the following page lists the supplies recommended for inclusion in your home health center. These products are inexpensive, easy to use and generally available at any drugstore or pharmacy.

Self-Care Supplies - continued

Self-Care Supplies

Dental disclosing tablets

First aid supplies:

- Adhesive strips-assorted (non-stick bandages are nice)
- Adhesive tape-one inch wide
- Butterfly bandages
- Cotton balls
- Elastic bandage-three inch
- Roller gauze bandage-two inch
- Safety pins
- Sterile gauze pads- two inch

Self-Care Ointments and Cleansers

You will need self-care supplies to clean up cuts, scrapes and sores. The chart below lists a number of products which will help prevent infection. In general, you should follow the instructions on the packaging. Keep out of reach of children.

Medications

Treat any medication with suspicion and respect. Medical drugs work by either mimicking or blocking chemical messengers in the body. When we use medicine, we are trying to either fool or help Mother Nature. While medicines can be one of our best and most powerful self-care aids, they can

SELF-CARE OINTMENTS and CLEANSERS

Product (Brand Name)	Purpose	Storage
Antibiotic creams (Bacitracin)	Abrasions Skin infections	Keep cool and dry. Discard if outdated.
Antiseptic Creams	Abrasions, cuts	Cool, dry
Hydrocortisone (Cortaid) (Caldecort) (Dermolate) (Lanacort)	Itching Poison ivy Limit use to two weeks.	Cool, dry
Hydrogen peroxide	Minor cuts Abrasions	Cool, dry. Discard if it fails to bubble when applied.
Petrolatum or petroleum jelly (Vaseline)	Dry skin Diaper rash	Anywhere
Rubbing alcohol 70%	Antiseptic Clean thermometer	Tightly closed

also be a source of complications and allergic reactions that undermine our health.

Basic guidelines for taking prescription and over-the-counter medications include:

- Use drugs only if non-drug approaches are not working.
- Know the benefits and side effects of a medication before taking it.
- Limit the medication to the minimum effective dose.
- Never take a prescription drug meant for someone else.
- Follow the prescription instructions exactly or let your doctor know why not.
- Keep medications in their original containers with the caps on tightly and stored according to directions.
- Do not take medications in front of small children. They are great mimics. Don't oversell the "candy" taste of children's drug products or leave children's vitamins accessible to small children.
- In addition to this book, every home would do well to have an up-to-date copy of a consumer's guide to medications. See Resource #A2 on page 268.

Over-the-Counter Medications

An over-the-counter (OTC) medication is any medical drug that can be purchased without a physician's prescription. There are hundreds of OTC drugs to choose from. Generally, your local pharmacist can be a great help in finding the one best suited to your needs.

Keep some OTC products at home in anticipation of possible need. Purchase others only after symptoms develop. The chart on the following page, OTC Drugs for Home Use, lists commonly used drugs and recommendations for stocking the drugs at home. More detailed descriptions of these OTC medications are discussed below.

Anti-Diarrheal Preparations

Because diarrhea often helps to clear the body of infection, try to avoid use of an anti-diarrheal for the first six hours. Then use only if the diarrhea causes cramping and discomfort.

There are two types of anti-diarrheal drugs: those which act to thicken the stool and those which slow intestinal spasm.

The *thickening mixtures* contain clay or fruit pectin and tend to absorb the bacteria and toxins in the intestine. Although they are safe in that they do not go into the system, they also absorb bacteria needed in digestion. Their continued use is not advised.

Good thickening products are those which contain kaolin (an inactive clay), attapulgite (another clay), or pectin.

Kaopectate and Kaopectate Concentrate contain kaolin and pectin. Diasorb contains attapulgite.

OTC Medications - cont.

Be sure to give a large enough dose. Anti-diarrheal preparations should be taken until the stool thickens; then they should be stopped immediately to avoid constipation.

Antispasmodic anti-diarrheal preparations stop the spasm of the intestine. Loperamide (Imodium A-D) is an example of this type of preparation.

Some products contain both thickening and antispasmodic ingredients: two examples are Donnagel and Parepectolin.

Precaution: Prevent Dehydration with Electrolytes
When anyone has diarrhea, there is a danger of dehydration from loss

OVER-THE-COUNTER MEDICATIONS FOR HOME USE

Keep on Hand at All Times		
Type of Drug	**Page**	**Comment**
Aspirin	253	For pain, fever and inflammation.
Acetaminophen	254	For pain and fever (especially with children).
Syrup of Ipecac	258	To start vomiting if poisoning occurs.

Buy as Needed		
Type of Drug	**Page**	**Comment**
Anti-diarrheal	251	To thicken stools or slow digestive spasms. Also consider electrolytes.
Antihistamines	255	For allergies and cold symptom relief. Also helpful for itching. (Also see hydrocortisone creams, page 250.)
Decongestants	255	To ease stuffy nose and head colds. Can be taken as nose drops or sprays. Not safe for children under 1 year of age, unless prescribed by physician.
Cough syrups:		
Expectorants	256	To thin and help clear the mucus.
Suppressants	257	To suppress the cough reflex.
Laxatives	257	Avoid if there is any chance of appendicitis. See page 35.
Ibuprofen	254	For pain and fever, particularly menstrual pain.

of body fluids and salts. You should attempt to have the person drink extra liquids after a few hours of giving nothing. Sometimes an electrolytically balanced solution is best.

To avoid dehydration from uncontrolled diarrhea, vomiting or perspiration, drink solutions similar to the body's fluids.

- Homemade electrolytes: 3 oz. water, 1 teaspoon sugar, 1 pinch salt.
- Supermarket: Gatorade.
- Pharmacy: Pedialyte, Lytren.

Aspirin and Acetaminophen

Aspirin is widely used for relieving pain and reducing fever in adults. It also reduces swelling and inflammation and is valuable for treating arthritis symptoms. Aspirin also relieves minor itching.

Consumers need to be aware of the potential dangers and side effects of aspirin.

- More childhood poisonings are caused by aspirin than by any other drug. Three to four grains per pound of body weight is a deadly dose. That's three to four baby aspirin per pound a child weighs.
- Aspirin should be avoided for children under age 15, unless recommended by a physician, because of the possible connection between aspirin and Reye's Syndrome.
- Aspirin can irritate the stomach lining and occasionally cause stomach bleeding.
- Some people are allergic to aspirin. (These people may also be allergic to ibuprofen.)

DOSAGE FOR ASPIRIN AND ACETAMINOPHEN*

Aspirin	Acetaminophen (Tylenol)	
Adults - 1 tablet (325mg.)	For liquid forms, follow the dosage instructions on the label.	
Adults - 1-3 tablets	Take every 3 hours, as needed.	
Aspirin should not be given to children under age 15, unless recommended by a physician.	Under 1 year	40-60 mg.
	1-3	60-120 mg.
	3-6	120-180 mg.
	6-12	180-325 mg.
	Adults	500-1000 mg.

Caution: Aspirin and acetaminophen overdose can be extremely harmful.

*Doses are approximate. What is important is to give enough to provide relief.

Aspirin/Acetaminophen - cont.

Acetaminophen does not seem to have the potential dangers aspirin has. There is less likelihood of allergic reaction. Acetaminophen does not irritate the stomach lining and is not linked to higher risks for Reye's Syndrome.

However, acetaminophen does not reduce swelling or inflammation and is not recommended for treatment of arthritis.

Ibuprofen is a third type of OTC fever and pain reliever. Ibuprofen is particularly effective in reducing menstrual cramp pain. Ibuprofen avoids the ringing-in-the-ears problems of aspirin but may create mild stomach upset and kidney problems. It is usually somewhat more expensive than aspirin.

When Not To Take Aspirin

- If suffering from gout
- If taking anticoagulants (blood thinners)
- For a hangover --- before or after alcohol. Aspirin, an acid, can irritate the already upset stomach.

Signs of Aspirin Poisoning (Salicylism)

- Ringing in the ears
- Rapid, deep breathing
- Visual disturbances
- Nausea
- Dizziness

Discontinue use if any of the above symptoms occur. Call a health professional if rapid, deep breathing, visual disturbances, nausea, or dizziness occurs.

In Case of Overdose

- Call a health professional, poison control center, or emergency room.
- Induce vomiting with syrup of ipecac.

Buying Hints

When buying aspirin, you need not get the most expensive brands, but sometimes the cheapest aspirin will deteriorate more rapidly than others. If it smells like vinegar, don't buy it or use it.

Additives to aspirin tablets may be useful, but they will not be more effective than aspirin in reducing pain. You run less risk of ill effects by taking the simplest drug possible.

Acetaminophen is available under brand names such as Tylenol, Liquiprin, and Tempra. Aspirin should be avoided for children unless recommended by a physician. Be sure to check the label for dosages and frequency of use.

Storage

Aspirin and acetaminophen should be stored in a locked cabinet. Keep dry and cool. Use childproof bottles, if possible. Do not refrigerate.

Shelf-Life

- Aspirin: one year. Discard when strong odor of vinegar is present.
- Acetaminophen: two years.

Aspirin and Heart Disease

Low-dose use of aspirin can help protect healthy people from heart attacks. People with uncontrolled high blood pressure should avoid the routine use of aspirin without consulting their doctors. For some, it increases the risk of bleeding strokes.

Cold Medications

Antibiotics will neither cure a cold nor relieve its symptoms.

Some over-the-counter products may provide temporary relief of cold symptoms but they are not necessary. Use them if they help you feel better or if they help you rest while recovering. Rest and liquids are probably the best treatments for colds.

Antihistamines

Antihistamines were originally developed to treat allergy symptoms. They are now included in most products for cold relief in combination with a decongestant. By drying up thc mucous membranes, antihistamines make the person more comfortable, whether the problem is a cold or an allergy.

Many cold preparations, such as Dristan, Coricidin, and Triaminic, contain both decongestants and antihistamines. Novahistine is safe for young children. Chlorpheniramine (Chlor-Trimeton) and diphenhydramine (Benadryl) are available over-the-counter as a pure antihistamine. Do *not* use antihistamines for children under four months. For children aged four months to one year, obtain a health professional's advice regarding correct dose.

Antihistamines are occasionally used to relieve itching and to relieve motion sickness if dimenhydrinate (Dramamine) or meclizine (Bonine) are not available. A product containing only antihistamines, without added decongestants, is best.

Precautions

The value of antihistamines in treating cold symptoms has not been proven. Some health professionals believe that, by drying the mucous membranes, antihistamines may prolong a cold. Moist membranes are needed to filter infection. Remember, these products dry *all* mucous membranes. Drink extra fluids when taking cold medications. Antihistamines can cause drowsiness or increased activity, depending on the individual.

Buying Hints

Ask your pharmacist for a suitable product; then read the label. Often, more ingredients mean simply more money, not more effectiveness. Time-release capsules can be more convenient, but they may also be more expensive. Store in a cool, dry place. Shelf-life: 1 year.

Decongestants

Decongestants make breathing easier by shrinking the swollen mucous membranes of the nose and allowing air to pass through the nose. Decongestants also help relieve a runny nose and provide some relief for postnasal drip, which can cause a sore throat. In some cases, early use of oral decongestants during a cold will prevent the eustachian tube from swelling and prevent ear infections.

Decongestants - continued

Decongestants can be taken orally, or used as nose drops, or as sprays. Oral decongestants, which are distributed through the bloodstream, are probably more effective and last longer. Sprays and drops provide immediate, temporary relief. Measurement of the dose is easier with drops.

Pseudoephedrine (Sudafed) is a good over-the-counter oral decongestant. *Do not give to infants under 1 year of age.*

Phenylephrine (Neo-Synephrine) (1/4% adults, 1/8% children) is an effective nasal solution for temporary relief.

Precautions
Decongestants can cause drowsiness in some people or increased activity in others.

Medicated nasal sprays or drops should not be used for more than three days nor more than three times a day. With continued use of nose drops, a kind of addiction to the drops known as the "rebound effect" may occur. The mucous membranes swell as in a cold. This can also cause loss of sense of smell.

The safest nasal drop for stuffy nose is a saline solution made at home. Saline nose drops will not cause a rebound effect. They provide comfort by keeping nasal tissues moist so they can work to filter the air. Saline nose drops are okay to use on infants with a stuffy nose. Put in drops, then suck out the mucus with a bulb aspirator.

Saline Nose Drops

1/4 teaspoon salt in 1 cup distilled water (too much salt will dehydrate nasal membranes).

Place in a clean bottle with dropper (available at drugstore). Place drops in affected nose as frequently as necessary. Discard and make a fresh solution weekly.

Inserting drops: have patient lie down, head hanging over the side of the bed. This way, the drops get farthest back. Try to prevent the dropper from touching the nose.

Storage
Most non-prescription tablets and capsules will last one year if stored in a cool, dry place. Nasal decongestants drops and sprays are generally good for up to one year.

Cough Preparations

Coughing is the body's method of expelling foreign substances and phlegm or mucus from the respiratory tract. Therefore, coughs are often useful and you usually don't want to eliminate them. Occasionally, however, coughs are severe enough to impair breathing or prevent rest.

Water and other liquids, such as fruit juices, are probably the best cough "syrup." They moisten and thin mucus so it can be coughed up more easily.

There are two kinds of cough preparations. The first, *expectorants*, help to thin the mucus, making it easier to "get it up."

Romilar and Robitussin are good expectorant cough syrups. Look for those containing guaifenesin.

The second kind of cough preparation is used to control or suppress a nagging cough. These are called *suppressants*. They actually suppress the cough reflex. These are for the dry, nagging, hacking cough that won't let you rest. Dextromethorphan is a good ingredient to look for in suppressant cough preparations. Cheracol-D and Robitussin-DM are effective.

Precautions
If a cough persists for more than five days, you should call a health professional.

Suppressant cough syrups work by suppressing the cough reflex. They can also suppress breathing and should be used with caution, especially with young children. Suppressants should not be used if the person has a constipation problem.

Buying Hints
Many cough preparations also contain ingredients for relief of other cold symptoms and several contain a large percentage of alcohol. Read the labels so you know what ingredients you are taking. It can be a waste of money and potentially harmful to take decongestants in several forms. There are many choices; your pharmacist can advise you.

The simplest *cough syrup* often can be made at home. It soothes irritated throat tissue. Mix one part lemon juice and two parts honey. This can be given to children over one year of age.

Cough drops are largely ineffective. The melting drops can soothe the throat, but so will water. Candy cough drops are just as effective as medicated over-the-counter drops. Cough drops are not advised for children under six, however, as they can go into the windpipe and cause choking.

Laxatives

Laxatives are widely overused by Americans. For guidelines, see Constipation on page 36. Laxatives often create more problems than they solve.

A laxative is defined as any compound which eases the passage and elimination of feces (bowel movement). Water is the simplest and best laxative. Increasing fluid intake is the first treatment to try for constipation. Also, increasing your roughage intake (bran, lettuce, leafy vegetables, and fruits such as prunes and apples) may provide relief. Often, simply increasing your activity level will stimulate bowel movement. If these natural remedies do not work, try the preparations described on page 258.

Precautions
No laxative should be taken if there is abdominal pain. If the problem is appendicitis, the stimulation of a laxative could rupture the appendix.

Do not take laxatives regularly. The regular use of laxatives decreases tone and sensation of the large intestine and develops dependency on the laxative.

Laxatives - continued

Increase water intake when taking any laxative.

Buying Hints

For infants: Add Maltsupex to the formula or give in a bottle. It is safe, not habit-forming and it acts as a stool softener. However, laxatives are *rarely* needed for infants and you should investigate the possible causes before trying any commercial remedy.

For children and adults: Mineral oil is a good lubricant. Do not force it down a child. If inhaled into the lungs, mineral oil can cause a type of pneumonia. Do not use regularly. Mineral oil slows the body's absorption of vitamins A, D, E, and K. Also, it can leak out the anus and be inconvenient. Docusate (Colace) is a stool softener safe for children. Peri-colace acts as a stimulant to force the contents of the intestines on through the digestive tract and to soften the stool.

Syrup of Ipecac

Syrup of ipecac (ip-uh-kack) is an over-the-counter drug which will cause a person to vomit quickly when it is swallowed.

In most cases of swallowed poison, the best treatment is to get the substance out of the victim's stomach as quickly as possible. Syrup of ipecac is excellent for this.

Sometimes, causing the patient to vomit can be harmful. *Do not* use ipecac if the patient has swallowed any of the following:

- Alkalis, such as dishwasher detergents or cleaning solutions. Instead use diluted vinegar and follow with water and milk to neutralize.
- Petroleum distillates such as furniture polish, kerosene, gasoline, oil-based paints, etc. Give water to dilute the poison without inducing vomiting.

Poisons

Do NOT Induce Vomiting

- Dishwasher detergent
- Gasoline, kerosene
- Draino
- Oven cleaner
- Oil-based paints
- Furniture polish
- Cleaning solutions

Induce Vomiting

- Laundry Soap
- Dishwashing liquid
- Plant food
- Aspirin
- Medications
- Ink
- Fingernail polish remover
- Rat poison

WITH ALL POISONINGS, CALL YOUR DOCTOR, EMERGENCY DEPARTMENT, OR POISON CONTROL CENTER IMMEDIATELY!

Dosage for Ipecac

1 to 3 years = 1 tablespoon. 3 to 6 years = 2 tablespoons. You must follow with at least 12 ounces of water. This is essential to ensure vomiting. Try to keep the patient walking around.

Repeat in 20 minutes if the person has not yet vomited. Repeat only once. When the poisoning victim vomits, have the person lie on his side with mouth lower than chest so the vomited material will not reenter the airway and cause more trouble. If the person leans over a toilet, be sure the chest is lower than the stomach.

The vomiting caused by ipecac is *very* violent and it should not be used in the following situations:

- If the victim is over five months pregnant.
- If the victim has a history of heart disease.
- If the child is under 12 months old.
- Anytime the gag reflex does not work properly. Examples of this condition are:
  - If the person is over 65.
  - If the victim has taken Valium.
  - If the victim is drunk.
  - If the person is drowsy.

IN ANY OF THESE CASES, CALL A HEALTH PROFESSIONAL IMMEDIATELY IF YOU SUSPECT A POISONING.

Shelf Life
Keep ipecac on hand and replace it every five years if you don't use it. If the bottle is opened, the product will be effective for one year.

Vitamins

A well-balanced diet usually provides more than enough of the vitamins and other nutrients the body needs to thrive. Still many people routinely use vitamin supplements "just to be on the safe side."

Consumers who take megadose vitamin supplements, particularly of the fat-soluble vitamins A, D, E and K run a high risk of toxic effects. Toxic build-ups are less likely with Vitamins B and C.

Vitamin Buyer's Guide
While it remains unproven whether or not vitamin and mineral supplements significantly improve health, those who choose to take them should consider the following guidelines.

1. Choose a balanced multiple-vitamin, rather than one or two specific nutrients, unless it has been medically prescribed. (Excessive levels of one nutrient can disrupt the body's balance and actually alter nutrient requirements.)
2. Choose a preparation that provides approximately 100% of the RDA (recommended dietary allowance) for recognized nutrients, in approximately equal proportions. Particularly avoid large doses of fat-soluble vitamins (A,D,E, and K).
3. Avoid preparations that claim to be "natural," "organic," or for "stress." The extra cost is not worth any purported benefit.
4. Choose a preparation with an expiration date on it. Some vitamin preparations lose potency with time. Hot, humid environments, such as bathrooms, accelerate this process.

Vitamins - continued

5. For most people, a well-balanced diet of fresh food provides all the vitamins needed for good health.

Prescription Drugs

Prescription medications are available only through a physician or certain other licensed health professionals. Generally, prescription drugs are more powerful than OTC medications and more likely to cause side effects. Discuss with your doctor the costs, risks and benefits of the drug before agreeing to the prescription. See Resource #A2 on page 268.

Once you decide that a drug is necessary for your illness, follow through by taking the drug as instructed. Be sure to ask your health professional for any special instructions about taking the drug: does four times a day mean during the waking hours only, or does it mean four times in 24 hours? You should know whether the medication should be taken with meals or on an empty stomach, and whether certain foods may lessen the drug's effectiveness.

Generally, "take with meals" means directly before, with, or after a meal. The medicine should at least be taken with some food, even if only a snack.

"Take without food" means the drug should be taken on an empty stomach. Take these drugs with water (not milk or juice) one hour before you eat or two hours after.

If you miss some doses, don't try to catch up by taking it all at once. Call your health professional to find out what to do.

Be sure that your physician knows what other drugs you are taking. Include OTC medications and vitamins. Other drugs may not only weaken the effect of a prescribed medication, but may interact with the drug and cause a serious reaction in your body.

Remember, too, that alcohol is a drug that can react with many medications. Alcohol and tranquilizers, for example, react together to become much more powerful and unpredictable.

Ask your physician or pharmacist what the expected side effects of the medication are. You will be less alarmed if you experience drowsiness or slight nausea if you know it is an expected side effect. If you have an unexpected reaction, or

Medicine Chest Spring Cleaning

Look inside your medicine chest and chances are you will find a history of diseases going back for years. Since you should never give a prescription drug to anyone other than the person it was prescribed for, and as most medications lose their potency after a few years, it is important to throw out any medication that:

- was prescribed for a particular illness that is now over.
- has an expiration date that has passed.
- has no label.

one that you feel is particularly severe for you, consult your health professional right away.

Antibiotics

Antibiotics are drugs that kill certain harmful bacteria which cause disease. By killing bacteria and limiting their multiplication, the antibiotics allow your own infection fighting system to cure you.

Antibiotics are only effective against bacteria; they have no effect on a virus. Therefore, *antibiotics have no use in curing the common cold* or any other virus-caused illness.

There are many different kinds of bacteria: some are helpful in our bodies, some are harmless, and some cause diseases. Different antibiotics attack different bacteria. Penicillin works against some bacteria, tetracycline against others. Ampicillin is a "broad spectrum antibiotic;" it kills many different types of bacteria, but it is closely related to penicillin.

An antibiotic will kill all the bacteria in the body which are sensitive to it --- whether they are harmful or helpful. Thus, the bacterial balance in your body may be destroyed while you are taking an antibiotic and you may develop stomach upset, a vaginal infection, or some other problem.

You should take antibiotics only when needed to fight a *bacterial* infection. There are several reasons for this. First, antibiotics can cause many side effects, most mild, some very severe. People react differently to drugs. If at any time you have *any* unexpected reaction to an antibiotic, tell your health professional *before* any other antibiotic is prescribed.

Second, bacteria build resistance to antibiotics. Taken too frequently, an antibiotic may be less effective. The indiscriminate use of antibiotics in some countries has already rendered some antibiotics useless.

Third, some people are allergic to antibiotics and may experience severe, life-threatening reactions.

Fourth, if the antibiotic is not useful in fighting the infection, why waste your time, money, energy and health?

When you and your health professional have decided that an antibiotic is necessary and you have a prescription, follow the instructions accurately.

Take the whole dosc for as many days as prescribed. Ask your health professional how long you should take the prescription. Antibiotics kill off many of the harmful bacteria quite quickly, so you are apt to feel better in a few days. You must continue to take the medication so it can continue to kill the bacteria until your body can control the infection. If you stop too soon, it is likely that only the weaker bacteria have been eliminated and that the stronger ones will survive and flourish.

Antibiotics - continued

Unless there are severe unexpected side effects, continue the dose for the full time prescribed.

When taking an antibiotic, as with any medication, you must follow instructions carefully. Taking a capsule with meals or an hour before can mean all the difference in effectiveness of certain antibiotics. Be sure you understand any special instructions about taking the medication. These *should* be on the bottle label, but ask your physician and your pharmacist if there are special instructions about taking an antibiotic. For example, some antibiotics are ineffective if taken with antacids. The chart below lists many antibiotics and precautions for their use.

Storage
Antibiotics should be stored in a dry, cool place. They will usually keep their potency for about a year. However, most are prescribed only for a specific illness in an amount to be completed during that illness. *NEVER* give an antibiotic prescribed for one person to another. Do not take an antibiotic for another illness without a health professional's instructions.

ANTIBIOTIC ADVICE

Antibiotic	Not affected by food	1 hour before or 2 hours after meals: empty stomach	With meals	Not with milk	Not with antacids
Ampicillin		X			
Amoxicillin	X				
Augmentin	X				
Cephalosporins:					
Cefaclor (Ceclor)	X				
Cefadroxil (Duricef)	X				
Cephalexin (Keflex)	X				
Cephradine (Velocef)	X				
CIPRO	X				
Dicloxacillin (Dynapen)		X			
Doxycycline		X			X
Erythromycin:					
E-Mycin, Ery-Tab	X				
ERYC		X			
Ilosone			X		
Minocycline (Minocin)					X
Nitrofurantoin			X		
Pediazole	X				
Penicillin G		X			
Penicillin VK	X				
Tetracycline		X		X	X
Bactrim, Septra	X				

Liquid antibiotics are always dated; most are good for two weeks if refrigerated, or one week if kept at room temperature.

Antibiotic Advice
Your physician or pharmacist should tell you when and with what foods to take a prescription, but if not, and you have forgotten to ask, refer to the chart on the preceding page. By following the instructions, you will ensure that your prescription is most effective.

Home Medical Tests

Medical testing is no longer limited to the laboratory. Many consumer products are now available which allow you to perform medical tests in your own home, at low cost and with a high degree of accuracy.

Home Urinalysis

Although medical labs routinely perform over one hundred tests on urine, a dozen or more urine tests can be done effectively at home. This is particularly helpful if you are monitoring the progression of an illness or the effectiveness of treatment. Currently available dip strip tests are listed below.

A more detailed description of these tests is included in "The People's Book of Medical Tests." See Resource #A3 on page 268.

Home Blood Glucose Monitoring

Diabetic patients can monitor their own blood sugar levels using a finger prick and test strip both with and without the use of glucose meters. For more information, call the American Diabetes Association or ask your pharmacist.

Home Throat Cultures

Throat cultures are needed to determine if the cause of a sore throat is viral or bacterial (strep). Because rheumatic fever often develops if strep throat is not treated with antibiotics, the test for strep is important. Collecting the culture specimen at home is inexpensive, convenient and may save an unnecessary visit to the doctor.

URINARY DIP STRIP TESTS

TEST	PURPOSE
Specific Gravity	Kidney function
pH	Acidity/alkalinity
Glucose	Diabetes
Ketones	Diabetes
Protein	Kidney disease
Bilirubin	Liver or bile duct disease
Urobilinogen	Liver or bile duct disease
Blood	Urinary tract disease
Leukocytes	Urinary tract infections
Home Pregnancy	Early confirmation of pregnancy

Home Throat Cultures - cont.

Ask your physician if you can learn how to do it yourself.

Home Medical Records

Your home health center is a good place to keep your family medical records. We recommend a three ring binder with dividers for each member of the family.

Each person should have a cover sheet with her immunization record, birth information and a list of any medication allergies. A sample immunization record with recommended immunization schedules is included on page 265. One is needed for each person in the family.

Pages should be added for each home physical exam (page 16) and for every significant illness. A drug inventory and record of doctors is also a good idea for anyone with continuing medical problems.

Sets of home medical record forms can be ordered from Healthwise, See Resource #B1 page 268.

Immunization Schedule

Immunizations provide protection against many serious diseases. They work by training the immune system to recognize and quickly attack diseases before they can cause any problems. The immunization schedule on page 265 should be followed closely for all children to insure protection against these diseases.

Reaction to Immunization

Reaction to immunizations should be recorded. It is not unusual for a baby to have a fever of 102-103° two to four hours after injection. The temperature should return to normal after 24 hours. Also, the leg or arm may be red, swollen, or hard where the injection was given. If the reaction seems to be excessive, tell your health professional and perhaps the next injection can be divided into two to three parts and given at two to three day intervals to lessen the reaction.

Diphtheria, Tetanus, and Pertussis (DTP)

DTP is an immunization for diphtheria, tetanus and pertussis, or whooping cough. This immunization is given as a series of three injections beginning at two months of age. They are spaced at two month intervals until all three injections are given. Boosters for diphtheria and tetanus (TD) are recommended every 10 years. The first one would be given at age 15. The part of the immunization for whooping cough is eliminated after age five.

Tetanus is a bacterial infection that can be fatal. The germ enters the body through cuts and thrives only in the absence of oxygen. So the deeper and narrower the wound, the greater the possibility of tetanus. Tetanus occurs not only from a rusty nail wound or animal bite, but also from flying objects from lawn mowers and innocent scratches from boards, rocks and

RECORD OF IMMUNIZATIONS

(Complete one for each family member)

Name ______________________ Date of Birth ____________________

Test	Age	Date Given	Reaction
DTP - Diphtheria/Tetanus/Pertussis (1st)	2 months		
(2nd)	4 months		
(3rd)	6 months		
DTP - Booster (1st)	15 months		
Booster (2nd)	5 years		
MMR - Measles/Mumps/Rubella (1st)	15 months		
(2nd)	12 years		
Polio (1st)	2 months		
(2nd)	4 months		
Polio - Booster (1st)	15 months		
Booster (2nd)	5 years		
HIB - Haemophilus Influenza-Type B	15 months to 5 years		
TD - Tetanus/Diphtheria	15 years		
TD - Boosters	every 10 yrs.		
Tuberculin Tests	on exposure		
Influenza Vaccine	annually after age 65		
Pneumococcal Vaccine	65 years		

Other

Comments

DTP - continued

metal. Once the tetanus infection does occur, the victim has only a 50% chance of survival. Since it is sometimes very difficult to tell if a wound is contaminated with tetanus, the only sure protection is immunization.

Active immunization is achieved by a basic series of three shots followed by a booster one year later. Routine boosters are then recommended every 10 years to keep the immunized state active. If you have a contaminated wound, you should get another shot if you haven't had one in the past five years.

If you have never been immunized against tetanus, it is a good idea to start the series of three active shots now, then have a booster every 10 years.

Measles, Mumps and Rubella (MMR)

MMR is an immunization for measles, mumps and rubella. It is now available as one shot although a few years ago each disease was immunized against separately. Room has been left on the form for you to record whichever way the immunizations were received.

It is important to immunize against measles (rubeola, red measles or regular measles), as it can lead to complications such as ear infections, pneumonia, encephalitis or even brain damage.

In some areas with many cases of measles, an early measles vaccine is provided at 9 months in addition to the 15 month MMR shot. Check with your health professional or public health department.

Mumps is another disease you should be immunized against because of its complications. It can lead to encephalitis, nerve deafness and sterility in males after puberty. Adult males who have never had mumps should be immunized. Female adults should also be immunized since mumps can go to the ovaries, which is very painful.

It is important to immunize against rubella (also called German, soft or mild measles) because it causes severe damage to the unborn child if a pregnant woman gets the disease in the first three months of pregnancy. All children should be immunized against this disease to prevent a pregnant woman from contracting it. If a woman plans to become pregnant, she should check her family medical records to see if she has had rubella or the immunization. If not, she can be tested by her health professional to determine this. If it is discovered that she has not had either the disease or the immunization, then she should be immunized. Sometimes, however, health professionals are reluctant to give the immunization because the woman should absolutely not get pregnant in the following three months while the vaccine is in her system. This should be discussed with the health professional.

Polio

Polio is rare today because of the effectiveness of polio vaccines.

There are two types of polio vaccine: live virus oral polio vaccine (OPV or Sabin) and inactivated virus vaccine (injectable, IPV or Salk).

The oral vaccine is generally recommended for children and adolescents. The injectable vaccine is recommended if the child or anyone in the same household has poor immunity production due to illness or medications. Unimmunized adults should consider immunization only if they plan to enter an area with high risk of exposure. In such cases, the injectable (IPV) vaccine is recommended.

The recommended sequence of doses for both OPV or IPV vaccine is given on page 265.

Haemophilus Influenza - Type B (HIB)

Each year there are 20,000 cases and over 1,000 deaths related to haemophilus influenza in the United States. About two-thirds of the deaths and severe complications (meningitis and cellulitis), occur in small children under 18 months of age. Unfortunately, HIB vaccine is safe for use only after the child reaches 18 months.

Every child 18 months to 5 years of age should be immunized to stop the spread of the disease. This is particularly true for children in day care centers and other settings where the chance of exposure is high.

Children over five and adults should be immunized only if they have sickle cell anemia or problems with their spleens.

Tuberculin Tests

A tuberculin test is not really an immunization, but rather a skin test for tuberculosis. A positive result does not necessarily mean that you have tuberculosis, but rather that the germ has entered the body. Usually your body defense mechanism will successfully combat the infection. If you have a positive reaction, a chest x-ray may be advisable. How often you should be tested depends on the prevalence of tuberculosis in your area or your exposure to the disease. Once a person has a positive reaction to a tuberculin test, the test should not be repeated. You will always have a positive reaction. Subsequent skin tests may cause more severe reactions.

Immunizations After Age 65

Annual influenza vaccinations are recommended for anyone age 65 or over. Younger people with chronic respiratory illnesses should also consider the vaccine.

A one-time pneumococcal vaccine is recommended for those 65 or over.

Others

The "others" category on the immunization record is for immunizations, such as smallpox, that are no longer needed and for immunizations that are recommended only for travel to certain foreign countries. Check with your health department before traveling to foreign countries.

Self-Care Resources

The most important self-care resource for the home is good information. Every household should invest in a basic health library. Many of the resources listed below can be found at your local bookstore. If not, ask the bookstore to order the ones you want.

Note: Many of the self-care resources listed below are available through:

Planetree Health Resource Center, 2040 Webster Street, San Francisco, CA 94115, (415) 923-3680

These are marked with an "*."

In addition to mailorder books, Planetree can prepare and mail "In-depth Research Packets" on the medical topic of your choice.

A. Three Books Every Home Should Have.

1. D.W. Kemper, et.al., *Healthwise Handbook*, (8th ed.), Healthwise, 1989. Available through Healthwise, Inc., P.O.1989, Boise, ID 83701, (208)345-1161
2. *J.W. Long, M.D., *The Essential Guide to Prescription Drugs, 1989: Everything You Need to Know for Safe Drug Use*, Harper and Row, 1989
3. *D. Sobel, M.D. and T. Ferguson, M.D., *The People's Books of Medical Tests,* Summit Books, 1985

B. General Purpose Resources

1. Home Medical Records (forms). Available through Healthwise, P.O. Box 1989, Boise, ID, 83701, (208)345-1161
2. *Medical SelfCare Magazine.* Available through Medical SelfCare Magazine, 255 Hope Street, Providence, RI, 02906, (401)351-4320
3. *SelfCare Catalog.* Call 800-345-3371 for a free catalog of self-care products.
4. D. Vickery, M.D., and J. Fries, M.D., *Take Care of Yourself,* Addison Wesley, 1986

Other Resources for Special Concerns

C. AIDS

1. **AIDS: A Self-Care Manual.* Available through AIDS Project, Los Angeles, 6721 Romaine St., Los Angeles, CA, 90038, (213)962-1600

D. Anxiety

1. C. Weeks, *Hope and Help for Your Nerves*, Bantam Books, NY, 1988
2. A. Seagrave and F. Covington, *Free From Fears*, Simon and Schuster, Poseidon Press, NY, 1988

E. Arthritis

1. *K. Long and J. Fries, M.D., *The Arthritis Helpbook*, Addison Wesley, 1986

F. Back Pain

1. *R. McKenzie, *Treat Your Own Back,* Spinal Publications, 1983
2. *R. Cailliet, M.D., *Low Back Pain Syndrome,* Davis Co., 1981

G. Children

1. R. Pantell, et.al., *Taking Care of Your Child,* Addison Wesley, 1984

H. Depression

1. D. Burns, *Feeling Good: The New Mood Therapy*, Wm. Morrow, 1980

I. Diabetes

1. *M. Moore, *Learning to Live Well with Diabetes*, Diabetes Center, 1985

J. Elder Care

1. D.W. Kemper, et.al., *Growing Younger Handbook (3rd ed.),* Healthwise, 1989. Available through Healthwise, P.O. Box 1989, Boise ID, 83701 (208)345-1161.
2. D.W. Kemper, et.al., *Growing Wiser: The Older Person's Guide to Mental Wellness*, Healthwise, 1986, P.O. Box 1989, Boise, ID, 83701, (208)345-1161
3. J. Fries, M.D., *Aging Well,* Addison Wesley, 1989

K. Fitness

1. *B. Anderson, *Stretching*, Shelter Publications, 1980

L. Medical Consumerism

1. C. Inlander and E. Weiner, *Take This Book to the Hospital With You,* Rodale Press, 1985
2. J. Green, "Minimizing Malpractice Risks by Role Clarification" in *Annals of Internal Medicine,* 109:3, August, 1988

M. Mental Self-Care

1. *D. Sobel and R. Ornstein, *The Healing Brain*, Simon and Schuster, 1987
2. *S. Locke, M.D., and D. Colligan, *The Healer Within*, New American Library, 1986
3. G.Emery and J. Campbell, *Rapid Relief From Emotional Distress,* Rawson Associates, 1986

N. Men's Health

1. *S. Rous, *Prostate Book: Sound Advice on Symptoms and Treatment,* Norton, 1988

O. Neck Pain

1. *R. McKenzie, *Treat Your Own Neck,* Spinal Publications, 1983

P. Newsletters

1. *HealthAction*. Available through Kelly Communications, 410 E. Water, Charlottesville, VA, 22901

2. *University of California, Berkeley Wellness Letter.* Available through P.O. Box 10922, Des Moines, IA, 50340
3. *Columbia University Health And Nutrition Newsletter.* Available through P.O. Box 5000, Ridgefield, NJ, 07657

Q. Smoking

1. *T. Ferguson, M.D., *The No-Nag, No-Guilt, Do-It-Your-Own-Way Guide to Quitting Smoking*, Putnam, 1987

R. Shyness

1. P. Zimbardo, *Shyness,* Addison Wesley, 1977

S. Stress

1. H. Benson and M. Klipper, *The Relaxation Response,* Avon Books, 1976

T. Wellness

1. D. Ardell, *High Level Wellness,* Ten Speed Press, 1986
2. D.W. Kemper, et.al., *Pathways: A Success Guide for a Healthy Life,* Healthwise, 1985. Available through Healthwise, P.O. Box 1989, Boise, ID, 83701 (208)345-1161
3. *R. Ryan and J. Travis, M.D., *Wellness Workbook,* Ten Speed Press, 1981

U. Women's Health

1. B. Hasselbring, et.al., *The Medical SelfCare Book of Women's Health,* Doubleday, 1987
2. C. Marshall, *From Here to Maternity* (4th ed.), Conmar Publishing, 1988
3. P. Simkin, et. al., *Pregnancy, Childbirth and the Newborn,* Meadowbrook, 1984

Index

D

E

F

G

H

I

M

R

S

T

U

V

W

X

Y

Z

EMERGENCY TELEPHONE NUMBERS

Ambulance ________________ Poison Control Center ________________

Hospital ________________ Police ________________

Fire ________________ Taxi ________________

Gas Company ________________ Electric Company ________________

Mental Health Emergency ________________

Family Doctor ________________ Name ________________

Pediatrician ________________ Name ________________

Friend/Relative ________________ Name ________________

Friend/Relative ________________ Name ________________

Name	Employer	Work Number
Wife ________________	________________	________________
Husband ________________	________________	________________
Friend ________________	________________	________________
Relative ________________	________________	________________